母语优势下的翻译策略研究

刘爱军 ◎著

中国书籍出版社
China Book Press

图书在版编目(CIP)数据

母语优势下的翻译策略研究 / 刘爱军著. -- 北京：中国书籍出版社, 2024.6. -- ISBN 978-7-5068-9931-4

Ⅰ. H315.9

中国国家版本馆 CIP 数据核字第 2024AB3492 号

母语优势下的翻译策略研究

刘爱军　著

丛书策划	谭　鹏　武　斌
责任编辑	毕　磊
责任印制	孙马飞　马　芝
封面设计	博健文化
出版发行	中国书籍出版社
地　　址	北京市丰台区三路居路 97 号（邮编：100073）
电　　话	（010）52257143（总编室）　（010）52257140（发行部）
电子邮箱	eo@chinabp.com.cn
经　　销	全国新华书店
印　　厂	三河市德贤弘印务有限公司
开　　本	710 毫米 × 1000 毫米　1/16
字　　数	273 千字
印　　张	17.25
版　　次	2025 年 1 月第 1 版
印　　次	2025 年 1 月第 1 次印刷
书　　号	ISBN 978-7-5068-9931-4
定　　价	98.00 元

版权所有　翻印必究

序

　　《母语优势下的翻译策略研究》是刘爱军博士基于他的博士论文而完成的一本专著,从选题、构思,到语料的搜集和整理,再到语料的统计分析,验证定性分析的观点,并基于此提出古典小说英译的策略建议,整个写作过程耗费了数年时间,是他多年研究的心得,也是多年所学的凝练和结晶。其较强的时代性和学术价值,在翻译研究领域,尤其是《三国演义》英译研究领域具有重要意义,值得仔细研读。

　　写作本书,不仅需要具备深厚的翻译研究功底,而且需要具有敏锐的翻译文本鉴赏能力,作者做到二者兼具实属不易。本书语料丰富,分析详尽,研究结论令人信服。

　　本书使用语料库的方法,对《三国演义》的经典英译进行了详尽的统计分析,从定量和定性的角度梳理了各自的风格特征,为《三国演义》的英译研究提供了客观、翔实的数据支撑。这些翔实的数据统计也为翻译理论研究、翻译实践以及翻译教学和批评提供了可资借鉴和参考的数据支持。与以往的研究相比,本书从词汇、句子、篇章三个层面探讨了《三国演义》经典英译的母语译者相较于非母语译者的区别性特征,为《三国演义》的英译研究提供了新的视角和维度。

　　本书的研究意义不仅在于对《三国演义》的经典英译进行了语料库的分析,而且在于其进一步验证了学界传统所认知的"母语优势",从定量和定性两方面说明了《三国演义》经典英译的母语译者和非母语译者在词汇、句子和篇章层面存在较大差异,进一步验证了母语思维对于译者风格的影响。

　　本书响应了国家推动中华文化走出去的目标,旨在提升中华传统文化软实力的影响,提升我国经典文学英译的接受度和传播效果,进一步推动中西文化的交流和融通,在厘清《三国演义》经典英译母语译者风格特征的基础上,探索研究母语优势下的翻译策略,为我国的文化走出去和文学外译提供翻译策略方面的参考。

  总之,本书对于《三国演义》英译研究,对于促进中华文化走出去和文学外译,对于推动中西文化交流和融通,以及提升中华文化软实力的影响具有重要的学术意义和参考价值。

上海外国语大学博士生导师 冯庆华

2023 年 11 月

目 录

第一章 绪　论 ………………………………………………… 1
  1.1 选题缘起 ………………………………………………… 1
  1.2 研究目的 ………………………………………………… 2
  1.3 研究内容、难点与意义 ………………………………… 3
  1.4 理论依据与研究方法 …………………………………… 4
  1.5 创新之处 ………………………………………………… 7
  1.6 本章小结 ………………………………………………… 7

第二章 文献综述 ……………………………………………… 9
  2.1 国外母语译者和非母语译者的研究 …………………… 9
  2.2 国内母语译者和非母语译者的研究 …………………… 10
  2.3 母语译者和非母语译者研究的现状述评 ……………… 11
  2.4 研究成果与展望 ………………………………………… 21
  2.5 语料库翻译学 …………………………………………… 23
  2.6 本章小结 ………………………………………………… 32

第三章 翻译理论研究对母语优势以及语言特征认知的要求 …… 33
  3.1 许渊冲翻译理论述略 …………………………………… 33
  3.2 高健的语言个性理论述略 ……………………………… 34
  3.3 本章小结 ………………………………………………… 35

第四章 古典小说英译的母语译者和非母语译者的定量比较研究 … 36
  4.1 古典小说英译的母语译者和非母语译者的定量比较研究：
     方法与范式 ……………………………………………… 36

· 1 ·

4.2　词汇层面 ……………………………………………… 43
　　4.3　句子层面 ……………………………………………… 194
　　4.4　篇章层面 ……………………………………………… 202
　　4.5　本章小结 ……………………………………………… 215
第五章　古典小说英译的母语译者和非母语译者的定性比较研究 … 217
　　5.1　方法与路径 …………………………………………… 217
　　5.2　战争场面描写英译比较 ……………………………… 220
　　5.3　否定词的英译比较 …………………………………… 225
　　5.4　动词的英译比较 ……………………………………… 230
　　5.5　自然环境描写的英译比较 …………………………… 236
　　5.6　本章小结 ……………………………………………… 239
第六章　母语译者的区别性特征对汉英翻译策略的启示 ………… 240
　　6.1　词汇层面的特征 ……………………………………… 240
　　6.2　对汉英翻译策略的启示 ……………………………… 247
　　6.3　句子层面的特征及翻译策略 ………………………… 250
　　6.4　篇章层面的特征及翻译策略 ………………………… 250
　　6.5　本章小结 ……………………………………………… 251
第七章　结　论 ………………………………………………………… 253
　　7.1　研究结论 ……………………………………………… 253
　　7.2　研究价值 ……………………………………………… 260
　　7.3　研究局限与展望 ……………………………………… 260
参考文献 ………………………………………………………………… 262

第一章 绪 论

"母语优势"一直以来是翻译界尤其是西方翻译界所持有的一种传统的经验认知。于1963年9月在南斯拉夫杜布罗夫尼克召开的国际翻译工作者联合会(The International Federation of Translators,即国内通称的"国际译联")第四次代表大会通过(1994年7月9日于奥斯陆修订)的《翻译工作者宪章》(The Translator's Charter)就翻译工作者的义务规定"翻译工作者应通晓原文,更重要的是要精通用来进行翻译的语言"(王承时,1985:41-43)。联合国教科文组织于1976年11月22日通过的《内罗毕宣言》即《关于翻译工作者和翻译作品的法律保护以及改善翻译工作者地位的实际方法的建议书》就规定"翻译工作者应尽可能从外语译到自己的母语,或译到一种掌握得与母语一样好的语言中"(裘克安,1984:43)。

本研究拟对我国经典文学名著《三国演义》以及经典散文等不同文体的母语译者和非母语译者的英译进行全面系统的统计分析,并结合定性的个案研究分析,探讨母语译者相较于非母语译者的风格特征,在此基础上,提出母语优势下的汉译英翻译策略建议,以期对我国的翻译研究和文学外译提供一些启示和参考。

1.1 选题缘起

本研究选题的确定源于三个因素。

一是偶然的发现使然。笔者在博士一年级时,偶然接触到了朱自清的散文名篇《匆匆》的五个英语译文,包括葛浩文译文和其他几位中国译者的译文。其中葛浩文是母语译者,其他四位中国译者是非母语译者,这引起了笔者极大的好奇和兴趣,便对这五个译文反复鉴赏,发现葛浩文的译文与其他四位中国译者的译文的确存在着一定的差异,而且其他四位中国译者之间也存在着一定的共性。这一发现激发了笔者继续此类研究的兴趣,遂萌生了继续系统研究母语译者风格特征的想法。

  二是导师的指引。冯庆华教授开设的《红楼梦翻译艺术研究》和《译者风格研究》两门博士课程,系统地阐述了语料库翻译学的研究方法,介绍了各种实用的语料库分析软件,并以具体的案例对于文本的研究方法和研究视角进行系统的指引和示范,为笔者的研究打下了坚实的基础。同时,导师的两门博士课程熏陶并深化了笔者对于翻译的认知,启发并引领笔者确立了研究方向和选题。

  三是对我国文化走出去的关注。随着我国文化走出去的需要日益增长和译出翻译的逐渐发展和兴盛,译出研究也越来越受到学界关注,也取得了丰硕的成果,笔者希望自己的研究也能为我国的文学外译提供一些启示或参考。

1.2 研究目的

  本研究目的有四:首先,在描写性翻译学研究的框架下,借助语料库统计软件对我国经典文学名著《三国演义》的母语译者和非母语译者的英译语料进行全面系统的统计分析,并结合定性的个案研究分析,探讨认知母语译者和非母语译者各自的风格特征;其次,在系统全面认知母语译者和非母语译者各自风格特征的基础上,对二者的风格特征进行比较研究,探讨二者之间是否存在差异,验证学界传统所认知的"母语优势";第三,对母语优势下的母语译者的风格特征以及非母语译者的风格特征进行系统的梳理,探究发现母语译者在词汇、句子、篇章层面的特征以及非母语译者的共性;第四,基于母语译者的词汇、句子、篇章层面的特征,提出母语优势下的汉英翻译策略,为我国的文化走出去和文学外译提供启示和参考。

第一章 绪 论

1.3 研究内容、难点与意义

研究内容有三：第一，建设我国古典名著《三国演义》的母语译者和非母语译者的英译语料库，并对语料进行降噪处理，使其成为语料库分析软件可处理的纯文本格式；第二，使用语料库分析软件对古典名著《三国演义》的母语译者和非母语译者的英译本进行词汇、句子、篇章层面的统计分析，结合定性研究，全面梳理母语译者相较于非母语译者风格特征，厘清母语优势在翻译中的具体特征；第三，在梳理母语译者相较于非母语译者风格特征的基础上，探索母语优势下的汉英翻译策略。

研究难点有二：第一，语料库的建设难度较大，虽然目前为止，我国的文学外译尤其是英译取得了长足进步和发展，许多名著都被进行了重译，呈现繁荣的景象，但多数名著的重译都是母语译者所翻，国内译者虽有进行重译的，但为数不多。第二，在大量的语料中，尤其是在不同的小说以及不同文体的译文中探索发现母语译者和非母语译者的差异，并使用语料库分析软件进行统计分析和验证，需要耗费较多的精力和时间；而且，使用语料库分析软件对通过鉴赏观察所发现的文本特征进行统计，涉及不少技术难题，需要反复探索验证。

研究意义有三个方面：第一，使用实证研究的方法，通过对《三国演义》的母语译者和非母语译者的译文进行比较研究，探索发现二者译文风格的差异，进一步验证学界传统所认知的"母语优势"。第二，对母语译者的风格特征和非母语译者的风格特征进行梳理，进一步厘清母语译者在词汇、句子、篇章层面的特征。这些通过语料库统计分析，并结合定性分析所探究的母语译者的风格特征以及非母语译者的风格特征是建立在实证研究基础上所得出的数据资料，可以为翻译理论研究探索以及翻译实践提供一定的可资借鉴和参考的数据支持；第三，在进一步厘清母语译者的风格特征的基础上，探索研究母语优势下的翻译策略，为我国的文化走出去和文学外译提供翻译策略方面的参考和支持。

1.4 理论依据与研究方法

本研究将以描写翻译学和语料库语言学为指导,在语料库翻译学框架内展开研究。描写翻译学推动了翻译研究的范式由规定性向描写性范式的转变,拓展的翻译研究的范围,扩大了翻译研究的视野。本研究将基于描写翻译学研究的描写范式,确定研究对象并筛选研究语料,使用语料库的方法展开研究。

1.4.1 理论依据

本研究借助描写翻译学和语料库语言学的研究成果,在语料库翻译学研究的框架内,厘清研究范围,构建研究框架,确定研究对象和研究范式。描写翻译学使翻译研究范式从"规定性"转变为"描写性",从概念上扩展了翻译研究的范围和视野,对翻译研究的深入发展和摆脱之前"规定性"的范式束缚具有重要意义,同时也是翻译研究发展不断深入的发展趋向和必然结果。描写翻译学与语料库语言学相结合的成果语料库翻译学为翻译研究提供了新的研究视角和研究方法,开拓出了新的研究空间;同时也为翻译研究的主观哲学思辨的质性分析提供了实证研究的验证方法。

1.4.1.1 描写翻译学

描写翻译学(Descriptive Translation Studies, DTS,也译作"描述翻译学")是翻译研究发展史上重要的突破和研究范式的创建,对于翻译研究的发展,尤其是对西方翻译学的建立与发展作出了重要贡献(韩子满,2005:98)。描写翻译学对于翻译研究一个重要的影响就是研究范式的转变,不仅极大地拓宽了翻译研究的视野和空间,也为翻译研究提供了新的方法论,而且对翻译研究的诸多方向和视角的深入研究和发展都有极大的助益和启发。描写翻译学的研究范式有助于翻译研究深

第一章 绪 论

化对翻译现象的认知,有助于对翻译现象进行更为全面的考察和研究,进而推动翻译研究不断发展。描写翻译研究使用具体的语言事实对翻译进行描述,能够更为全面和客观地阐释说明主观思辨和感悟的质性判断,给予其有力的数据和事实支持,使研究结论更为可信和客观,同时可以用客观的数据和事实去验证基于经验所提出的假设和预测。

1.4.1.2 语料库语言学

语料库语言学20世纪中叶在欧美开始兴起和发展,迄今已有半个多世纪的历史,随着计算机科学的发展而得到快速普及并逐步走向成熟。语料库语言学突破了以往的语言学家主观感悟的内省式和诱导式的研究方法,使用语料库的方法对真实具体的语言事实进行统计分析,从中发现语言的某些现象或使用规律,其研究具有实证性。语料库语言学主要借助计算机统计工具对特定语料的语篇特征、句法特征、词汇特征等进行统计分析,采用概率统计法得出结论。语料库语言学对于语言学研究以及翻译研究的发展都具有重要意义,其拓宽了研究的视野,并提供了更为科学便捷的研究方法,对语言学和翻译学的深入发展起了重大的推动作用。语料库语言学为翻译学的发展和研究提供了新的基础研究方法,为翻译研究注入了新的动力。

1.4.1.3 语料库翻译学

语料库翻译学是描写翻译学与语料库语言学相结合而发展的产物,是翻译研究发展的重要突破,其概念最早是由 Mona Baker 于1996年提出的。自此以后,语料库翻译学发展迅猛,取得了丰硕成果。语料库翻译学以语料库为研究基础,使用计算机技术对大量真实的语言材料进行统计分析,探索发现特定语料中的一些语言特征,是一种使用语料库统计工具对翻译语料进行描写和分析的方法,为翻译研究提供了新的研究方法,拓宽了翻译研究的范围和视野。传统的翻译研究以研究者自身的主观感悟以及哲学思辨的质性分析为主,缺乏客观的数据支持,一些假设和预测无法得到有效验证。语料库翻译学则为此提供了有效的研究方法和工具,可以对诸多的哲学思辨的质性分析和评判提供客观、可信的数据支持,使所得出的结论更为科学、客观,增强了翻译研究的科学性。

1.4.2 研究方法

本研究在描写翻译学的框架下，使用语料库翻译学的研究方法，对研究文本进行描写和分析，进而运用理论论证的方法，探究母语优势下的汉英翻译策略。具体通过创建具有代表性的不同文体的我国文学英译的母语译者和非母语译者的语料库以及英文的参照语料库，借助语料库分析软件 Wconcord 和 PowerConc，采用定量分析与定性个案研究相结合的方法进行分析和研究。主要采用定量分析、定性抽样分析、多维度比较研究、理论论证等方法进行研究。以英文原文的语料库为参照，通过比较研究母语译者和非母语译者的风格特征，探究母语译者和非母语译者的差异，在此基础上，运用理论论证的方法，探究二者差异的成因，进而提出母语优势下的汉英翻译策略。

1.4.2.1 语料库统计分析：假设验证过程

本研究自建我国古典小说《三国演义》的母语译者和非母语译者的英译语料库以及由英文原文经典小说和散文组成的参照语料库。使用语料库分析软件对语料库进行定量统计和分析，统计的项目包括高频词、特色词、类符、形符、标点符号、固定搭配、常用句式等，以参照语料库为参照，探究母语译者和非母语译者的差异，验证学界传统所认知的母语优势，并探究分析母语优势在词汇、句子、篇章层面的特征，为后续母语优势下翻译策略的探究奠定基础。

1.4.2.2 译本定性研究

定量研究与定性研究相辅相成、互为表里。定性研究重在对文本进行质性描述和分析，定量研究重在文本进行量化的描述和分析；定性分析的质性描述要靠定量分析的数据来支撑，定量分析要靠定性分析对数据反映的特征和意义进行质性阐释。为弥补定量研究的不足，本研究采用定量分析与定性个案分析相结合的方法。定性个案分析主要采用抽样研究的方法，对涉及母语译者和非母语译者差异明显的几个视角的具体表述进行抽样研究分析。古典小说英译的抽样研究的项目主要包括战争场面描写的英译、自然环境描写的英译、否定词的英译、动词的英译,结合定量研究所统计的数据,全面比较分析母语译者和非母语译者的差异。

1.4.2.3 理论论证

本研究以描写翻译学为基础,使用语料库研究方法所得出的数据,运用传统译学理论以及翻译研究的最新成果探究母语译者和非母语译者差异背后的原因以及制约非母语译者的翻译策略机制,尝试提出母语优势下的汉英翻译策略。

1.5　创新之处

本研究的创新之处有三：第一,研究语料新。本研究不仅包括我国的经典文学名著《三国演义》的经典英译,还将第一个由中国人翻译的《三国演义》的英文全译本与英美译本纳入研究。第二,研究视角新。与以往的研究相比,本研究拟从母语译者和非母语译者的视角来对《三国演义》的英译进行比较研究,以期发现母语译者相较于非母语译者的区别性特征。第三,应用内容新。基于母语译者相较于非母语译者的区别性特征,对我国文学外译的翻译策略进行探讨,为我国的文化走出去,尤其是文学外译提供参考,并为翻译研究提供新的数据支持。

1.6　本章小结

本章首先陈述了选题缘由,继而明确了研究目标,确定了研究内容,对研究意义和研究难点进行了梳理。确立了研究的理论基础,包括描写翻译学、语料库语言学、语料库翻译学。基于本研究的研究目的、研究内容和研究难点等,制订了研究方法,包括语料库统计分析、定性抽样分析、多维度比较研究、理论论证等方法。在此基础上,本研究拟对外国文学英译的母语译者和非母语译者的风格特征进行比较研究,验证学界传统所认知的母语优势,进而探究母语优势下的汉英翻译策略。

第二章 文献综述

母语译者和非母语译者的比较研究由于所涉及的诸多因素,比如母语和本族语者的概念的不确定性,译者个人的能力、风格、所采取的翻译策略的差异以及译者所处的社会条件、文化语境、政治因素等的差异使其在翻译领域相对于其他视角的研究更为复杂,因而在翻译研究领域一直较少有人涉足。但随着全球化的不断发展和深入,随着我国对外开放的不断深入和文化走出去的需求不断增长,对于母语译者和非母语译者差异的研究越来越成为一种客观要求。同时,翻译事业的发展和繁荣为我们开展二者差异的研究客观上提供了丰富的研究语料;翻译研究成果的不断积累和研究方法手段的不断创新以及研究视野的不断拓展,也使得人们对这一翻译研究领域进行更为深入的探索成为可能。

2.1 国外母语译者和非母语译者的研究

母语译者和非母语译者的比较研究在翻译研究领域一直都较少有人去关注并进行深入系统地探索研究。母语原则在国外一直是一种约定俗成的原则,也被学界所广泛接受,一直以来都较少有人对其进行深入研究。近年来,有个别的研究者开始对其进行关注并进行了一些研究,但总体来说,不论是研究视角还是研究成果都相对较少。

在国外,"虽然非母语翻译的实践历史悠久,但以非母语为视角来进行专门的系统研究则不多见,"(马士奎,2012:23)只有相关的零星评价和论述。主要的代表人物有纽马克和莫娜·贝克(Mona Baker)等。纽马克在《翻译问题探讨》(*Approaches to Translation*)和《翻译教程》(*A Textbook of Translation*)等翻译理论著作中有零星的议论；莫娜·贝克(Mona Baker)主编的《翻译研究百科全书》(*Routledge Encyclopedia of Translation Studies*)对非母语翻译的命名、历史、现状以及相关研究背景进行了较为详尽的评述。

近年来国外比较有影响的相关实证研究的成果是斯图阿特·坎贝尔(Stuart Campbell)的《母语向第二语言的翻译》(*Translation into the Second Language*)和耐克·K. 波科恩(Nike K. Pokorn)的《挑战传统原则——译入非母语》(*Challenging the Traditional Axioms: Translation into a Non-mother Tongue*)。坎贝尔的《母语向第二语言的翻译》主要探讨的是从母语译入第二语言(非母语)的过程中与二语习得相关的翻译能力问题。

波科恩的《挑战传统原则——译入非母语》则属于真正意义上的研究母语译者和非母语译者差异的实证研究。该书以斯洛文尼亚著名作家伊万·参卡尔(Ivan Cankar)的19篇作品的英译为研究语料，对母语译者和非母语译者的差异进行了研究，得出结论，认为母语译者的身份并不能保证译文的质量，母语译者的译文并非总是天然优于非母语译者的译文。这些结论无疑是基于对语料的详细分析基础上的，是值得肯定的，对我们的研究也极具参考价值。

2.2　国内母语译者和非母语译者的研究

国内的翻译研究一直以来对于从译者的母语或非母语的视角进行研究的比较少，只有为数不多的文章和少量专著。随着翻译事业和翻译研究的不断进步和发展，尤其是文学外译的发展，对于从译者的母语或非母语的视角进行的研究也逐渐获得学界的关注。

国内的翻译研究一直以来并没有明确区分母语和非母语的视角，近些年来随着我国文化走出去以及文学外译的发展和繁荣，对文学外译的研究开始逐渐兴起，以非母语或母语和非母语的差异为视角的研究也开始出现。文军、潘月的《母语向第二语言的翻译》评介一文对坎贝尔的《母语向第二语言的翻译》(*Translation into the Second Language*)进行了简要的介绍和评介。王恩冕的《从母语译入外语：东亚三国的经验对比》一文对东亚三国（中国、日本、韩国）口译员的母语译入外语的现状进行了对比分析，并针对我国口译员所存在的问题提出了解决的对策和方法。马士奎的《从母语译入外语：国外非母语翻译实践和理论考察》一文对国外非母语翻译的实践和理论研究进行了梳理，比较详尽地介绍了国外非母语翻译研究的现状。余静的《〈挑战传统原则——译入非母语〉述评》一文对波科恩的专著《挑战传统原则——译入非母语》进行了较为详尽的介绍。

潘文国教授的《译入与译出——谈中国译者从事汉籍英译的意义》和王建开教授的《母语者还是外语者：中国文学对外传播的译者资格之争——兼谈高校英语教师的能力转型》从母语译者在母语语言和母语文化方面的优势肯定了母语译者的优势。王建国教授、何自然教授的《重过程，还是重结果？——译者的母语对英译文本的影响》主要从语用学的角度论证了在语用原则上汉语重过程和英语重结果的差异，从而阐释了把母语翻译成外语远比把外语翻译成母语要难的论点，从语用学的角度论证了母语优势，具有重要意义。李美教授的专著《母语与翻译》使用多位著名翻译家的译作为例，使用定性分析的方法论述了母语译者的优势。黄立波教授的《译出还是译入：翻译方向探究——基于语料库的翻译文体考察》一文以语料库的方法，研究发现母语译者和非母语译者在语际显化程度上有差异。关于母语优势的问题，上述研究实际上从不同的角度，包括文化的角度、语用学研究的角度，以及定性分析和语料库定量分析的实证研究的视角论证了学界传统所认知的母语优势。

2.3 母语译者和非母语译者研究的现状述评

对于母语译者和非母语译者的研究总体来说，数量较少，而且多为就某一视角或某一论点所展开的研究论述，进行系统论述的专门论著比较少见。国外比较有影响和代表性的有斯图阿特·坎贝尔（Stuart Campbell）的《母语向第二语言的翻译》（*Translation into the Second Language*）和耐克·K.波科恩（Nike K. Pokorn）的《挑战传统原则——

译入非母语》(Challenging the Traditional Axioms: Translation into a Non-mother Tongue),国内的有李美教授的《母语与翻译》。

关于母语译者和非母语译者研究的论文虽然数量较少,但所涉及的研究视角则比较多,主要包括关于从母语到外语翻译的译者资格的问题、关于母语优势的问题、关于母语译者和非母语译者翻译的优劣的问题、关于非母语译者在目的语表达及应用方面的问题等视角。

由于母语译者和非母语译者的研究在表现形式上是译者的文化身份所决定并以此为依据来划分的译者资格的问题,但其研究所涉及的因素则是多方面的,包括母语和非母语、母语文化和非母语文化、思维模式、翻译过程、翻译批评、翻译策略、语言学等,以此所衍生的研究视角也是多样的,因此,多数研究都是以围绕其中的一个问题为主,同时也会涉及其他视角的研究。

2.3.1 母语优势问题的研究述评

母语译者和非母语译者研究就其研究的对象来说,所研究的是以文化来决定并以此为依据来划分的译者本身,即母语译者和非母语译者。基于翻译实践以及翻译理论研究的历史经验所形成的母语优势的常识,一些研究是以译者的资格问题为视角来展开论述的,并从文化和翻译现状的客观需求等方面为依据来论证自己的观点。包括潘文国教授的《译入与译出——谈中国译者从事汉籍英译的意义》、王建开教授的《母语者还是外语者:中国文学对外传播的译者资格之争——兼谈高校英语教师的能力转型》都属于此类研究。

关于母语优势问题的研究,王建国教授、何自然教授的《重过程,还是重结果?——译者的母语对英译文本的影响》、李美教授的专著《母语与翻译》、黄立波教授的《译出还是译入:翻译方向探究——基于语料库的翻译文体考察》都是围绕母语优势问题展开来研究的。

潘文国教授的《译入与译出——谈中国译者从事汉籍英译的意义》一文针对英国汉学家格雷厄姆(Graham)为代表的一些学者的汉籍英译只能由英语译者译入,而不能由汉语学者译出的观点所主张的三点理由,从三十年来国际政治与翻译理论、语言学理论的发展出发逐一进行了批驳;针对译出的诉求,文章认为从语言和文学角度看,译入的优势是明显的,但从文化的角度看,译入和译出同等重要,并从三方面论述

第二章 文献综述

了文化对翻译的干预,指出译出的重要性(潘文国,2004:40-43)。潘文国教授在某种程度和意义上也认同西方翻译界传统的观点,即以格雷厄姆(Graham)为代表的一些学者对于汉籍英译所持的观点:翻译只能是译入母语、而不是译出母语的问题。潘文国教授认为"一般来说,这个说法是正确的,从接受美学的角度来看更是如此。"因为"译入的翻译,母语使用者具有天然的优势,因为他最熟悉、最有发言权,也最理解语言中的一些微妙之处。"(潘文国,2004:41)针对一般情况而言,潘文国教授强调,母语译者在目的语方面有优势,非母语译者在源语方面有优势,两者兼备最好,但这样的情况比较少见;而且不能走极端,是不可取的,"翻译必须以'译入'为主只是'一般'情况下的正确说法,并不是金科玉律。"(潘文国,2004:42)

王建开教授的《母语者还是外语者:中国文学对外传播的译者资格之争——兼谈高校英语教师的能力转型》一文以翔实的译例对我国文学英译的英语母语译者的优势、国外汉学家的文化劣势、中国译者的双语及源语文化优势以及合作翻译中虽然中外各有长短,需要相互取长补短,但从现实出发,文学英译只能主要依靠国内译者的特征进行了论述,得出结论认为我国的文学英译还要靠我们自己(王建开,2016:81-84)。王建开教授的研究主要是针对我国文学外译的译者资格进行论述的,其论述我国文学外译主要靠我国自己的译者即非母语译者的主要依据是我国文学外译的现状。

王建开教授从历史议论和文学英译的母语译者两个方面论述了母语译者的优势。从历史议论的视角,王建开教授认为翻译实践要求译者应该译入具有语言优势的一方,而多数情况下,译者的母语要强于外语,"在长期的实践历史中,这样的认识得到普遍认可"(王建开 2016:81),而且经过长期的历史积淀,逐渐形成翻译界的行业规定,包括国际译联的《翻译工作者宪章》(*The Translator's Charter*)以及联合国教科文组织所通过的《内罗毕宣言》即《关于翻译工作者和翻译作品的法律保护以及改善翻译工作者地位的实际方法的建议书》等都认为翻译应该是从外语译入到母语或者掌握得与母语一样好的语言。这一论述以翻译实践的历史以及在翻译实践经验基础上所形成的行业规定为依据,从事实上肯定了翻译中的母语优势。从文学英译的母语译者的视角,王建开教授以国外汉学家的英译为例,论述了英语母语译者所译的汉语文学作品译文流畅,不乏文笔优美者,成为译入语本国文学作品的一部分,并产生了长期影响(王建开,2016:81)。王建开教授的研究以母语译者英译的汉语诗歌及其在国外享有的很高声誉并被收入各种英美文学丛书、选集和文库的事实为例,论述了母语译者在汉籍英译中的母语优势。

　　王建国、何自然的《重过程,还是重结果?——译者的母语对英译文本的影响》一文通过论证"汉语存在过程取向的语用习惯,英语存在结果取向的语用原则"的差异,得出结论认为"把母语翻译成外语远比把外语翻译成母语要难,汉→英翻译最恰当的译者应该是英语为母语者",同时提出:"译者需要了解汉语重过程、英语重结果的语用原则,从而在翻译过程中注意思维方式方面的有效转换,做到有效表达。"(王建国、何自然,2014:10-11)

　　王建国、何自然的研究是目前为数不多的使用实证的方法从理论上证明非母语翻译与母语翻译相比难度要大的研究。笔者认为这一研究是目前对于母语翻译和非母语翻译比较研究领域中最为重要的贡献,对于翻译研究尤其是我国目前的文化走出去和文学外译具有重要的理论价值。一直以来,西方翻译界在传统上一直有约定俗成的母语翻译的原则,认为翻译只能由从外语译入母语,即"译入",而非由母语译入外语,即"译出",因为母语者对于目的语即译入语和母语文化的掌握要更为全面和细腻。母语优势一直以来也是被我国翻译界所承认的。但长期以来,母语译者相较于非母语译者的优势如何在理论上予以研究并论证揭示还是非常少见的,王建国、何自然的研究从语用学的视角在理论上论证并揭示了英语母语译者在思维模式上和非母语译者的不同。具体来说,王建国教授和何自然教授的研究发现非母语译者即汉语为母语的译者杨宪益虽然"在很大程度上表现出了精湛的英语语感,但其有时在译文中会不自觉地表现出汉语的语用倾向来"(王建国、何自然,2014:10)。王建国教授和何自然教授通过研究发现汉语存在过程取向的语用习惯,英语存在结果取向的语用原则。这一发现对于我们的汉籍英译具有重要的参考价值,尤其是对于我们汉籍英译的非母语译者,即我们中国自己的译者而言是重要的指导意义的。王建国教授和何自然教授的研究发现对于我们的翻译研究和实践具有双重意义。在理论上,基于其论证并揭示了汉语重过程,而英语重结果的语用原则差异,他们的研究至少在语用学视角下揭示了汉英两种语言的差异,从而在思维方式上对母语译者和非母语译者造成了不同的影响,使长期以来学界所持的翻译

第二章 文献综述

母语原则获得了某种理论支持,而非仅是一种约定俗成的习惯和原则,这是这一研究在理论方面所具有的重要意义。同时,这一研究所论证并揭示的英汉两种语言在语用原则方面的差异为我们的翻译实践提供了一定的参考价值,又具有实践指导意义。

王建国教授和何自然教授的研究也从侧面证明潘文国教授关于母语优势的观点以及其关于非母语译者在目的语表达及应用方面的问题的论述,尤其是对于后者的侧面支持具有更为重要的意义。关于非母语译者在目的语表达及应用方面,潘文国教授认为中国译者作为非母语译者在汉籍英译中也有精品问世,而且随着翻译理论研究和实践的不断发展和进步,我国译者的译作质量会不断进步和提高,随之会有更多的精品问世。王建国教授和何自然教授的研究则是我国翻译理论研究发展的成果,也是我国翻译理论研究不断进步的具体体现,其对我国翻译实践的发展和进步都具有重要的参考价值。这说明随着我国在翻译领域研究的不断进步和发展,我们对于翻译的研究和认知不是一成不变的,而是不断发展进步的,而且随着其他相关领域和学科的发展对翻译研究和实践的不断推动,我们对翻译的研究和认知将随之进步,并推动翻译实践的发展进步。这对于肯定我国文化走出去和文学外译中我国译者的作用和贡献具有重要意义。同时从翻译实践的角度来说,王建国教授和何自然教授的研究对于非母语译者的翻译的推动,尤其是对于我们的汉籍英译的推动具有更为重要的指导作用和参考价值。

虽然王建国教授和何自然教授的研究只是从语用学较为单一和细微的视角来进行研究论证的,但其对于我们把一直以来的母语优势从感性认识上升到理性认识具有重要意义。

此外,王建国教授和何自然教授在其文中针对基于在语用原则上汉语重过程和英语重结果的差异所提出的对翻译中归化和异化的界限进行恰当界定的问题,并提出:"翻译中划分归化和异化,最好只是针对如何处理特定的文化负载词而言,不能任意扩大两者的界限。"(王建国、何自然,2014:11)王建国教授和何自然教授所提出的这一界定虽然只是对归化和异化的界限,笔者以为在翻译研究领域意义重大,具有以下几重意义:首先,这一界定是王建国教授和何自然教授的研究从语用学视角对于翻译研究进行的推动和发展,对于我们深入认知汉籍英译所涉及的源语言和目的语汉英两种语言以及翻译时如何在两种语言之间进行转换提供了一定的参考和原则指导,对于推动和提升我们的翻译实践具有重要的参考意义；其次，以往我们对于翻译中直译和意译以及归化和异化的翻译策略的界定往往是基于译文对于原文词汇和表层结构的改变的程度来进行判断和界定的，而王建国教授和何自然教授把归化和异化界定在文化负载词的范畴，说明他们的研究认为归化和异化应该仅限于如何处理文化负载词的范围，而不应包括如何处理原文的非文化负载词汇和表层结构的范围。这一对于翻译策略归化和异化的界定事实上指出了译文对于原文非文化负载词汇和表层结构的改变程度以及如何改变不属于归化和异化的翻译策略范畴，从而在事实上说明如何对原文的非文化负载词和表层结构进行处理应该遵循目的语的某种语言规范和原则，而这种目的语的语言规范和原则是基于对目的语的语言的深入认知上的。

王建国教授和何自然教授提出这一对于归化和异化范畴的界定是基于他们的研究发现：汉语和英语在语用原则上汉语重过程而英语重结果的差异。按照两位教授对于归化和异化的范畴所提出的界定，如果在汉籍英译时，简单地将译文保留原文的词汇和表层结构归类为异化，依照目的语英语的语言结构改变原文的表层结构归类为归化是不可取的。因为保留原文的词汇和表层结构的异化翻译策略将使译文在语用原则上与目的语英语的重结果的原则不相符，从而给译文再现原文的内容到风格的效果带来影响。这一界定是对归化和异化翻译策略研究的推进和深化，突破了仅依据译文对原文的词汇和表层结构所做改变的程度来进行归化和异化界定的原则，有助于我们进一步研究和认知翻译策略，尤其是我国文学外译的翻译策略。

李美教授的专著《母语与翻译》以母语译者戴乃迭为例，对其译作的词句、语篇和文化层面的再创造进行了分析，发现其译作在母语优势下具有增删得体、措辞工巧、尽脱窠臼、变通有法、整合到位以及段落分合与连贯到位等特征。

李美教授的专著《母语与翻译》是为数不多的专门论述母语优势及其对翻译的影响的专著，是翻译领域从实证的角度研究论述母语优势，尤其是母语译者在翻译中的优势专著。李美教授的专著《母语与翻译》出版于 2008 年，时间上要早于王建国教授和何自然教授的《重过程，还是重结果？——译者的母语对英译文本的影响》一文。李美教授的研究主要是用定性的方法以多位著名翻译家的译作为例，通过翔实的译例分析和比较，论述了母语译者相较于非母语译者的一些翻译特征和优势；

第二章 文献综述

而王建国教授和何自然教授的研究是从语用学的角度,以《红楼梦》杨译和霍译为例来研究论述了汉语重过程,英语重结果的语用差异,从而论证了把母语译成外语要比把外语译成母语要难,以语用学的视角,从理论上论证了母语译者相较于非母语译者在语言上具有优势。二者的研究在视角上与方法上是不同的,李美教授的研究主要是以定性的方法论述母语译者的翻译中的优势,而王建国教授和何自然教授的研究主要是以语用学的视角论述母语译者的优势。二者的共同点是从不同的视角论述了翻译界,尤其是西方翻译界长期以来所持有的翻译应从外语译入母语,而非从母语译入外语的传统翻译的母语原则的合理性的一面,从理论的角度和实证的角度论证了翻译界长期以来所持有的母语译者的母语优势的传统认知。

李美教授的研究在翻译研究领域尤其是母语译者和非母语译者的比较领域具有重要意义。李美教授的研究论证使长期以来学界所持的翻译母语原则获得了实证研究的支持,而非仅是一种约定俗成的习惯和原则,这是这一研究在理论方面所具有的重要意义。李美教授的研究使我们对于母语优势的认知有了实证的支撑,同时为我们研究翻译领域中的母语优势提供了实证支撑。李美教授的研究为我们在翻译研究领域进一步研究汉籍英译的目的语英语具有一定的参考价值,同时也为我们在汉籍英译中如何进一步提高译作质量,使我们的汉籍英译的翻译实践不断进步,提供了一定的参考,对我们的汉籍英译的实践具有一定的参考价值和指导意义。

李美教授的研究还具有以下几重意义和特征。李美教授的研究对象不仅涉及汉语作品的英译,也涉及英语作品的汉译;不仅研究汉语作品英译的母语译者的译作,也研究英语作品汉译的母语译者的作品,包括汉英两种作品的双向译作;对于母语译者的研究所涉及的母语译者不仅包括英语为母语的译者,也包括汉语为母语的译者,具有更广泛的代表性,其所得出的结论也更具有说服力。李美教授的研究所选用的译作涉及的文体多样,不仅包括文学作品中最为常见的小说,还包括散文、戏剧和诗歌。其研究以文学的多种文体的母语译者和非母语译者的译作为例,论述了母语译者的优势,所使用的译作文体的多样性使其研究所得出的结论具有代表性和说服力。

2.3.2 优劣问题的研究述评

关于母语译者和非母语译者翻译优劣的问题,首先我们要明确的是母语优势并不等于母语译者翻译的优秀,二者是不能画等号的,母语优势只是影响译文的多个因素之一,并不最终决定译文的质量。潘文国教授的《译入与译出——谈中国译者从事汉籍英译的意义》、王建开教授的《母语者还是外语者:中国文学对外传播的译者资格之争——兼谈高校英语教师的能力转型》都对此有所涉及。

关于母语译者和非母语译者翻译的优劣问题,潘文国教授认为"中国的译者有译得好的,有译得不好的;西方的译者也有译得好的,有译得不好的;大家应该在同一起跑线上共同竞争。先验地规定谁有资格译谁没有资格译是不可取的。"(潘文国,2004:41)应该说潘文国教授的观点客观地指出了母语译者和非母语译者翻译优劣问题的实质不在于译者的身份,而在于译者个人本身。翻译过程本身的复杂性决定了影响译文质量的因素也复杂多样,除了译者本身的素养以外,翻译所处的社会环境、文化语境、时代背景、政治因素、读者的需求、出版社以及资助人等都是影响翻译最终产品和质量的不可忽略的因素。但相较于这些外在的因素,影响翻译质量的最根本和最重要的因素无疑还是译者本身。就影响译者翻译过程的诸多因素:源语的素养、源语的文化素养、目的语的素养、目的语的文化素养、对原文的理解、所采取的翻译策略、翻译的目的、译者个人的翻译能力以及译者个人的倾向性等因素来看,母语译者一般来说对于目的语的掌握和目的语的文化素养相对来说更好,非母语译者一般来说对于源语的掌握和源语的文化素养相对来说更好,二者各有优势。因此,就影响译者翻译过程的诸多因素来看,并非母语译者或非母语译者各自占有的优势相对于另一方要多,而是二者各有优势,因此不能得出母语译者的译作质量就一定优于非母语译者,或非母语译者的译作质量就一定优于母语译者,译作的质量并非取决于译者的身份,而是取决于包括译者个人的翻译能力和素养在内的诸多内在和外在的因素,而且主要取决于译者个人的翻译能力和素养这一内在因素。

关于母语译者和非母语译者翻译的优劣问题,王建开教授的研究也有涉及。王建开教授认为母语译者和非母语译者各有优势和劣势,母语译者在目的语语言和文化方面有优势,非母语译者在源语语言和文化方面有优势。在承认母语译者优势的前提下,认为国外的汉学家即我国文学作品英译的母语译者在理解原文方面相较于非母语译者存在劣势,其译文存在望文生义等误读的情况,同时认为我国译者即非母语译者在理解原文语言及文化方面存在优势,并以具体的译例为佐证。"从实际情况来看,中国译者的译本远非不忍卒读,母语译者的译本也并非无懈可击。"(王建开,2016:84)

2.3.3 目的语表达及应用方面的研究述评

关于非母语译者在目的语表达及应用方面的问题,潘文国教授在承认母语译者在目的语和文化方面占有优势的前提下,认为非母语译者可以在"汉籍英译这一领域中占有一席之地"(潘文国,2004:41)。潘文国教授承认母语译者的目的语语言和文化的优势,认为这是一般而言的情况,因为在汉籍英译的具体实践中,中国译者也有翻译的精品问世,而且随着国内译者在这一领域的不断探索和翻译事业的发展,我国译者的译作质量在不断提高,"一批质量高的或比较高的精品正在逐渐问世"(潘文国,2004:41)。此外潘文国教授还指出事实上,目前西方各大图书馆的英译中国文学作品,多数的译者为海外的中国人。潘文国教授以目前汉籍英译翻译实践的现状为依据,指出非母语译者在翻译领域中应有的地位,在事实上否认了西方翻译界的传统观点,即翻译应由母语译者来承担,而非母语译者,从而肯定了非母语译者在翻译实践上的可能性和应有的地位,肯定了译作的质量并非取决于译者的身份,而主要取决于译者自身的翻译能力。在我国现阶段大力推动文化走出去的环境下,潘文国教授的研究对从理论上确立我国译者在我国文学作品外译中的地位具有重要的意义。

此外,值得我们关注的是王建开教授的研究提到了许渊冲先生的翻译,肯定了许渊冲先生卓越的翻译,尤其是外国文学作品的英译成就,在事实上肯定了非母语译者的译作质量和文学外译的资格,即我国文学外译主要靠我国自己的译者不仅是基于我国文学外译的规模所需,同时也基于我国自己的译者较高的译作质量。这也在事实上回答了关于非母语译者在目的语表达及应用方面的问题,即非母语译者虽然在语言及文化方面与母语译者相比存在劣势,但这不是绝对的,非母语译者也可以译出高质量的译作和精品,非母语译者在语言表达及应用方面可以通过不断的提高使其不再成为翻译中的劣势。李美教授的研究以著名翻译家许渊冲先生的翻译为例,论述了非母语译者的译作亦可以是高质量的精品,以实证的方法论证了非母语译者也可以高质量地完成从母语译入外语的译出翻译,从而论证了译作的质量并非由译者的身份所决定,在事实上回答了关于母语译者和非母语译者翻译的优劣问题,在承认母语优势的基础上,认为译作的质量并非取决于译者的身份,非母语译者同样可以用高质量的译作完成译出。关于母语优势的问题,李美教授以实证的方法论证了母语译者在目的语方面的语言及文化优势,肯定了西方翻译界长期以来所持有的"母语原则"的理论基础即母语译者在母语方面的优势。关于非母语译者在目的语表达及应用方面的问题,李美教授以著名翻译家许渊冲先生的翻译为例事实上同样予以了回答,非母语译者可以在从母语译入外语的译出中译出高质量甚至精品的译作,而且,随着对翻译研究的不断深入和发展,翻译实践也会不断进步,"并不是我们中国人天生就做不好汉外翻译,而是,我们距离做好这份工作还有一段继续努力跋涉的征程。"(李美,2008:311)

2.3.4 译者资格问题的研究述评

潘文国教授以目前汉籍英译翻译实践的现状为依据,指出非母语译者在翻译领域中应有的地位,在事实上否认了西方翻译界的传统观点,即翻译应由母语译者来承担,而非母语译者,从而肯定了非母语译者在翻译实践上的可能性和应有的地位,肯定了译作的质量并非取决于译者的身份,而主要取决于译者自身的翻译能力。在我国现阶段大力推动文化走出去的环境下,潘文国教授的研究对从理论上确立我国译者在我国文学作品外译中的地位具有重要的意义。

王建开教授的《母语者还是外语者:中国文学对外传播的译者资格之争——兼谈高校英语教师的能力转型》主要从两个方面论述了我国译者必须参与外国文学作品外译的译者资格问题。一是我国译者在源语语言和源语文化方面具有优势,二是我国文学作品数量巨大、内容丰富仅靠母语译者是无法完成任务的,必须主要由我国译者来参与承担文学外译的任务。潘文国教授的研究和王建开教授的研究分别以充分的事实为依据从文化操控、非母语译者对于源语语言及文化方面的优势、我国文学外译的现状论证了我国译者对外国文学作品进行外译的资格和应有的地位,从理论上确立了我国译者的文学外译的译者资格。

此外,值得我们关注的是王建开教授的研究提到了许渊冲先生的翻译,肯定了许渊冲先生卓越的翻译,尤其是外国文学作品的英译成就,在事实上肯定了非母语译者的译作质量和文学外译的资格,即我国文学外译主要靠我国自己的译者不仅是基于我国文学外译的规模所需,同时也基于我国自己的译者较高的译作质量。

2.4 研究成果与展望

学界关于母语译者和非母语译者的研究成果,本研究将以其研究的视角为依据,分别进行论述。关于译者资格的问题,潘文国教授的《译入与译出——谈中国译者从事汉籍英译的意义》主要从两个方面论证了我国译者在我国文学作品外译中的译者资格地位:一是从文化操控的角度进行了论证,认为我国文学作品的外译必须有我国自己的译者参与;二是我国译者随着翻译理论研究和实践的进步,译作质量会逐步提高,未来会有更多精品问世。

关于母语优势的问题,潘文国教授的《译入与译出——谈中国译者从事汉籍英译的意义》和王建开教授的《母语者还是外语者:中国文学对外传播的译者资格之争——兼谈高校英语教师的能力转型》从母语译者在母语语言和母语文化方面的优势肯定了母语译者的优势。王建国教授、何自然教授的《重过程,还是重结果?——译者的母语对英译文本的影响》主要从语用学的角度论证了在语用原则上汉语重过程和英语重结果的差异,从而阐释了把母语翻译成外语远比把外语翻译成母语要难的论点,从语用学的角度论证了母语优势,具有重要意义。李美教授的专著《母语与翻译》使用多位著名翻译家的译作为例,使用定性分析的方法论述了母语译者的优势。黄立波教授的《译出还是译入:翻译方向探究——基于语料库的翻译文体考察》一文以语料库的方法,研究发现母语译者和非母语译者在语际显化程度上有差异。关于母语优势的问题,上述研究实际上从不同的角度,包括文化的角度、语用学研究的角度，以及定性分析和语料库定量分析的实证研究的视角论证了学界传统所认知的母语优势。

关于母语译者和非母语译者翻译的优劣问题，潘文国教授的研究以先验地认定译者的资格问题不可取为依据，事实上肯定了译作的质量主要取决于译者自己个人的翻译素养和能力；王建开教授的研究以母语译者和非母语译者各自的语言和文化优势为依据，论证了两者各有优势。

关于非母语译者在目的语表达及应用方面的问题，潘文国教授以发展的视角论述了我国译者在文学外译中，随着翻译理论研究和实践的进步，译作质量会逐步提高，未来会有更多精品问世，并以我国译者的文学外译的高质量为事实依据，肯定了我国译者文学外译。王建开教授的研究和李美教授的研究都对许渊冲的翻译成就有所论述。其中，李美教授的研究是以专门的章节对许渊冲先生的研究进行论述。二者都以许渊冲的翻译所取得的国内国际公认的成就的事实论证了非母语译者在目的语表达及应用方面并不是取决于译者的文化身份。这些研究成果为本研究的展开奠定了坚实的基础。上述关于母语译者和非母语译者多个视角研究之间的关系是密切相关的，彼此互为支撑，在研究的过程中不能将彼此完全割裂开来。区别母语译者和非母语译者其身份的依据就是语言的母语属性，基于此，母语译者和非母语译者的研究本质上是研究母语对翻译的影响，因此，母语译者和非母语译者的研究问题都是由母语的两个核心特征——母语思维和母语文化对翻译的影响而衍生的。母语优势的问题视角、母语译者和非母语译者翻译的优劣的问题视角、母语译者和非母语译者翻译优劣的问题视角、母语译者和非母语译者差异的问题视角以及译者资格问题的视角都是基于母语思维和母语文化对翻译的影响而衍生的研究视角。

综合以上母语译者和非母语译者的研究成果，我们可以总结归纳为以下四条。

第一，文化角度、语用学研究、定性分析都指向并论证了学界传统所认知的母语优势。

第二，译作的质量并非取决于译者的文化身份，母语优势只是影响翻译的因素之一。

第三，把母语翻译成外语远比把外语翻译成母语要难。

第四，非母语译者的非母语劣势某种程度上虽然客观存在，但并非不可克服。

以上这些研究结果说明了母语译者和非母语译者研究的复杂性,同时也说明这一研究还有很大的空间有待于我们去探讨。

2.5 语料库翻译学

语料库翻译学是指以语料库为基础,以真实的双语语料或翻译语料为研究对象,以数据统计和理论分析为研究方法,依据语言学、文学和文化理论及翻译学理论,系统分析翻译本质、翻译过程和翻译现象等内容的研究。(胡开宝,2011:1)根据王克非的定义,语料库翻译学是以语言理论和翻译理论为研究上的指导,以概率和统计为手段,以大规模双语真实语料库为对象,采用语内对比与语际对比相结合的方法,对翻译现象进行历时或共时的描写和翻译,探索翻译本质的一种翻译学研究方法。(王克非,2012:4)语料库翻译学以描写翻译学和语料库语言学为理论来源和基础,为翻译研究提供了新的研究方法和广阔的研究空间。

2.5.1 理论基础一:描写翻译学

描写翻译学的概念最早由詹姆斯·霍姆斯(James S. Holmes)在哥本哈根召开的第3届国际应用语言学会议上发表了一篇名为《翻译研究的名与实》的论文中提出。在文中对霍姆斯对翻译学的研究目标、研究范围以及学科内的划分提出了详细的构想,被西方译学界认为是"翻译学学科的创建宣言"。(Gentzler,1993:92)霍姆斯认为,翻译研究包括"纯"研究(pure studies)和应用研究两部分,"纯"研究又包括两个分支:描写翻译研究和理论翻译研究。

2.5.1.1 描写翻译研究区别于传统翻译研究的特征:描写性(descriptive)

描写翻译研究核心的特征就是"描写性"(descriptive)以区别于传统翻译研究的"规范性"(prescriptive)特征。基于对翻译的本质、翻译的过程、翻译研究所涉及的范围等相关概念的认知和局限,传统翻译研究重在研究译文如何达成与源语文本的对等或等效。传统翻译研究所提出的翻译理论或翻译原则都是为如何实现对等或等效而服务的,其性质多为规范性的。这些研究重点关注译文是否忠实于原文或与原文是否对等,着重探究翻译的"忠实"问题、翻译的"方法"问题、翻译的"标准"问题等。传统翻译研究的主要理论和成果的代表包括泰特勒的"翻译三原则"、奈达的"动态对等"、严复的"信、达、雅"、傅雷的"神似"、钱钟书的"化境"等。

但随着翻译理论研究和实践的不断发展和深入,学界发现,传统的翻译理论越来越难以解释翻译当中出现的复杂现象,包括译文的多样性,译者的主体性,社会、文化等文本之外的相关因素对翻译的影响和制约等,即传统翻译理论无法解释或涵盖翻译中的所有现象或事实,说明传统的翻译理论相对翻译这一现象或事实本身,其研究的范围和视野以及手段和方法已经呈现出局限性和不足,翻译研究需要扩大研究范围和视野以及使用新的研究方法来阐释翻译现象并探索新的翻译理论来推动翻译研究和实践的发展。基于此种研究历史语境,以及与翻译相关的其他学科研究的不断发展,描写翻译学及其一个分支——语料库翻译学便应运而生。

随着描写翻译学的出现,翻译学研究的范式也随之发生了转变,描写翻译学相对于传统翻译学的研究范式,由传统的"规定性"转变为"描写性"。描写翻译学突破了传统翻译研究的以源语文本为依归,探究译文如何达成对于源语文本的忠实的束缚,侧重描述译文,借助于其他学科的研究成果,从目的语的文化、社会、译者,以及影响翻译或译者的所有因素对翻译过程或译文进行阐释和说明。描写性相对于规定性,主要在于由在原文和译文之间探究转换的方法以达成译文和原文的对等或等效的范畴,转变为对译文以影响和制约译文及译文生成过程的阐释和说明。基于此,描写性翻译研究不再局限于源语文本和译文之间的相互转换,而是把翻译行为和译文放在一个更为宏大和真实的历史的、社会的、文化的时空进行考察和研究,使翻译研究对于翻译行为和译文等的翻译事实的认知更为全面和真实,其研究的视角更为多样,对翻译现象的解释力更强。

第二章 文献综述

2.5.1.2 描写翻译研究的对象和范围

随着研究范式的转变,描写翻译学相对于传统翻译研究的研究对象也发生了转变,研究的范围和视野相对于传统翻译学也得到了极大拓展。描写翻译学的研究对象从传统翻译学的以原文为依归的翻译的"忠实"问题、翻译的"方法"问题、翻译的"标准"问题等转为以译文为核心的影响翻译的目的语的社会与文化、翻译的目的、翻译批评、翻译的选择、翻译的社会功能、译者、译文的细节及多样性等。描写翻译学的研究范围也从传统翻译学研究的主要以原文和译文的文本层面的比照所涉及的词汇、句法、语法、语篇、语用、功能等转变为以译文为核心的影响翻译行为的所有相关学科和领域及其与翻译行为之间的相互影响和制约的事实。描写翻译学相较于传统翻译研究的研究对象的转变与研究范围的转变密切相关,相辅相成。

2.5.1.3 描写翻译研究对于翻译研究的意义

描写翻译研究对于翻译研究的发展具有重要意义和极大的推动作用。第一,描写翻译研究以极大的研究范围和包容性推进了翻译研究对于翻译的认知。描写翻译研究一个重要的观点就是翻译不是在真空中进行的语言转换,而是受到各种语言文化因素制约的社会行为和文化历史现象。描写翻译研究的这一观点是把翻译行为的事实放在整个社会的文化和历史的时间和空间之中来考察,使其对于翻译行为的认知相较于传统的翻译研究更为真实和客观。第二,描写翻译研究相较于传统翻译研究的研究范式的转变为翻译研究提供了新的研究视角和研究方法,这些新视角和新方法在翻译研究中的使用推进了翻译研究在各维度和方向的进步和发展,同时促进了传统翻译研究的进步和发展。尤其是翻译研究新方法——语料库方法,广泛应用于翻译研究对于翻译语言、翻译共性、翻译规范、译者风格、翻译教学、翻译实践的研究,有力促进了翻译研究的发展。第三,描写翻译研究相较于传统翻译研究的研究对象的转变和研究范围的拓展为翻译研究提供了广阔的空间和视野。描写翻译研究将翻译研究的研究范围从传统译学的主要以原文和译文的文本层面的比照所涉及的语言学及文化领域转变为以译文为核心的影响翻译行为的所有相关学科和领域,尤其是描写翻译研究中的规范理论将社会学视角与翻译研究相融合,使社会学研究渗入、融合进了翻译研究领域,翻译研究的视野得到了极大拓展,研究内容和视角也随之更为丰富和多样。描写翻译研究的重要内容关于翻译规则的探究也极大拓展了翻译研究的空间,丰富了研究的内容和研究视角的多样性。第四,描写翻译研究从目的语出发,所提出的"假定的翻译"的概念,对于描写翻译学在翻译研究中的地位的确立具有重要意义,同时对于翻译研究的学科的独立性和科学性的确立也具有重要的促进作用。

2.5.2 理论基础二:语料库语言学

语料库语言学是语料库翻译学的重要基础之一。语料库语言学为语料库翻译学提供了对特定语料进行实证研究的研究方法即语料库方法,使翻译研究不再停留于内省式的主观哲学思辨的质性层面,使用语料库的方法可以对特定的语料进行定量的统计分析,从而发现特定语料的文本特征。语料库的研究方法使翻译对文本不仅可以进行定性研究,也可以进行定量研究,同时也可以使用定量研究对定性研究进行验证和佐证,使其更为科学和客观。

语料库语言学是指利用语料库观察和分析语言事实,并依据这些事实证实或证伪现有言学理论,或提出新的观点、理论的研究。(胡开宝,2012:63)语料库语言学主张"系统地对大量的文本语料进行审视,使我们有可能发现一些之前从未有机会发现的语言事实"(Sinclair,1991)。语料库语言学以大量精心采集而来的真实文本(authentic texts)为研究素材,主要通过概率统计的方法得出结论,因此语料库语言学从本质上讲是实证性的(empirical)(梁茂成、李文中、许家金,2010:3)。正是采用真实的语言素材,为研究对象,使语料库语言学的研究是基于真实可靠的语言事实,因而,其研究所得出的结论也就更为客观和可信。

语料库语言学研究的两个重要基础:一是语料库,二是语料库统计工具即语料库统计分析软件。语料库语言学家 John Sinclair(1991)将语料库定义为"A collection of naturally-occurring language text, chosen to characterize a state or variety of a language."。在实践中,语料库的分类比较复杂,一般来说,基于不同的标准和目的有不同的分类。常见的语料库类型有单语语料库、双语或多语语料库、平行语料库、可比语料库、通用语料库、专用语料库等。此外,根据语言传播媒介的

第二章 文献综述

不同,可以分为口语语料库和笔语语料库;根据语言产出者的身份的不同,可以分为本族语者语料库和学习者语料库;根据语料产出年代的不同,可以分为共时语料库和历时语料库;以及依照研究目的的不同而划分的其他语料库。总之,语料库种类繁多,但都是为一定的研究目的而服务的。

一般,为了一定的研究目的需要自建语料库。自建语料库需要依据研究目的明确语料库的规模、代表性和内容等因素。随着语料库语言学以及计算机技术的进步与发展,出现了越来越多的大型的种类不同的有影响力的语料库。20世纪60年代,Nelson Francis和Henry Kucera在美国创建了首个美国英语书面语语料库,布朗语料库(BROWN),也是世界上最早的计算机语料库。国内最早建成的语料库是20世纪80年代由上海交通大学的杨惠中教授创建的上海交通大学科技英语语料库(JDEST),总库容近400万英语词。1995年,英国曼彻斯特大学的Mona Baker教授创建了世界上第一个翻译语料库翻译英语语料库(TEC),其库容为2000多万英语词。1994年,由牛津出版社、朗文出版公司、牛津大学计算机服务中心以及大英图书馆等机构联合开发的英语国家语料库(BNC),总库容超过1亿英语词。美国杨百翰大学的Mark Davies创建的美国当代英语语料库(COCA)是目前为止世界上最大的英语平衡语料库,其总库容为5.2亿英语词。这些语料库的建成和应用极大地推动了语料库语言学和语料库翻译学的发展,也标志着计算机技术的进步和发展推动了语料库技术的发展和成熟,从而推动了语料库语言学和语料库翻译学的发展和进步。

语料库的创建和统计分析涉及语料库技术。语料库技术是指在语料库的创建和应用过程中所使用的技术,即与语料格式转换、语料降噪、语料对齐、语料库检索、检索统计结果和分析等相关的技术(管新潮、陶友兰,2017:16)。格式转换工具包括PDF文档转换工具和其他的格式转换工具,常用的PDF文档转换工具有Adobe Acrobat 9 Pro、ABBYY FineReader 12和金山PDF转换器V6.2等,此外,WORD和EXCEL软件也是非常有效的语料格式转换工具。语料降噪是指消除语料中多余的字符或影响语料对齐的字符、公式、图表等,以提高语料库统计分析的效用(管新潮、陶友兰,2017:20)。常用的语料降噪工具主要有WORD软件和EmEditor软件。用于语料对齐工具比较多,常用的主要有SDL Trados 2011的WinAlign、ABBYY Aligner、Tmxmall

对齐工具、ParaConc 软件 View Corpus Alignment 等。常用的语料标注软件有 TreeTagger 等。常用的语料库检索和统计分析工具主要有 Wconcord、WordSmith、AntConc、ParaConc、PowerGREP、Power Conc 等。

  语料库语言学的研究与其所依赖的研究工具以及计算机技术密切相关。在语料库语言学的研究中,语料的收集和整理、语料的加工以及语料的统计分析都有赖于其研究工具以及计算机技术提供技术支持和服务,其发展与进步极大程度上受到语料库研究工具以及计算机技术发展与进步程度的制约。语料库语言学自诞生之初受制于计算机技术水平相对滞后的制约,进步速度较慢。自 20 世纪 60 年代以来,随着计算机技术的快速发展和进步,语料库的建库速度和规模也随之取得了长足的进步,语料库技术尤其是语料库检索和统计分析工具更是在近年来飞速发展和进步,对于语料的检索分析已由传统的索引行分析、词表分析、主题词分析发展到了多维度分析(multidimensional analysis)、多因素分析(multifactorial analysis)、聚类分析(cluster analysis)等。

  计算机技术以及语料库研究工具的发展和进步推动语料库语言学研究的不断进步,同时也推动了与语料库语言学密切相关的语料库翻译学的不断进步和发展。由于诸多类型不同的大型语料库的建立和语料库检索和统计工具的飞速发展,为语料库翻译学的研究提供了规模庞大,种类繁多,适用于不同研究目的的真实的语言素材以及高效、统计内容复杂的统计手段,极大地推动力语料库翻译研究的发展和进步。语料库语言学在语料库和语料库方面的进步也为语料库翻译研究深入认知和发现特定语料库的文本特征,进而为翻译在文化、社会、历时、共时等视角的更为深入的研究提供了更为充实的数据支撑,推动了翻译理论研究和实践的进步。

  描写性翻译学主张采用真实的翻译文本或语言事实为研究对象,对客观存在的翻译行为和翻译文本进行描写研究。语料库语言学也主张采用大量真实的语言文本为研究素材,以确保研究基于真实的语言事实,并以语料库统计软件进行数据统计,从而确保研究结论的客观性和科学性。描写性翻译学和语料库语言学在研究素材真实性上的一致性使语料库翻译学获得了二者融合的必要条件。描写性翻译学为语料库翻译学提供了研究的方向,语料库语言学为语料库翻译学提供了必要的研究方法和真实的语言素材,加上二者在研究素材真实性上的一致性为融合所提供的必要条件,语料库翻译学的诞生便成为必然。

第二章 文献综述

2.5.3 语料库翻译学研究的主要概念及特征

语料库翻译研究作为新出现和发展的翻译学研究分支，涉及其研究的学科定位的一些相关概念直接关系到其研究的科学性以及研究方法和研究内容是否合理等问题。对于这些概念的定义就显得尤为重要。首先是学科属性的定位，即语料库翻译学的方法论和研究范式的定位。语料库翻译学不是一种翻译理论，而是一种译学研究方法论，同时也是一种译学研究范式。

语料库翻译学的方法论的定位使语料库翻译研究具有了明确的研究方法论属性，在翻译研究中语料库的研究方法被明确为一种科学的全新的研究方法。以往的翻译研究主要依靠内省式或诱导式的研究方法。内省式和诱导式的研究方法主要依靠研究者自己个人的主观判断和直觉为出发点而做出某种假设，然后以少量的例证或有限的实验去予以验证，难免具有主观片面性，科学性和客观性相对不足。语料库的研究方法以大量真实的文本或语言事实为素材，运用计算机技术对文本进行数据统计，并以此为依据对文本进行分析，与以往的研究方法相比，由于有了具体的数据作支撑，其所得出的结论更为科学和客观。语料库翻译学是一种全新的研究范式。

纵观译学研究历史，译学研究范式经历了四次重要转变，即语文学范式、语言学范式、文化范式和语料库翻译学范式（胡开宝，2012：61）。语料库翻译学具备了范式所要求的要素，包括翻译学界所公认的研究方法，即语料库方法，以翻译文本内容作为目的语文化的事实，并具有独特属性，具有自己的研究领域等。这些要素都使语料库翻译学具备了研究范式科学定位所需要的特征。

语料库翻译学因为其在基于描写性翻译学和语料库语言学都以客观语境中的语言事实为研究素材的共性的基础上，以描写性翻译学为框架，融合了语料库语言的研究方法，因而具有以下一些区别于以往的传统翻译研究的特征。

第一，语料库翻译研究具有实证性特征。语料库翻译研究是以真实的语言素材，借助语料库技术，尤其是语料检索和统计分析工具对大量的语料进行统计分析，结合定性分析，发现其文本特征，总结或验证翻译中的规律性特征，其结论具有科学性和客观性。

第二,语料库翻译研究具有自下而上与自上而下的方法相结合的特征。自下而上的方法是指在分析真实语料和数据统计的基础上,归纳出关于研究的一般结论或抽象理论。自上而下的方法与自下而上方法相反,具体表现为首先提出某一理论框架或理论假设,然后根据这一框架或假设确定研究的步骤与方法,依据适当的证据支持或反驳某一理论或假设(胡开宝,2012:64)。语料库翻译研究主要以语料库为基础进行研究,可以分为两种研究方式:基于语料库的翻译研究和语料库驱动下的翻译研究。如果是以特定语料的统计数据为依据,提取或总结出关于翻译的一般规律或提出某一翻译理论假设或发现某一翻译事实,则属于语料库驱动下的翻译研究,使用了自下而上的方法;如果事先依据主观哲学思辨、某一理论或通过对特定语料的观察,提出某一预测或假定,然后依据对特定语料统计分析所得出的数据并结合定性分析进行验证或归纳出某一翻译规律或翻译理论或翻译事实,则属于基于语料库的翻译研究,使用了自下而上和自上而下相结合的方法。

第三,语料库翻译研究具有多层次的描写与多视角的解释并重的特征。语料库翻译研究并不排斥除了语料库方法之外的其他研究方法,相反语料库方法只是语料库翻译研究的一种主要方法,这种方法需要其他研究方法的补充,才能更为完整和全面地解释翻译现象或事实,并探究翻译现象或事实背后的成因。描写性翻译学是语料库的来源之一,或者说语料库翻译学脱胎于描写性翻译学,所以描写性是语料库翻译学的一个重要特征。对特定的翻译语料或大量翻译事实进行多视角、多层次、多维度的描写是语料库翻译研究不可或缺的描写性特征,语料库方法和这些多视角、多层次、多维度的描写之间是密切相关、相辅相成、互为支撑的关系。多视角、多层次、多维度的描写为语料库方法提供了研究方向和对现象进行阐释和解释的空间,语料库方法为多视角、多层次、多维度的描写提供了数据支撑的科学性和客观性。

第四,语料库翻译研究具有定量研究方法的应用的特征。定量分析是使用语料库统计工具对特定语料或文本进行统计来获得的关于语料或文本的数据,并对获取的数据信息进行分析来总结归纳出一定的翻译规律或翻译事实。语料库翻译研究以语料库为基础,使用语料库统计分析工具对特定文本进行数据统计,以期发现关于文本的词汇、句子、语篇层面的特征。通过语料库统计工具对语料或文本所获得的数据分析所得出的结论因为有语料或文本的具体数据作支撑,其结论具有科学性和客观性。定量分析为语料库翻译研究提供了科学性和客观性的主要支撑,这是语料库翻译研究区别于以往翻译研究的主观内省式或诱导式方法的重要特征。用于反映语料或文本词汇特征的统计项目主要包括形符、类符、标准形符/类符比、形符/类符比、特定词汇的频数和使用频率等;用于反映语料或文本句子特征的统计项目主要包括平均句长、平均句段长、具体句式结构的频数和使用频率等;用于反映词汇和句式特征的统计项目也可以用来反映语料或文本的语篇特征。语料或文本的统计项目还包括反映搭配显著性的数据搭配序列频数与节点词频数之比、搭配词的相对频数、Z值、T值等,或用于检验相互比较的数据之间差异是否具有显著性的数据卡方检验和对数似然比等。

2.5.4 语料库翻译学的研究方法:语料库方法

语料库翻译学研究的研究方法是语料库方法。语料库方法是指以语料库为研究平台,基于语料分析和数据统计,提出有关理论假设,证实或证伪现有假设的研究方法。(胡开宝,2007:60)语料库方法使用大量的真实的自然文本,进行数据统计和分析,并结合定性分析的方法来分析文本的特征,属于一种实证性的研究方法。语料库的研究方法基于其研究素材的真实性和统计数据的客观性,其所发现的文本特征以及相关的结论相较于其他研究方法更具有科学性和客观性。

根据语料库方法所涉及的两个重要研究基础,就是语料库和语料库统计工具即语料库统计分析软件。这两个研究基础要素在 2.4.2 理论基础二:语料库语言学已有详细介绍,这里不再赘述。除了语料库和语料库统计分析软件之外,语料库研究方法最重要的是研究视角和统计内容。语料库和语料库统计分析软件本质上都属于研究工具属性,是语料库研究的外在物质条件,对研究起辅助性作用。研究视角和统计内容则是由特定研究目的所决定的,决定着研究及研究结果的创新性。语料库翻译学研究的主要推动力"语料库翻译学研究还注重在描写基础上对翻译事实或数据体现的规律性特征进行解释,探索这些规律的前因后果""任何研究的价值或魅力不仅仅在于它可以回答'什么'和'如何'的问题,而且在于它能够解答'为什么'的问题"(胡开宝,2007:64-67)。

2.6 本章小结

本章主要对国内外母语译者和非母语译者的比较研究进行了梳理并对本研究的研究理论基础进行了简要介绍。国内外对于母语译者和非母语译者的相关研究比较少，笔者从母语优势、译者的翻译资格、母语译者和非母语译者翻译的优劣问题、非母语译者在目的语表达及应用方面的问题四个视角对母语译者和非母语译者相关的研究进行了梳理。通过以上四个视角的梳理，笔者发现研究结果显示：文化角度、语用学研究、定性分析都指向并论证了学界传统所认知的母语优势；译作的质量并非取决于译者的文化身份，母语优势只是影响翻译的因素之一；把母语翻译成外语远比把外语翻译成母语要难；非母语译者的非母语劣势某种程度上虽然客观存在，但并非不可克服。以上这些研究结果说明了关于母语译者和非母语译者研究的复杂性，同时也说明这一研究还有很大的空间有待于我们去探讨。本章对本研究的理论基础语料库翻译学进行了简要介绍。对语料库翻译学的两大理论基础描写性翻译学和语料库语言学、语料库翻译研究的主要概念及特征、语料库翻译学的研究方法语料库方法进行了重点介绍。

第三章 翻译理论研究对母语优势以及语言特征认知的要求

我国的翻译理论自近代以来随着大量翻译实践活动的发展和繁荣而不断地发展和进步,翻译理论和实践相互促进,相伴发展,同时又以实践对理论的推动为主向前发展,我国翻译理论的发展表现出明显的实践推动的特征。许渊冲的竞胜理论和高健的语性理论是我国翻译理论的重要成果和代表,是两位翻译家在多年的大量翻译实践的基础上总结提炼的翻译规律。许渊冲在翻译实践和理论方面的成就已为国内和国际翻译界所公认,高健则是国内知名的翻译家,其成果亦为学界所公认。下面笔者就以许渊冲和高健两位译家的翻译理论为例探讨。

3.1 许渊冲翻译理论述略

许渊冲在《再谈中国学派的文学翻译理论》一文中结合我国传统哲学中老子和孔子的一些思想和理念对于翻译理论从本体论到目的论进行了系统的总结和概括。这一总结和概括基于其多年的翻译实践,基于其对我国传统哲学中老子和孔子的一些思想和理念的传承和应用,以及我国翻译领域长期以来尤其是近代以来在大量实践基础上积累和总结的翻译研究成果,同时也是对我国传统文化的继承、发展和应用。笔者以为,中国学派的文学翻译理论最重要的一个特征是实践性,其源于实践而又反作用于实践,因而对实践的指导意义也最为强烈。

许渊冲认为:"中国学派的译论来源是老子提出的'本体论',孔子提出的'认识论''方法论'和'目的论'。"就其本体论来说,许渊冲指出"文学翻译的本体是解决'信'和'美'的矛盾","翻译之道既不是'求信'也不是'求美',而是求'信美'相结合之道",并进一步指出:"'求信'并不是忠实于原文的文字,而是忠实于文字所写的更真、更美的现实。"(许渊冲,2012:89)这里的本体论实际上包含了两层意义:首先,译文不应该追求对原文表层结构的忠实,而应该忠实于原文所反映的现实;其次,要做到"信美"相结合之道,就要做到认知并发挥目的语的优势并进行再创造。就其认识论来说,许渊冲指出"'从心所欲'是发挥主观能动性,发挥创造力,是艺术",而发挥主观能动性和创造力,就要求对目的语具体的语言特征有深入的认知。这是充分发挥其优势进行再创造的前提条件。就其目的论来说,许渊冲指出"'三之论'是说译文目的是使读者知道原文内容,喜欢译文文字,读后感到愉快",说明其目的是要达到再现原作的风格,尤其是文学美的属性,使目的语读者产生共鸣。从中我们可以发现,其目的论暗含了译文要符合译入语思维模式及其具体语言使用特征的要求。中国学派的文学翻译理论的本体论、认识论和目的论实际上揭示了文学翻译的创造性和艺术性两个本质属性,而其核心则是认知并发挥目的语的优势。这就要求我们在翻译研究领域不断认知和发现目的语的语言特点和优势,从而最大限度地发挥其优势。

3.2 高健的语言个性理论述略

  高健的语言个性理论同样要求我们在翻译中深入认知并充分应用目的语的语言特征。高健认为:"每种语言都有它自己所独具的性格、习性、脾气、癖好、气质,都有它自己所独具的倾向、性能、潜力、可能性、局限性以及优势与不足等""由于每种语言都有上述各不相同的个性,他们在各自的运用与发展过程中于是逐渐物化为多种多样纷繁不一的具体语言特征。"(高健,1999:57)根据高健对语言个性的定义,我们可以发现,语言个性所包含的特征都在运用与发展的过程中物化为多种多样纷繁不一的具体的语言特征,所以我们要进一步深入认知一种语言的个性,尤其是其所独具的性格、习性、气质,或倾向、性能、局限性以及优势与不足等,除了宏观地对语言进行研究外,更重要的还需要对语言的具体特征通过语料库的方法进行研究。语言的具体特征可以反映和体现语言个性的各个侧面,通过语料库的方法我们不仅可以认知其具体的语言特征,而且还可以认知这些具体的语言特征是如何承载和体现语言个性的。在翻译中,对于目的语这两方面进一步的认知对推进我们的翻译研究和实践,尤其是对我们的文化走出去和文学外译具有重要意义。

3.3 本章小结

本章研究简要从我国翻译理论研究的视角阐述了翻译理论对于我们进一步认知汉英翻译的目的语英语的要求,许渊冲中国学派的文学翻译理论和高健的语言个性理论的核心观点都是基于汉英两种语言的差异而提出的翻译理论,是两位翻译家在多年翻译实践基础上的提炼和总结。

从许渊冲中国学派的文学翻译理论到高健的语言个性理论都对我们认知目的语的语言特征提出了要求,从翻译的创造性和艺术性来说,认知目的语的语言特征并在翻译中充分发挥其优势,应用其特点成为翻译的内在要求。我们对于译文在语言层面的基本要求不能仅停留在语法正确和语言规范的层面,"由于汉译外不仅仅是将中文翻译成符合语法要求的外语,更是需要翻译成符合外国人阅读习惯与表达要求的外语"(管新潮,陶友兰,2017:159),因此我们应努力探索目的语的具体语言特征,为我国的文化走出去和文学外译提供参考。语料库研究方法以及文本分析软件的出现和不断发展为我们探索并发现语言的具体特征,不断深化对语言具体特征的认知提供了有效的研究方法和强有力的研究工具。

第四章 古典小说英译的母语译者和非母语译者的定量比较研究

4.1 古典小说英译的母语译者和非母语译者的定量比较研究：方法与范式

关于学界传统所认知的母语优势已经被学界的诸多学者从文化、语用学的视角以及定性研究和定量研究分别予以论证，其在本研究的第二章节的文献综述中已经予以了详细论述。进一步发现母语译者相较于非母语译者的区别性特征，认知母语优势的具体特征，需要详细制订研究方法，确定研究的范式，进一步提高对母语译者和非母语译者的定量研究的科学性，并确保定量统计所获得数据的准确性和客观性。

4.1.1 研究目标

本章拟通过对《三国演义》的母语译者和非母语译者的英译本进行定量研究，从词汇、句子、篇章三个层面统计分析母语译者和非母语译者的风格特征，对母语译者和非母语译者的风格特征进行系统的定量描写；进一步系统地厘清母语译者相较于非母语译者的区别性特征，为提出母语优势下的汉英翻译策略奠定基础。

第四章　古典小说英译的母语译者和非母语译者的定量比较研究

4.1.2 语料库

为了在更大范围内验证母语译者的优势,探究其相较于非母语译者的区别性特征,本研究使用自建语料库,选取我国古典四大名著《三国演义》的公认的有影响力的母语译者和非母语译者的英译本为研究语料。《三国演义》是我国古典四大名著,古典小说的代表,广为流传,在我国文学尤其是小说史上具有极其重要的地位,是我国文学的经典作品。《三国演义》是元末明初罗贯中在《三国志》以及广为流传的关于三国的民间故事的基础上创作而成的,是我国第一部长篇章回体历史小说,结构宏伟,语言精湛,是我国古典历史演义小说的杰作。《三国演义》是一部历史小说,同时也是一部文化小说,因其艺术成就和文化影响力,在世界范围内尤其在东亚和东南亚地区广为流传,已经被翻译成英、法、日、俄、德等多国文字。《三国演义》描写了从东汉末年到西晋初年近100年的历史风云,描写了诸多宏伟的历史场景,涉及社会的各个方面,是一部描写了以政治军事为主的涵盖生活、文化、人文、习俗等多方面的历史画卷,内容丰富庞杂,涉及的语言描写也极为丰富。基于《三国演义》在我国文学史上的地位、小说内容所涵盖范围的广泛性和复杂性、语言描写的丰富性和高超的艺术成就,其英译对于我国古典小说以及我国古典文学的英译都具有一定的代表性,其母语译者和非母语译者的英译本对于我国考察我国古典文学英译母语译者相较于非母语译者的区别性特征也具有典型的代表性。

基于上述原因,本研究选取《三国演义》英译本的母语译者和非母语译者的公认的有影响的优秀译本为研究语料和考察对象,对其进行语料库统计分析,提取关于文本特征的数据,进行定量分析,以期发现二者的区别性特征。《三国演义》到目前为止,公认的有影响的共有3个全译本和2个节译本,全译本包括C.H. Brewitt-Taylor(邓罗)译本 Romance of the Three Kingdoms、Moss Roberts(罗慕士)译本 Three Kingdoms 和虞苏美译本 The Three Kingdoms,节译本包括杨宪益、戴乃迭节译的《三国演义》第43～50回译文和张亦文节译的第43～50回译文。

邓罗(C.H. Brewitt-Taylor,1857—1938)曾于19世纪末20世纪初担任中国海关税务司,1880年秋来到中国,1889年11月在《中国评论》上发表其译自《三国演义》第29回"小霸王怒斩于吉,碧眼儿坐领江东"的"The death of Sun Tse",开始了其《三国演义》的英译事业。之后陆续翻译了《三国演义》的一些章节,并在《中国评论》上发表,包括译自第68回"甘宁百骑劫魏营,左慈掷杯戏曹操"的"Conjuring"和节译自第8回"王司徒巧使连环计,董太师大闹凤仪亭"的"A Deep-Laid Plot and a Love Scene"。1925年,邓罗的《三国演义》英文全译本Romance of the Three Kingdoms问世,由上海别发洋行发行,这是《三国演义》的第一部英文全译本,对于《三国演义》后续的翻译和在国外的传播具有重要意义。邓罗英译本所选用的底本为毛宗岗父子点评本。现存《三国演义》主要有两个版本,一个是嘉靖本(1522年版本),即明代嘉靖元年(1522年)序列本,另一个是清代康熙年间毛纶毛宗岗父子全面整理修订之后的点评本,即毛宗岗父子点评本。嘉靖本是现存《三国演义》的最早版本,是明代嘉靖元年(1522年)序列本,题名《三国志通俗演义》,分24卷,每卷10回,共240回。毛宗岗父子点评本由毛纶毛宗岗父子于清代康熙年间对明代版本进行全面整理,修订为120回。毛宗岗父子点评本与嘉靖本相比,删去了许多历史文献信息,文字更为通俗易懂,自出现以来,"结束了以往一切旧本流传的局面,以一种崭新的定本流传后世"(郑铁生,2000:3),成为到目前为止最为流行的版本,占据了市场的主流。

莫斯·罗慕士(Moss Roberts,1937—),是美国汉学家,1937年7月出生于美国纽约的布鲁克林,于1960年在美国哥伦比亚大学英文专业硕士学位,1966年完成了其博士论文《孔子〈论语〉中形而上学的语境》(The Metaphysical Context of Confucius' Analects)获中文专业博士学位,现任纽约大学东亚系教授。罗慕士从1970年开始《三国演义》的翻译,最初翻译完成的是《三国演义》的选译本,共选译46回,于1976年由潘塞恩图书公司(Pantheon Books)出版,题名为《三国演义:中国的壮丽史诗》(Three Kingdoms: China's Epic Drama)。1983年来中国访问时,受外文出版社的邀请,开始《三国演义》全译本: Three Kingdoms: A Historical Novel 的翻译,于1991年由加利福尼亚大学出版社和外文出版社共同在美国出版,1994年由外文出版社在中国大陆首次出版。从1970年开始的选译本的翻译,到1991年全译本的出版,完成《三国演义》全译本的翻译前后共花费了罗慕士15年的时间。罗慕士翻译的《三国演义》的全译本所依据的底本也是120回本的毛宗岗

第四章　古典小说英译的母语译者和非母语译者的定量比较研究

父子点评本。除了《三国演义》之外，罗慕士还翻译了毛泽东的读书笔记《苏联经济学批判》(Critique of Soviet Economics)和《道德经》(Dao De Jing: The Book of the Way)等。《三国演义》全译本的翻译无疑是奠定其翻译成就和翻译家身份最重要的译作。罗慕士学识渊博、学养深厚，对于中国文化、文学、历史、哲学等都有一定的研究，这些都为其《三国演义》的翻译奠定了坚实的基础，也对其《三国演义》的翻译产生了深刻的影响。

虞苏美(1940—2019)是华东师范大学英语语言文学系教授，著名文学翻译家。浙江镇海人，1964年毕业于华东师范大学外语系，并留校任教。1980毕业于英国伦敦大学教育学院，获教育硕士学位。出版有多种颇具影响力的英语教材和英汉译著。虞苏美是第一位将《三国演义》全本翻译成英语的中国人，这在《三国演义》英译史上具有重要意义。其所翻译完成的《三国演义》英文全译本：The Three Kingdoms 于2014年由新加坡塔特尔出版公司(Tuttle Publishing)出版，2017年由上海外语教育出版社以英汉对照版出版。虞苏美的《三国演义》英文全译本所依据的底本也是120回本的毛宗岗父子点评本。

杨宪益(1915—2009)祖籍江苏淮安，出生于天津，是我国著名的翻译家、外国文学专家、文化史学者、诗人，是中国作协名誉顾问，中国文联委员，外文文学会、中国大百科全书编委会、红楼梦学会等学术团体主要成员，历任英文杂志《中国文学》(Chinese Literature)翻译专家、主编、顾问。1993年获香港大学名誉文学博士学位，2009年被中国翻译协会授予"翻译文化终身成就奖"。杨宪益在翻译事业上取得了巨大成就，译作甚多，影响广泛，在国内外享有盛誉。其翻译"涵盖诗词、戏剧、小说、史学等方面的著作百余部(篇)，从《诗经》到中国现当代文学，时间跨度长达两千六百多年，总计一千多万字"。(党争胜、冯正斌，2019：110)翻译的我国文学作品主要包括：《红楼梦》《聊斋志异》《儒林外史》《镜花缘》《老残游记》《魏晋南北朝小说选》《唐代传奇选》《乐府》《诗经》《楚辞》《汉魏六朝诗文选》《史记选》《资治通鉴》《唐宋诗歌散文选》《文心雕龙》《长生殿》《牡丹亭》《关汉卿杂剧选》《鲁迅选集》等。杨宪益所发起并主持的"熊猫丛书"，为我国的文学外译工作作出了重要贡献。其《红楼梦》英译：A Dream of Red Mansions 无疑是其诸多译作中最有影响的一部，到目前为止依然是《红楼梦》这部我国最伟大的古典小说之一的公认的最好的最有影响力的两部英文全译本之一,为其带来了国内外的广泛声誉。

对于我国四大古典文学名著,除了《红楼梦》之外,杨宪益还对《西游记》和《三国演义》进行了节译。对《西游记》节译了从第59回到第61回共3回的内容,对《三国演义》节译了从第43回到第50回共8回的内容。这两个节译都是杨宪益与其夫人戴乃迭合译的。《三国演义》的节译于1962年在《中国文学》第1、2期上发表,这两个节译之后都收录在《三部古典小说节译》(*Excerpts from three classical Chinese novels*)中,1981年由《中国文学》杂志社出版,中国国际图书贸易总公司出版(中国国际书店)发行。杨宪益《三国演义》的节译本所依据的底本也是120回本的毛宗岗父子点评本。

张亦文(？—)是加拿大籍华裔教授,其所翻译的《三国演义》的节译本所选取的是第43回到第50回共8回的内容,于1972年由香港文心出版社出版,1985年由中国友谊出版公司以英汉对照的形式出版发行。张亦文的节译本所依据的底本也是120回本的毛宗岗父子点评本。

本研究将分别对《三国演义》的3个英文全译本的母语译者和非母语译者的译本以及两位母语译者的英文全译本的第43～50回内容和两位非母语译者的节译本分别进行比较研究。为了研究的方便,本研究将把邓罗译本简称为邓译,罗慕士译本简称为罗译,虞苏美译本简称为虞译,节选自邓罗译本的第43～50回内容简称为邓译本(节译),节选自罗慕士译本的第43～50回内容简称为罗译本(节译),杨宪益、戴乃迭节译的《三国演义》第43～50回译文简称为杨译本(节译),张亦文节译的《三国演义》第43～50回译文简称为张译本(节译)。

4.1.3 语料库工具与统计方法

本研究采用3款语料库工具:用于语料词性标注的TreeTagger for Windows 3.0,用于语料统计分析的Wconcord和PowerConc 1.0 beta 25b。TreeTagger和PowerConc 1.0 beta 25b均是由北京外国语大学开发的绿色免费软件。语料标注软件主要用于建库前对语料进行词性标注,语料库统计软件主要用来对语料库进行研究目的所需的数据统计。

第四章 古典小说英译的母语译者和非母语译者的定量比较研究

4.1.4 研究方法与步骤

学界传统所认知的母语优势是一种基于翻译长期的实践历史的经验在某种程度上被学界的诸多学者从文化视角、语用学视角以及定性和定量的实证研究分别予以论证。要进一步验证翻译中的母语优势,并探究母语译者相较于非母语译者的区别性特征,需要进一步扩大研究范围,使用语料库方法,全面系统地对研究语料进行统计分析,以期验证和探究母语优势及其特征。

使用语料库方法对母语优势进行研究是使用定量分析和定性分析相结合的方法,通过对母语译者和非母语译者的译文特征进行定量的统计分析,依据二者相关数据的差异性和显著性,结合使用相关理论对母语优势以及母语译者相较于非母语译者的区别性特征进行归纳总结,进而在此基础上探究母语优势下的汉英翻译策略。

使用语料库方法进行研究最显著的特征就是使用语料库以及语料库工具进行定量的统计分析,并结合定性分析获得相关结论。语料库方法相较于以往的翻译研究方法,增强了结论的科学性和客观性,有效避免了传统翻译研究的感悟式、印象式的主观性和个案描写、主观哲学思辨的片面性。使用语料库方法进行研究不仅基于较大规模的语言事实——语料库,而且基于语料库统计工具对文本统计所获得的翔实的数据上,有效保证了其所得出结论的科学性和客观性。基于语料库翻译研究的基本特征:自上而下和自下而上相结合以及多层次的描写和多维度的阐释并重,本研究采用的基本研究步骤为:定向观察、定量分析和统计、定性阐释。

定向观察:基于学界传统所认知的母语优势的假设,《三国演义》的母语译者的英译本 Moss Roberts(罗慕士)译本 *Three Kingdoms* 和非母语译者的英译本杨宪益、戴乃迭节译的《三国演义》第43~50回译文和张亦文节译的第43~50回译文分别进行文本细读、整体观察和母语译者和非母语译者译本的鉴赏比较,以期发现和捕捉两者之间的差异性特征,形成初步假设,为下一步的定量统计分析奠定基础。

定量统计和分析:依据定向观察所形成的初步假设的基础上,创建研究语料库,并根据假设对语料库进行定量统计,获取研究语料的文本特征所需的相关数据。具体来说,就是创建《三国演义》中文原文以及母语译者和非母语译者的英译本的语料库,杨宪益、戴乃迭节译的《三国演义》第 43～50 回译文和张亦文节译《三国演义》的第 43～50 回译文。同时把所创建的研究语料库处理成为语料库统计软件可识别的电子版本,并进行降噪处理和词性标注,为后续的语料库软件统计分析奠定基础。本研究将使用词性标注软件对研究语料进行词性标注,语料库统计分析软件 Wconcord 对研究语料进行形符、类符、主体词、累计词频、平均句长等项目的数据统计,使用 PowerConc 对研究语料进行关键词、高频词、特色词、独特词,以及句式结构和篇章层面的特征项目进行数据统计,获取相关文本的数据特征,并以所获取的数据为基础对研究语料进行定量分析。定量分析所获得的各研究语料的各个层面的数据是各研究语料的文本特征的数据体现。语料文本特征的数据特征反映了文本的风格特征,同一源语文本的不同译者的译文其风格特征的差异由其词汇使用的用词、词频、分布、排列组合以及句式的结构等来决定和体现的。母语译者和非母语译者各自在文本统计的数据上的特征反映了各自文本的风格特征,基于此,就可以探究发现母语优势下母语译者相较于非母语译者的区别性特征。

定性阐释:语料库翻译研究是使用语料库的方法进行翻译研究的一种翻译研究范式。语料库方法为翻译研究提供了基于语料库和语料库技术的定量研究的方法,为语料库翻译研究的实证性、科学性和客观性奠定了基础,但语料库翻译研究并不排斥定性研究的方法,相反,语料库翻译研究需要定性的质性研究为定量研究的数据提供定性的阐释。定量分析与定性分析两者相辅相成、互为支撑。对语料进行统计分析所得的数据特征需要进行定性分析的阐释,以论述描写语料的数据特征所反映的文本的质性特征。同时,语料库翻译学的多层次的描写和多视角的阐释并重的特征要求对定量研究的数据或事实所反映的翻译规律进行解释,并探索其成因。基于此,对研究语料进行定量研究和定性研究相结合的分析之后,需要对非母语译者特征的成因进行分析探究,进而提出母语优势下的汉英翻译策略。对于研究语料进行定性分析将在本研究的第五章进行,对于非母语译者特征的成因分析以及探究母语优势下的汉英翻译策略将在本研究的第六章进行。

第四章 古典小说英译的母语译者和非母语译者的定量比较研究

4.2 词汇层面

　　词汇在语言中的重要性不言而喻,其是构成短语、句子和篇章的基本单位,也是构成意义的基本单位。关于词汇的重要论述见于语言学、翻译学等各类著作中。词汇是语言的基本要素之一,有其自身复杂的精密结构,构成语言的一个组织层面。人类思维离不开概念,而概念的语言形式主要表现为词汇(汪榕培、王之江,2008:5)。词汇是体现文本风格和特征的重要因素,词汇的使用风格和特征是文本风格和特征的重要指标。文本是作者个体创作或译者个体的翻译创造活动的产物,就文本创作而言,文本的词汇特征体现的是作者个体的语言使用风格和特征,是作者个体的创作能力、文化素养、思想倾向、意识形态、语言能力和使用习惯等因素综合所形成的写作风格的结果;就译者翻译而言,译文的词汇特征体现的是译者个体的翻译风格和语言使用特征,是译者个体的翻译能力和素养、翻译策略、翻译风格、思想倾向性、意识形态、语言使用的风格、思维模式和母语文化等因素综合所形成的译者风格的具体表现。就母语译者和非母语译者而言,二者在思维模式和母语文化的不同,应该在译文的词汇层面有所体现和反映,母语译者的母语优势应该在译文的词汇层面有所体现和反映。

　　基于此,母语译者译文的高频词、关键词、特色词与非母语译者的译文相比,应该有一定的差异。母语译者译文的词汇特征体现和反映的不仅是译者的整体风格,更为重要的是母语译者译文的高频词、关键词、特色词应该体现和反映母语译者的思维模式和翻译文化观。

　　本章拟通过使用 PowerConc 和 Wconcord 等语料库分析软件对《三国演义》两位母语译者和一位非母语译者的全译本,以及《三国演义》从第43回到第50回共8回的两位母语译者和两位非母语译者的节译本在词汇、句子、篇章等层面进行统计分析和比较研究,考察我国古典小说英译中母语译者相较于非母语译者在词汇、句子、篇章等层面的差异,以期发现母语译者相较于非母语译者的区别性特征,为探究非母语译者的特征成因以及母语优势下的汉英翻译策略提供数据支撑，从而为我国的文化走出去，尤其是古典小说的文学外译提供翻译策略方面的原则指导和参考奠定基础。

4.2.1 形符

表1.《三国演义》三个英文全译本形符类符

	邓译本	罗译本	虞译本
形符数	594696	549417	591730
类符数	14209	16163	13785

表2.《三国演义》四个英文节译本形符类符

	邓译本	罗译本	杨译本	张译本
形符数	36476	33202	30099	32474
类符数	4231	4789	3211	3839

形符数(tokens)指一个文本内所有单词的总和，形符数的大小反映了文本的单词总数的大小。就特定文本的译本来说，形符数的大小反映了译文所使用的词汇总量以及译文文本的长度。形符数的大小无疑与译者的风格密切相关，很大程度上受译者风格的影响。不同的译者基于对于原文的理解的不同，尤其是文学作品原文的精神内涵和风格上的细腻微妙之处的鉴赏和体验上的差异，以及在翻译过程中译者如何使用目的语对其所理解的原文的精神内涵和风格上的细腻微妙之处进行再现便会呈现出不同的表现和差异。这些不同的译者基于其不同翻译风格以及其他各种因素的制约和影响，对同一原作的不同的处理方法表现为译文在词汇、句式以及篇章等层面的不同，有些表现不明显，有些表现比较明显。影响译文风格的因素还包括文化语境、政治因素、时代因素、出版社以及赞助商等。但这些因素当中，起主要作用的因素应该是译者自身因素，包括译者的翻译风格以及所采取的翻译策略、文化的倾向性等。就母语译者和非母语译者来说，各自的思维模式对其译文的风格特征也具有重要影响。下面本研究将从形符数的视角来对母语译者和非母语译者的译文进行比较分析。

从《三国演义》三个英文全译本的形符数的统计来看，我们可以发

第四章　古典小说英译的母语译者和非母语译者的定量比较研究

现邓译本的形符数为594696,罗译本的形符数为549417,虞译本的形符数为591730。三位译者的形符数基本相当,差异不大。尤其是邓译本和虞译本基本接近,邓译本只比虞译本多2966,就总数为接近60万的译文来说,不到3000的单词数所占比例比较小。罗译本与虞译本相比,其形符数则少了4万多,数量差异还是比较明显的,在一定程度上反映了两位译者翻译风格上的差异。

从《三国演义》四个英文节译本的形符数的统计来看,我们可以发现邓译本(节译)的形符数为36849,罗译本(节译)的形符数为33866,杨译本(节译)的形符数为26206,张译本(节译)的形符数为32587。四位译者的形符数的差异还是比较明显的。尤其是邓译本(节译)与杨译本(节译)和张译本(节译)相比,其形符数明显要大于其他两位。邓译本(节译)的形符数比杨译本(节译)的形符数多10643,比张译本(节译)的形符数多4262;罗译本(节译)的形符数比杨译本(节译)的多7660,比张译本(节译)的多1279。

从表1和表2的统计来看,母语译者和非母语译者在形符数方面并不存在明显差异,即译者在形符数方面的差异并不是绝对由译者的母语译者或非母语译者的文化身份来决定,既存在母语译者的形符数低于非母语译者的情况,也存在非母语译者的形符数低于母语译者的情况。

但从总体上来看,不论从《三国演义》的全译本来考察,还是从《三国演义》的节译本来考察,两位母语译者的形符数总体上都比较多,三位非母语译者的形符数既有多也有少。《三国演义》英文全译本的两位母语译者的译文,其中一位的形符数比非母语译者的多,另一位的形符数比非母语译者的形符数少;但一个显著的特征是三位译者的形符数都比较多,并不存在某位译者的形符数显著偏少的特征;《三国演义》英文节译本的两位母语译者的形符数比两位非母语译者的形符数要多,而且差异比较显著。从《三国演义》英文节译本的四位译者的译文来看,母语译者的形符数大于非母语译者的形符数是母语译者和非母语译者之间的一个显著差异。

如果再以译本所产生的时间顺序来考察,我们可以发现,杨译本由杨宪益、戴乃迭夫妇翻译完成的,并于1962年刊载于《中国文学》第1、2月号,可以肯定,杨译本最晚于1962年翻译完成(陈琳,2016:46);张译本由张亦文翻译完成,于1972年由香港文心出版社发行,由此也可以肯定张译本最晚于1972年翻译完成；虞译本是由虞苏美翻译完成，2014年由新加坡塔特尔出版公司（Tuttle Publishing）出版，2017年由上海外语教育出版社发行，由此也可以肯定虞译本最晚于2014年翻译完成；邓译本由邓罗翻译完成，于1925年由上海别发洋行发行，由此可以肯定邓译本最晚于1925年翻译完成，事实上，邓译本的全文英译稿曾经顺利完成，但在义和团运动中遭毁（Cannon，2009：154）；罗译本由罗慕士翻译完成，其从1970年就开始了《三国演义》的相关翻译，经过十几年努力完成全译本的翻译，并于1991年在英国出版发行。

在包括全译本和节译本在内的5个译本中，虞译本是最晚出现的，其翻译有可能对其他4个译本进行了借鉴，尤其是从两位母语译者的全译本中借鉴了母语译者的某些翻译方法和策略，同时，作为非母语译者对于杨译本和张译本两位非母语译者的译本的某些非母语译者的特征可以进行避免。此外，在从1925年《三国演义》的第一部全译本出版发行到2017年的近百年的时间里，尤其是随着我国翻译事业的发展与繁荣，我国的翻译理论研究和实践也不断发展与进步，进一步推动了我国译者在汉英翻译实践方面的发展，所以我国译者所完成的汉籍英译的译文出现某些母语译者在母语优势下的某些特征便成为可能。我国译者汉籍英译所呈现的这一特征也与潘文国教授在其《译入与译出——谈中国译者从事汉籍英译的意义》一文中在论及我国译者的汉籍英译的译文质量时所提出的随着国内译者在翻译领域的不断探索和翻译事业的发展，我国译者的译作质量在不断提高的论断相吻合。

基于以上对《三国演义》的全译本和节译本的母语译者和非母语译者的译本的形符数的统计和比较分析，我们可以认为特定文本的译文的形符数的多少并非取决于译者的文化身份，但一般来说，母语译者译文的形符数具有较强的倾向性，非母语译者译文的形符数具有较少的倾向性。这只是基于《三国演义》的母语译者和非母语译者的两个全译本和三个节译本以及《红楼梦》的母语译者和非母语译者的两个全译本作为参照所得出的结论。

《三国演义》英译的母语译者形符数相较于非母语译者较高的特征也可以从散文英译中得到佐证。本研究选取流传广泛的朱自清的经典散文《匆匆》《荷塘月色》《背影》的母语译者和非母语译者的英译为参照语料。《匆匆》的英译包括葛浩文译文、张培基译文、朱纯深译文和张梦井译文；《荷塘月色》的英译包括葛浩文译文、朱纯深译文、杨宪益译

第四章 古典小说英译的母语译者和非母语译者的定量比较研究

文和徐英才译文；《背影》的英译包括葛浩文译文、杨宪益译文、徐英才译文和张培基译文。为了研究的方便，本研究把葛浩文的《匆匆》《荷塘月色》《背影》的译文简称为葛译；徐英才的《荷塘月色》和《背影》的译文以及《匆匆》的张梦井译文统称为徐译；杨宪益的《荷塘月色》和《背影》的译文以及《匆匆》的张培基译文统称为杨译；朱纯深的《匆匆》和《荷塘月色》的译文以及《背影》的张培基译文统称为朱译。本研究使用 Wconcord 对《匆匆》《背影》《荷塘月色》的葛译和其他四位中国译者的英译本分别进行了统计，其结果如表 3 和表 4 所示。

表 3. 朱自清散文英译语料情况

原文(单位：字)		译文(单位：词)			
		葛译	徐译	杨译	朱译
《匆匆》	544	480	439	475	463
《荷塘月色》	1184	1218	1126	942	1100
《背影》	1141	1254	1150	978	1131
合计	2869	2952	2715	2395	2694

表 4. 朱自清散文英译总体用词情况

译文	形符数	类符数
葛译	2934	945
徐译	2694	899
杨译	2368	812
朱译	2675	905

形符数和类符数是反映译文特征的两个重要指标。根据 Wconcord 的统计，《匆匆》《背影》和《荷塘月色》的葛译形符数为 2934，类符数为 945；徐译的形符数为 2694，类符数为 899；杨译的形符数为 2368，类符数为 812；朱译的形符数为 2675，类符数为 905。《匆匆》《背影》《荷塘月色》原文的形符数为 2872，类符数为 737。

从以上统计结果来看，葛译的形符数和类符数的数据最大。形符数体现的是文本的长度，类符数体现的是文本的词汇丰富程度。形符数越高，说明文本字数越多，文本越长，反之亦然；类符数越高，说明文本词汇越丰富，反之亦然。一般来说，由于汉语注重意合，英语注重形合，汉译英的文本要比汉语原文本要长。我们发现葛译的形符数体现了这一特征,其形符数要多于其他三位译者,分别比徐译、杨译和朱译高出240,566和259。与原文2872的总形符数相比,葛译与徐译、杨译和朱译的形符数差异比较显著。

同时,徐译、杨译和朱译的形符数少于原文的形符数,分别比原文低178,504和197,与原文的形符数相比,差异比较显著。徐译和朱译的形符数相差不大,杨译的形符数最少。这表明从形符数的视角来看,三位译者的译文与通常的汉译英的文本要比原文长的情况不同。下面结合具体例句来看。

例1:

原文:这几天心里颇不宁静。今晚在院子里坐着乘凉,忽然想起日日走过的荷塘,在这满月的光里,总该另有一番样子吧。(46字)

葛译: These past few days I have been exceedingly restless. This evening, as I sat in my courtyard enjoying the cool night air, I suddenly thought of the lotus pond along which I was used to taking daily walks, and I imagined that it must look quite different under the light of this full moon.(54词)

徐译: I feel very restless these days. Tonight, while I sit in our yard and enjoy the cool air, it strikes me that the lotus pool that I pass by every day must look different under this full moon.(38词)

杨译: The last few days have found me very restless. This evening as I sat in the yard to enjoy the cool, it struck me how different the lotus pool I pass every day must look under a full moon.(39词)

朱译: I have felt quite upset recently. Tonight, when I was sitting in the yard enjoying the cool, it occurred to me that the Lotus Pond, which I pass by every day, must assume quite a different look in such moonlit night.(41词)

四位译者的译文都是公认的经典译文,从内容到风格都是佳译典范。但我们进一步研究会发现,四位译者的译文还是存在一定差异的。不论从字数、用词,还是句式结构上,葛译与其他三位译者都存在一定差异,而其他三位译者则在这几方面都大体相似。首先来看其他三位译者的译文,侧重于对内容和意义的忠实,译文是以原文的内容和意义为主线展开的。所以,在译文的字数、用词和句式结构上,三位译者大体相似。葛译恰当的用词和句式的灵活构造使葛译在准确再现原文意义的

第四章　古典小说英译的母语译者和非母语译者的定量比较研究

基础上,行文更加流畅,对于原文的口吻和节奏的再现更为充实、饱满和细腻,整体上使译文更为自然和地道。相比较而言,其他三位译者的译文则略显拘谨。葛译与其他三位译者这一翻译风格的差异与我们所统计的形符数和类符数的差异相一致。

葛浩文作为母语译者和其他三位作为非母语译者在形符数方面的差异佐证了母语译者形符数较高的特征,这一特征也可以我国的经典文学名著《红楼梦》的两个英译本得到佐证。霍克斯译本和杨宪益译本是迄今为止公认的成就最高,最有影响力的两个译本。笔者使用 PowerConc 对霍克斯译本和杨宪益译本分别进行统计发现,同样是母语译者和非母语译者,霍克斯译本的形符数为 849200,远多于杨宪益译本的 643724。这说明母语译者和非母语译者在形符数方面的差异并不是偶然现象。下面是参照语料《红楼梦》霍译和杨译以及《三国演义》英译的相关例子。

例 2:.

原文(霍译蓝本):宝玉看见袭人两眼微红,粉光融滑,因悄问袭人道:"好好的哭什么?"袭人笑道:"谁哭来着?才迷了眼揉的。"因此便遮掩过了。因见宝玉穿着大红金蟒狐腋箭袖,外罩石青貂裘排穗褂,说道:"你特为往这里来,又换新衣裳,他们就不问你往哪里去吗?"宝玉道:"原是珍大爷请过去看戏换的。"袭人点头,又道:"坐一坐就回去罢,这个地方儿不是你来的。"宝玉笑道:"你就家去才好呢,我还替你留着好东西呢。"袭人笑道:"悄悄儿的罢!叫他们听着做什么?"一面伸手从宝玉项上将通灵玉摘下来,向他妹妹们笑道:"你们见识见识。时常说起来都当稀罕,恨不能一见,今儿可尽力儿瞧瞧。再瞧什么稀罕物儿,也不过是这么着了。"说毕递与他们,传看了一遍,仍与宝玉挂好。又命他哥哥去雇一辆干干净净、严严紧紧的车,送宝玉回去。花自芳道:"有我送去,骑马也不妨了。"袭人道:"不为不妨,为的是碰见人。"花自芳忙去雇了一辆车来,众人也不好相留,只得送宝玉出去。袭人又抓些果子给茗烟,又把些钱给他买花爆放,叫他:"别告诉人,连你也有不是。"一面说着,一直送宝玉至门前,看着上车,放下车帘。茗烟二人牵马跟随。来至宁府街,茗烟命住车,向花自芳道:"须得我和二爷还到东府里混一混,才过去得呢,看大家疑惑。"花自芳听说有理,忙将宝玉抱下车来,送上马去。宝玉笑说:"倒难为你了。"于是仍进了后门来,俱不在话下。(568 字)

· 49 ·

原文(杨译蓝本)：宝玉看见袭人两眼微红，粉光融滑，因悄问袭人："好好的哭什么？"袭人笑道："何尝哭，才迷了眼揉的。"因此便遮掩过了。当下宝玉穿着大红金蟒狐腋箭袖，外罩石青貂裘排穗褂。袭人道："你特为往这里来又换新服，他们就不问你往哪去的？"宝玉笑道："珍大爷那里去看戏换的。"袭人点头。又道："坐一坐就回去罢，这个地方不是你来的。"宝玉笑道："你就家去才好呢，我还替你留着好东西呢。"袭人悄笑道："悄悄的，叫他们听着什么意思。"一面又伸手从宝玉项上将通灵玉摘了下来，向他姊妹们笑道："你们见识见识。时常说起来都当希罕，恨不能一见，今儿可尽力瞧了。再瞧什么稀罕物儿，也不过是这么个东西。"说毕，递与他们传看了一遍，仍与宝玉挂好。又命他哥哥去或雇一乘小轿，或雇一辆小车，送宝玉回去。花自芳道："有我送去，骑马也不妨了。"袭人道："不为不妨，为的是碰见人。"花自芳忙去雇了一顶小轿来，众人也不敢相留，只得送宝玉出去，袭人又抓果子与茗烟，又把些钱与他买花炮放，教他"不可告诉人，连你也有不是。"一直送宝玉至门前，看着上轿，放下轿帘。花，茗二人牵马跟随。来至宁府街，茗烟命住轿，向花自芳道："须等我同二爷还到东府里混一混，才好过去的，不然人家就疑惑了。"花自芳听说有理，忙将宝玉抱出轿来，送上马去。宝玉笑说："倒难为你了。"于是仍进后门来。俱不在话下。（562字）

霍译：Baoyu noticed that Aroma's eyes were slightly red and that there were recent tear-stains on her powdered cheeks.

"Why have you been crying?" He spoke the words in an undertone as she handed him the pine nuts.

"Who's been crying?" said Aroma with a feigned laugh. "I've just been rubbing my eyes"

Her little fiction was successful, for he made no further comment.

Baoyu was wearing his dark-red gown with the pattern of golden dragons and white fox-fur lining, and a sable-lined slate-blue jacket with fringed edges.

"Fancy!" said Aroma, "you got yourself all dressed up just to come and see us. Didn't anyone ask you where you were going?"

"No," said Baoyu. "Actually I changed because I was going to Cousin Zhen's. He invited me over to watch the players." Aroma nodded.

第四章　古典小说英译的母语译者和非母语译者的定量比较研究

"You'd better go back after you've sat a bit longer," she said. "This is really no place for you here." "You shouldn't be too long, either," said Baoyu with a smile. "I've got something nice waiting for you when you get back"

"Sh!" said Aroma. "Do you want them all to hear you?"

As she said this, she reached out and took the Magic Jade from his neck.

"Here's something that will interest you all," she said, holding it out to the others. "You know how often you've spoken about that wonderful lade of Master Bao's and said how much you'd give for a look at it? Well, here it is! Now you can look to your heart's content. There you are, that's all it is! Not so wonderful, really, is it?"

They passed it from hand to hand, and when it had gone full circle and all had examined it, she hung it once more round his neck. Aroma told her elder brother to go out and hire the cleanest, smartest looking cab he could find to take Baoyu home in.

"I can see him safely back," said Hua Zi-fang. "He won't come to any harm on horseback."

"It's not a question of whether he'll come to any harm or not," said Aroma, " I'm afraid someone might see him."

Hua Zi-fang hurried out to hire a cab. The rest of the company, realizing that Baoyu had no real business to be there, made no effort to detain him and rose to see him off. Aroma snatched up a handful of sweetmeats for Tealeaf. She also gave him a few coppers to buy fireworks with.

"Mind you don't tell anyone about this visit!" she said. "You'll be in trouble yourself if they find out about it."

She escorted Baoyu to the gate and saw him into the cab, pulling the blind down on him as soon as he was inside. Tealeaf and her brother followed behind it with the horse. When they arrived outside the Ning-guo mansion, Tealeaf told the cabbie to stop.

"We'd better go in here for a bit before going home," he explained to Aroma's brother. "Otherwise they might get suspicious."

Hua Zi-fang acknowledged the sense of this precaution, and lifting Baoyu from the cab, helped him up on to his horse.

"Thank you for your trouble," said Baoyu with a winning smile as he rode into the rear gate of the Ning-guo mansion.

And there, for the time being, we shall leave him. (550 词)

杨译: He noticed that her eyes were red and there were traces of tears on her powdered cheeks. "Why have you been crying?" he whispered.

"Who's been crying?" she retorted cheerfully. "I've just been rubbing my eyes." In this way she glossed the matter over.

Xiren saw that Baoyu was wearing his red archer's tunic embroidered with golden dragons and lined with fox-fur under a fringed bluish-grey sable coat. "Surely you didn't change into these new clothes just to come here?" she said. "Did no one ask where you were going?"

"No, I changed to go to Cousin Zhen's to watch some operas."

She nodded. "Well, after a short rest you'd better go back. This is no place for you.

"I wish you'd come home now," coaxed Baoyu. "I've kept something good for you."

"Hush!" she whispered. "What will the others think if they hear?" She reached out to take the magic jade from his neck and turning to her cousins said with a smile, "Look! Here's the wonderful thing that you've heard so much about. You've always wanted to see this rarity. Now's your chance for a really good look. There's nothing so very special about it, is there?"

After passing the jade around for their inspection she fastened it on Baoyu's neck again, then asked her brother to hire a sedan-chair or a small carriage and escort Baoyu home.

"I can see him back quite safely on horseback," said Zifang.

"That's not the point. I'm afraid of his meeting someone."

Then Zifang hurried out to hire a sedan-chair, and not daring to detain Baoyu they saw him out. Xiren gave Mingyan some sweetmeats

第四章 古典小说英译的母语译者和非母语译者的定量比较研究

and money to buy firecrackers, warning him that he must keep this visit secret if he wanted to steer clear of trouble. She saw Baoyu out of the gate, watched him get into the chair and lowered its curtains. Her brother and Mingyan followed behind with the horse.

When they reached the street where the Ning Mansion stood, Mingyan ordered the chair to stop and told Zifang, "We must look in here for a while before going home, if we don't want people to suspect anything."

Since this made good sense, Zifang handed Baoyu out and helped him to mount his horse, while the boy apologized for troubling him. Then they slipped through the back gate, and there we will leave them. (396词)

例3：

原文：司徒杨彪曰："关中残破零落；今无故捐宗庙，弃皇陵，恐百姓惊动；天下动之至易，安之至难。望丞相鉴察。"卓怒曰："汝阻国家大计耶？"太尉黄琬曰："杨司徒之言是也。往者王莽篡逆，更始赤眉之时，焚烧长安，尽为瓦砾之地；更兼人民流移，百无一二。今弃宫室而就荒地，非所宜也。"卓曰："关东贼起，天下播乱。长安有崤函之险；更近陇右，木石砖瓦，克日可办，宫室营造，不须月馀。汝等再休乱言。"司徒荀爽谏曰："丞相若欲迁都，百姓骚动不宁矣。"卓大怒曰："吾为天下计，岂惜小民哉！"即日罢杨彪、黄琬、荀爽为庶民。（245字）

邓译：Yang Biao, Minister of the Interior, said, "I pray you reflect. The Land Within the Passes is all destruction. There is no reason to renounce the ancestral temples and abandon the imperial tombs here. I fear the people will be alarmed. It is easy to alarm them but difficult to pacify them." "Do you oppose the state plans?" said Dong Zhuo angrily. Another official, Grand Commander Huang Wan, supported his colleague, "In the era of Recommencement (AD 23-25), Fan Chong of the Red Eyebrows rebels burned Changan to the ground and reduced the place to broken tiles. The inhabitants scattered all but a few. It is wrong to abandon these palaces here for a wasteland." Dong Zhuo replied, "The East of the Passes is full of sedition, and all the empire is in rebellion. The city of Changan is protected by the Yaohan

Mountains and the Hangu Pass. Moreover, it is near Longyou, whence can be easily brought timber, stone, brick, and building materials. In a month or so palaces can be erected. So an end to your wild words!" Yet Minister of Works Xun Shuang raised another protest against disturbing the people, but Dong Zhuo overbore him also. "How can I stop to consider a few common people when my scheme affects the empire?" said Dong Zhuo. "A Han on the west, a Han on the east. The deer (emperor) in Changan shall worry least." That day the three objectors — Yang Biao, Huang Wan, and Xun Shuang — were removed from their offices and reduced to the rank of commoners. (263 词）

罗译: Minister of the Interior Yang Biao objected: "The whole Guanzhong region is devastated. We will throw the common people into panic if we abandon the imperial family temples and mausoleums here for no good reason. It is easy enough to disturb the peace of the realm; nothing is harder than preserving it. I only hope that the prime minister will reflect carefully." Angrily, Dong Zhuo shot back, "Are you going to stand in the way of the dynasty's plan for survival?" Grand Commandant Huang Wan said, "I agree with Minister of the Interior Yang. At the end of Wang Mang's usurpation, in the reign period Recommencement [Geng Shi, A. D. 23-25], the Red Eyebrow rebels burned Chang'an, reducing the city to rubble. After the exodus, of every hundred inhabitants only one or two remained. So I would question the wisdom of abandoning this city of palaces and dwellings for a wasteland." To this objection Dong Zhuo replied, "Here, east of the land within the passes, rebellion is rife. Anarchy is loose in the land. Chang'an, however, is well protected by the forbidding Yao Mountains and Hangu Pass. What's more, it is close to the region west of the Longyou Hills, where timber, stone, brick, and tile are readily obtainable. A new palace shouldn't take more than a month to construct—so enough of your absurd arguments." At this point Minister of Works Xun Shuang also protested: "If the capital is moved, the population will be thrown into commotion." "I am planning for an empire!" Zhuo bellowed. "I can't be bothered about the ruck." That

第四章　古典小说英译的母语译者和非母语译者的定量比较研究

day he deprived the three critics of rank, reducing them to commoner status.（278 词）

虞译: Three high-ranking officials voiced their opposition to the move, saying that the city of Chang'an had been burned down during a previous rebellion and that it would not be right to abandon the imperial tombs and ancestral temples. They also argued that the move would alarm the people so greatly that it would be difficult to pacify them again. But Dong Zhuo paid no heed to any of them and that day all three were stripped of their official ranks and reduced to common folk.（85 词）

例 4：

原文：众诸侯内有济北相鲍信，寻思孙坚既为前部，怕他夺了头功，暗拨其弟鲍忠，先将马步军三千，径抄小路，直到关下搦战。华雄引铁骑五百，飞下关来，大喝："贼将休走！"鲍忠急待退，被华雄手起刀落，斩于马下，生擒将校极多。华雄遣人赍鲍忠首级，来相府报捷。卓加雄为都督。

却说孙坚引四将直至关前。哪四将？第一个，右北平土垠人，姓程名普，字德谋，使一条铁脊蛇矛；第二个，姓黄名盖，字公覆，零陵人也，使铁鞭；第三个，姓韩名当，字义公，辽西令支人也，使一口大刀；第四个，姓祖名茂，字大荣，吴郡富春人也，使双刀。孙坚披烂银铠，裹赤帻，横古锭刀，骑花鬃马，指关上而骂曰："助恶匹夫，何不早降？"华雄副将胡轸引兵五千，出关迎战。程普飞马挺矛，直取胡轸。斗不数合，程普刺中胡轸咽喉，死于马下。坚挥军直杀至关前，关上矢石如雨。孙坚引兵回至梁东屯住，使人于袁绍处报捷，就于袁术处催粮。

或说术曰："孙坚乃江东猛虎，若打破洛阳，杀了董卓，正是除狼而得虎也。今不与粮，彼军必散。"术听之，不发粮草。孙坚军缺食，军中自乱。细作报上关来。李肃为华雄谋曰："今夜我引一军，从小路下关，袭孙坚寨后；将军击其前寨：坚可擒矣。"雄从之，传令军士饱餐，乘夜下关。

是夜月白风清。到坚寨时，已是半夜，鼓噪直进。坚慌忙披挂上马，正遇华雄。双马相交，斗不数合，后面李肃军到，竟天价放起火来。坚军乱窜，众将各自混战，止有祖茂跟定孙坚，突围而走。背后华雄追来。坚取箭，连放两箭，皆被华雄躲过。再放第三箭时，因用力太猛，拽折了

· 55 ·

鹊画弓，只得弃弓纵马而奔。祖茂曰："主公头上赤帻射目，为贼所识认，可脱帻与某戴之。"坚就脱帻换茂盔，分两路而走。雄军只望赤帻者追赶，坚乃从小路得脱。祖茂被华雄追急，将赤帻挂于人家烧不尽的庭柱上，却入树林潜躲。华雄军于月下遥见赤帻，四面围定，不敢近前，用箭射之，方知是计，遂向前取了赤帻。祖茂于林后杀出，挥双刀欲劈华雄；雄大喝一声，将祖茂一刀砍于马下。杀至天明，雄方引兵上关。

程普、黄盖、韩当都来寻见孙坚，再收拾军马屯扎。坚为折了茂，伤感不已，星夜遣人报知袁绍。绍大惊曰："不想孙文台败于华雄之手。"便聚众诸侯商议。众人都到，只有公孙瓒后至，绍请入帐列坐。绍曰："前日鲍将军之弟不遵调遣，擅自进兵，杀身丧命，折了许多军士；今者孙文台又败于华雄：挫动锐气，为之奈何？"诸侯并皆不语。绍举目遍视，见公孙瓒背后立着三人，容貌异常，都在那里冷笑。绍问曰："公孙太守背后何人？"瓒呼玄德出曰："此吾自幼同舍兄弟，平原令刘备是也。"曹操曰："莫非破黄巾刘玄德乎？"瓒曰："然。"即令刘玄德拜见。瓒将玄德功劳，并其出身，细说一遍。绍曰："既是汉室宗派，取坐来。"命坐，备逊谢。绍曰："吾非敬汝名爵，吾敬汝是帝室之胄耳。"玄德乃坐于末位，关、张叉手侍立于后。（1147字）

邓译：Among the feudal lords, Bao Xin, the Lord of Jibei, was jealous lest the chosen Van Leader Sun Jian should win too great honors. Wherefore Bao Xin endeavored to meet the foe first, and so he secretly dispatched his brother, Bao Zhong, with three thousand by a bye road. As soon as this small force reached the Pass, they offered battle.

Fast reacting, Hua Xiong at the head of five hundred armored horsemen swept down from the Pass, crying, "Flee not, rebel!" But Bao Zhong was afraid and turned back. Hua Xiong came on, his arm rose, the sword fell, and Bao Zhong was cut down from his horse. Most of Bao Zhong's company were captured. Bao Zhong's head was sent to the Prime Minister's palace. Hua Xiong was promoted to Commander-in-Chief. Sun Jian presently approached the Pass. He had four generals: Cheng Pu of Tuyin whose weapon was an iron-spined lance with snake-headed blade; Huang Gai of Lingling who wielded an iron whip; Han Dang of Lingzhi using a heavy saber; and Zu Mao of Wujun who fought with a pair of swords. Commander Sun Jian wore a

第四章 古典小说英译的母语译者和非母语译者的定量比较研究

helmet of fine silver wrapped round with a purple turban. He carried across his body his sword of ancient ingot iron and rode a dappled horse with flowing mane. Sun Jian advanced to the Pass and hailed the defenders, crying, "Helpers of a villain! Be quick to surrender!"

Hua Xiong bade Hu Zhen lead five thousand out against Sun Jian. Cheng Pu with the snaky lance rode out from Sun Jian's side and engaged. After a very few bouts, Cheng Pu killed Hu Zhen on the spot by a thrust through the throat. Then Sun Jian gave the signal for the main army to advance. But from the Pass, Hua Xiong's troops rained down showers of stones, which proved too much for the assailants, and they retired into camp at Liangdong. Sun Jian sent the report of victory to Yuan Shao. Sun Jian also sent an urgent message for supplies to the commissary. But a counselor said to the Controller Yuan Shu, "This Sun Jian is a very tiger in the east. Should he take the capital and destroy Dong Zhuo, we should have a tiger in place of a wolf. Do not send him grain. Starve his troops, and that will decide the fate of that army."

And Yuan Shu gave ears to the detractor and sent no grain or forage. Soon Sun Jian's hungry soldiers showed their disaffection by indiscipline, and the spies bore the news to the defenders of the Pass. Li Su made a plot with Hua Xiong, saying, "We will launch tonight a speedy attack against Sun Jian in front and rear so that we can capture him." Hua Xiong agreed and prepared for the attack. So the soldiers of the attacking force were told off and given a full meal. At dark they left the Pass and crept by secret paths to the rear of Sun Jian's camp. The moon was bright and the wind cool. They arrived about midnight and the drums beat an immediate attack. Sun Jian hastily donned his fighting gear and rode out. He ran straight into Hua Xiong and the two warriors engaged. But before they had exchanged many passes, Li Su's army came up from behind and set fire to whatever would burn.

Sun Jian's army were thrown into confusion and fled in disorder. A melee ensued, and soon only Zu Mao was left at Sun Jian's side. These two broke through the Pass and fled. Hua Xiong coming in hot pursuit, Sun Jian took his bow and let fly two arrows in quick succession, but both missed. He fitted a third arrow to the string, but drew the bow so fiercely that it snapped. He cast the bow to the earth and set off at full gallop. Then spoke Zu Mao, "My lord's purple turban is a mark that the rebels will too easily recognize. Give it to me, and I will wear it!"

So Sun Jian exchanged his silver helmet with the turban for his general's headpiece, and the two men parted, riding different ways. The pursuers looking only for the purple turban went after its wearer, and Sun Jian escaped along a by-road. Zu Mao, hotly pursued, then tore off the headdress which he hung on the post of a half-burned house as he passed and dashed into the thick woods. Hua Xiong's troops seeing the purple turban standing motionless dared not approach, but they surrounded it on every side and shot at it with arrows. Presently they discovered the trick, went up and seized it. This was the moment that Zu Mao awaited. At once he rushed forth, his two swords whirling about, and dashed at the leader. But Hua Xiong was too quick. With a loud yell, Hua Xiong slashed at Zu Mao and cut him down the horse. Hua Xiong and Li Su continued the slaughter till the day broke, and they led their troops back to the Pass.

Cheng Pu, Huang Gai, and Han Dang in time found their chief and the soldiers gathered. Sun Jian was much grieved at the loss of Zu Mao. When news of the disaster reached Yuan Shao, he was greatly chagrined and called all the lords to a council. They assembled and Gongsun Zan was the last to arrive. When all were seated in the tent Yuan Shao said, "The brother of General Bao Xin, disobeying the rules we made for our guidance, rashly went to attack the enemy: He was slain and with him many of our soldiers. Now Sun Jian has been defeated. Thus our fighting spirit has suffered and what is to be done?" Everyone was silent. Lifting his eyes, Yuan Shao looked round from one to another till he came to Gongsun Zan, and then he remarked three men who stood behind Gongsun Zan's seat. They were of striking appearance as they stood there, all three smiling cynically.

第四章　古典小说英译的母语译者和非母语译者的定量比较研究

"Who are those men behind you?" said Yuan Shao. Gongsun Zan told Liu Bei to come forward, and said, "This is Liu Bei, Magistrate of Pingyuan and a brother of mine who shared my humble cottage when we were students." "It must be the Liu Bei who broke up the Yellow Scarves rebellion," said Cao Cao. "It is he," said Gongsun Zan, and he ordered Liu Bei to make his obeisance to the assembly, to whom Liu Bei then related his services and his origin, all in full detail.

"Since he is of the Han line, he should be seated," said Yuan Shao, and he bade Liu Bei sit. Liu Bei modestly thanked him, declining. Said Yuan Shao, "This consideration is not for your fame and office. I respect you as a scion of the imperial family." So Liu Bei took his seat in the lowest place of the long line of lords. And his two brothers with folded arms took their stations behind him. （1170 词）

罗译：Among the insurgent lords led by Yuan Shao was the lord of Jibei, Bao Xin. Anxious lest Sun Jian's vanguard win the highest honors, he secretly sent his brother Bao Zhong ahead to the pass. Taking side paths to avoid detection, Bao Zhong arrived with three thousand men and incited the enemy to battle. Hua Xiong responded quickly. Racing to the pass with five hundred armored shock cavalry, he shouted, "Rebel! Stand where you are!" Bao Zhong tried desperately to turn back but fell to a stroke of Hua Xiong's blade. Many of his commanders were taken alive. The victor sent Bao Zhong's head to the prime minister and reported the triumph. Dong Zhuo made Xiong his chief commander. Unaware of this defeat, Sun Jian was advancing to the pass. He had four commanders: Cheng Pu (Demou) from Tuyin in Youbeiping, wielding a steel-spined spear with snakeheaded blade; Huang Gai (Gongfu) of Lingling, wielding an iron whip; Han Dang (Yi-gong) from Lingzhi in Liaoxi, wielding a great backsword; and Zu Mao (Darong) from Fuchun in Wujun, wielding a pair of swords-of-war. Sun Jian donned his silver-sheened armor and red hood, and belted on a well-tempered sword. From his crenellemaned horse he pointed to the pass and shouted directly to Hua Xiong, "Surrender, you wretched slave to villainy."

Hua Xiong's lieutenant commander, Hu Zhen, led five thousand men out of the pass to do battle. Cheng Pu came on with leveled spear and pierced Hu Zhen's throat. Down he went. Sun Jian waved his men on toward the heart of the pass, but they suffered a heavy pelting with stones and arrows and withdrew to Liangdong. Sun Jian sent one messenger to Yuan Shao to report the victory and another to Yuan Shu for grain.

Concerning Sun Jian's request someone advised Yuan Shu: "Sun Jian is the tiger of the east. If he takes the capital and kills Dong Zhuo, we'll be facing a tiger instead of a wolf. Deny the grain and watch his army fall apart." Yuan Shu, persuaded, sent no supplies. Sun Jian's men became uncontrollable, and word of it soon reached the government camp at the pass. Dong Zhuo's adviser, Li Su, plotted the next step with Hua Xiong. "Tonight," said Su, "I'll take a company of men by side paths down from the pass and strike from the rear. You attack their forward positions. Jian can surely be captured." Hua Xiong approved and ordered his men to be fed well in preparation for the action. The moon was bright and the breeze refreshing when Hua Xiong reached Sun Jian's camp. At midnight his men stormed in, howling and shrieking. Sun Jian donned his armor, leaped to horse, and took on Hua Xiong. As they tangled, Li Su struck from the rear, ordering his men to set fires wherever they could. Sun Jian's army fled, though some commanders skirmished individually. Zu Mao alone stuck by Sun Jian. The two dashed from the battleground, pursued by Hua Xiong. Xiong dodged two arrows and kept pace. SunJian shot a third, but drew so hard his bow split. He threw it aside and rode for his life.

"Your red hood's a perfect target," cried Zu Mao. "I'll wear it." The men switched headgear and took flight by different roads. Xiong's soldiers spotted the bright color in the distance and gave chase. Sun Jian followed a side road and got away. Zu Mao, hard-pressed, hung the hood on a half-burned piece of timber and hid in a nearby copse. Catching the moonlight, the hood attracted Hua Xiong's men, and they circled it. No one dared advance, but after someone shot at it,

第四章　古典小说英译的母语译者和非母语译者的定量比较研究

they discovered the ruse and went for the headdress. At that moment Zu Mao came slashing out of the wood, wielding both his swords. But his object, Hua Xiong, uttering fierce cries, delivered a single fatal swordstroke that dropped Zu Mao from his horse.

The slaughter continued until morning. Then Hua Xiong brought his men back to the pass. Sun Jian's remaining commanders, Cheng Pu, Huang Gai, and Han Dang, found their leader and rounded up their men. Sun Jian grieved over the loss of Zu Mao and sent a messenger to report to Yuan Shao. Stunned at the defeat of Sun Jian by Hua Xiong, Yuan Shao called the lords into session. Gongsun Zan reached the meeting late, and Yuan Shao invited him to sit among the lords. "The other day," Yuan Shao began, "General Bao Xin's younger brother ignored orders and advanced without authority. He himself was killed, and we lost many men. Now Sun Jian has been beaten. Our edge is blunted, our mettle dulled.

What is our next step to be?" Not one of the lords replied. The war-ruler scanned the audience. Behind Gongsun Zan three extraordinarylooking strangers stood smiling grimly. Yuan Shao asked who they were. Gongsun Zan had Xuande step forward. "This is Liu Bei," he said, "magistrate at Pingyuan. We were fellow students and like brothers even then." "Not the one who helped break the Yellow Scarves?" asked Cao Cao. "The very one," answered Gongsun Zan. He told Xuande to salute Yuan Shao and Cao Cao and then proceeded to describe his protege's origins and accomplishments. "Since he belongs to a branch of the imperial family," Yuan Shao concluded, "let him come forward and be seated." But Xuande modestly declined. 11 "It is not your name or rank I salute," insisted Shao, "but your lineage." With that, Xuande took his place at the end of the line. Lord Guan and Zhang Fei posted themselves behind him, hands folded on their chests. （936 词）

虞译：Among the lords serving Yuan Shao was Bao Xin, who was jealous lest the chosen van leader, Sun Jian, should win the honor of the victory of the first battle. Determined to meet the foe first, he secretly dispatched his brother Bao Zhong with 3,000 horse and foot soldiers to get to the pass by a back road.

As soon as this small force reached their destination they offered battle. Hua Xiong, at the head of five hundred mail-clad horsemen, swept down from the pass to meet them. Frightened, Bao Zhong hastened to turn back but it was too late. Hua Xiong raised his arm and the great sword fell, cutting his victim down from his horse. Many of his men were captured. The poor man's head was sent to Dong Zhuo as proof of the victory and Hua Xiong was duly promoted to an even higher rank.

Soon Sun Jian also approached the pass. He had four subordinate officers with him: Cheng Pu, whose weapon was an iron-spined spear; Huang Gai, who wielded an iron whip; Han Dang, a swordsman; and Zu Mao, who fought with double swords. Sun Jian himself donned fine silver armor and wore a red turban wrapped around his head. He carried across his body his sword of ancient ingot iron and rode a dappled horse with flowing mane. He advanced to the pass and shouted up at its defenders: "Surrender, you lackeys of Dong Zhuo!" Down from the pass came Hu Zhen with 5,000 men to respond to the challenge. Cheng Pu with the snaky lance rode out to fight against him. After only a few bouts, Hu Zhen was killed by a thrust through his throat. Then Sun Jian led his army to push forward, but from the pass rained down showers of stones that proved too much for the assailants and they retired into their camp at Liangdong. A messenger was sent to announce the victory to Yuan Shao and also to ask Yuan Shu for immediate supplies of grain. But some of his advisors said to Yuan Shu, "Sun Jian is a very tiger. If he should take the capital and destroy Dong Zhuo, it would be like driving out a wolf to bring in a tiger. Do not send him grain and his army will fall apart." Yuan Shu listened to this and sent no grain or forage. Soon, chaos emerged among the hungry soldiers under Sun Jian and spies reported the news to the pass defenders, who decided upon a speedy attack on Sun Jian from the front and rear. They hoped to capture him in this way.

第四章　古典小说英译的母语译者和非母语译者的定量比较研究

　　Hua Xiong gave his soldiers a large meal and told them to be ready to set out when darkness fell. That night the moon was bright and the wind cool. By midnight his troops had reached Sun Jian's camp. Then they beat drums and shouted loudly as they pressed forward. Sun Jian hastily put on his fighting gear and rode out. He ran straight into Hua Xiong and the two immediately engaged in battle. After they had exchanged a few passes, another army came up from the rear and set fire to whatever would burn. Sun Jian's men were thrown into great confusion and fled like rats. A general melee ensued and soon only Zu Mao was at his chief's side. The two of them broke through the enemy's encirclement and fled. Hua Xiong came in hot pursuit. Sun Jian took his bow and let fly two arrows in quick succession but both missed. When he fitted a third arrow to the string he drew the bow so fiercely that it snapped. He had to give it up and rode off at full speed. Zu Mao said, "My lord, the red turban around your forehead is a mark that the enemy recognizes easily. Take it off and let me wear it." So they exchanged their headpieces and parted. The pursuers went only after the wearer of the red turban. So Sun Jian was able to escape through a bypath. Zu Mao, hotly pursued, tore off the headpiece and hung it on the post of a half-burned house. Then he dashed into the thick woods to hide. Seeing the turban from a distance, Hua Xiong's men dared not approach it but instead encircled from every side and shot at it with arrows. Before long the deception was discovered and they went up to seize the turban. This was the moment Zu Mao was waiting for. He rushed out of the woods and swinging his double swords, dashed at Hua Xiong. But his enemy was too powerful for him. With a loud yell, Hua Xiong cut him down from his horse. The killing continued till daybreak and it was only then that the victor led his men back to the pass.

　　Sun Jian's three other chief officers finally joined him. They collected the remaining soldiers and encamped again. He was much grieved at the loss of the faithful Zu Mao. When news of the disaster was reported to Yuan Shao he was greatly alarmed and called all the lords to a council. All came, with Gongsun Zan being the last to arrive. Yuan Shao invited them to sit inside his tent and said: "First it was General Bao's brother who disobeyed the orders and rashly went to attack the enemy. He ended up getting himself slain and with him many of our soldiers. Now General Sun has also been defeated. Our fighting spirit has suffered from these two losses. What do you think we should do?"

Everyone was silent. Lifting his eyes, Yuan Shao looked from one to another till he came to Gongsun Zan and noted the three unusual-looking men behind his seat. All three were smiling cynically.

"Who are those men behind you?" he asked. Gongsun Zan asked Liu Bei to come forth and said, "This is Liu Bei, Magistrate of Pingyuan and an old friend of mine. We used to live under the same roof." "He must be the Liu Bei who defeated the Yellow Turban rebels," said Cao Cao. "Yes, he is," replied Gongsun Zan. And he asked Liu Bei to pay his respects to the assembly, to whom he then related in full detail Liu Bei's services and his origin of birth. "He should be seated since he is of the Han line," said Yuan Shao and he bade Liu Bei sit down. Liu Bei thanked him modestly. Yuan Shao said, "This consideration is not for your fame or your office. I respect you as a scion of the imperial family." So Liu Bei took his seat at the end of the long line of lords while his two brothers stood behind him with folded arms. （1128词）

例5：

原文：却说鲁肃、孔明辞了玄德、刘琦，登舟望柴桑郡来。二人在舟中共议，鲁肃谓孔明曰："先生见孙将军，切不可实言曹操兵多将广。"孔明曰："不须子敬叮咛，亮自有对答之语。"及船到岸，肃请孔明于馆驿中暂歇，先自往见孙权。权正聚文武于堂上议事，闻鲁肃回，急召入问曰："子敬往江夏，体探虚实若何？"肃曰："已知其略，尚容徐禀。"权将曹操檄文示肃曰："操昨遣使赍文至此，孤先发遣来使，自今会众商议未定。"肃接檄文观看。其略曰：

孤近承帝命，奉词伐罪。旌麾南指，刘琮束手，荆襄之民，望风归顺。今统雄兵百万，上将千员，欲与将军会猎于江夏，共伐刘备，同分土地，永结盟好。幸勿观望，速赐回音。

第四章　古典小说英译的母语译者和非母语译者的定量比较研究

鲁肃看毕曰："主公尊意若何？"权曰："未有定论。"张昭曰："曹操拥百万之众，借天子之名，以征四方，拒之不顺。且主公大势，可以拒操者，长江也。今操既得荆州，长江之险，已与我共之矣，势不可敌。以愚之计，不如纳降，为万安之策。"众谋士皆曰："子布之言，正合天意。"孙权沉吟不语。张昭又曰："主公不必多疑，如降操，则东吴民安，江南六郡可保矣。"孙权低头不语。

须臾，权起更衣，鲁肃随于权后。权知肃意，乃执肃手而言曰："卿欲如何？"肃曰："恰才众人所言，深误将军。众人皆可降曹操，惟将军不可降曹操。"权曰："何以言之？"肃曰："如肃等降操，当以肃还乡党，累官故不失州郡也。将军降操，欲安所归乎？位不过封侯，车不过一乘，骑不过一匹，从不过数人，岂得南面称孤哉？众人之意，各自为己，不可听也。将军宜早定大计。"权叹曰："诸人议论，大失孤望。子敬开说大计，正与吾见相同，此天以子敬赐我也。但操新得袁绍之众，近又得荆州之兵，恐势大，难以抵敌。"肃曰："肃至江夏，引诸葛瑾之弟诸葛亮在此，主公可问之，便知虚实。"权曰："卧龙先生在此乎？"肃曰："现在馆驿中安歇。"权曰："今日天晚，且未相见。来日聚文武于帐下，先教见我江东英俊，然后升堂议事。"肃领命而去。

次日，至馆驿中见孔明，又嘱曰："今见我主，切不可言曹操兵多。"孔明笑曰："亮自见机而变，决不有误。"肃乃引孔明至幕下，早见张昭、顾雍等一班文武二十余人，峨冠博带，整衣端坐。孔明逐一相见，各问姓名。施礼已毕，坐于客位。

张昭等见孔明丰神飘洒，器宇轩昂，料到此人必来游说。张昭先以言挑之曰："昭乃江东微末之士，久闻先生高卧隆中，自比管、乐，此语果有之乎？"孔明曰："此亮平生小可之比也。"昭曰："近闻刘豫州三顾先生于草庐之中，幸得先生，以为如鱼得水，思欲席卷荆襄。今一旦以属曹操，未审是何主见？"孔明自思："张昭乃孙权手下第一个谋士，若不先难倒他，如何说得孙权？"遂答曰："吾观取汉上之地，易如反掌。我主刘豫州躬行仁义，不忍夺同宗之基业，故力辞之。刘琮孺子，听信佞言，暗自投降，致使曹操得以猖獗。今我主屯兵江夏，别有良图，非等闲可知也。"

昭曰："若此，是先生言行相违也。先生自比管、乐，管仲相桓公，霸诸侯，一匡天下；乐毅扶持微弱之燕，下齐七十余城：此二人者，真济世之才也。先生在草庐之中，但笑傲风月，抱膝危坐。今既从事刘豫州，当

· 65 ·

为生灵兴利除害,剿灭乱贼。且刘豫州未得先生之前,尚且纵横寰宇,割据城池。今得先生,人皆仰望,虽三尺童蒙,亦谓彪虎生翼,将见汉室复兴,曹氏即灭矣;朝廷旧臣,山林隐士,无不拭目而待,以为拂高天之云翳,仰日月之光辉,拯民于水火之中,措天下于衽席之上,在此时也。何先生自归豫州,曹兵一出,弃甲抛戈,望风而窜?上不能报刘表以安庶民,下不能辅孤子而据疆土,乃弃新野,走樊城,败当阳,奔夏口,无容身之地。是豫州既得先生之后,反不如其初也。管仲、乐毅果如是乎?愚直之言,幸勿见怪。"

  孔明听罢,哑然而笑曰:"鹏飞万里,其志岂群鸟能识哉?譬如人染沉疴,当先用糜粥以饮之,和药以服之,待其腑脏调和,形体渐安,然后用肉食以补之,猛药以治之,则病根尽去,人得全生也。若不待气脉和缓,便投以猛药厚味,欲求安保,诚为难矣。吾主刘豫州向日军败于汝南,寄迹刘表,兵不满千,将止关、张、赵云而已,此正如病势尪羸已极之时也。新野山僻小县,人民稀少,粮食鲜薄,豫州不过暂借以容身,岂真将坐守于此耶?夫以甲兵不完,城郭不固,军不经练,粮不继日,然而博望烧屯,白河用水,使夏侯惇、曹仁辈心惊胆裂,窃谓管仲、乐毅之用兵,未必过此。至于刘琮降操,豫州实出不知;且又不忍乘乱夺同宗之基业,此真大仁大义也。当阳之败,豫州见有数十万赴义之民扶老携幼相随,不忍弃之,日行十里,不思进取江陵,甘与同败,此亦大仁大义也。寡不敌众,胜负乃其常事。昔高皇数败于项羽,而垓下一战成功,此非韩信之良谋乎?夫信久事高皇,未尝累胜。盖国家大计,社稷安危,是有主谋。非比夸辩之徒,虚誉欺人:坐议立谈,无人可及;临机应变,百无一能。诚为天下笑耳。"这一篇言语,说得张昭并无一言回答。(1962字)

  邓译:In the boat on the way to Chaisang, the two travelers beguiled the time by discussing affairs. Lu Su impressed upon his companion, saying, "When you see my master, do not reveal the truth about the magnitude of Cao Cao's army." "You do not have to remind me," replied Zhuge Liang, "but I shall know how to reply." When the boat arrived, Zhuge Liang was lodged in the guests' quarters, and Lu Su went alone to see his master. Lu Su found Sun Quan actually at a council, assembled to consider the situation. Lu Su was summoned thereto and questioned at once upon what he had discovered. "I know the general outline, but I want a little time to prepare my report,"

第四章 古典小说英译的母语译者和非母语译者的定量比较研究

replied Lu Su. Then Sun Quan produced Cao Cao's letter and gave it to Lu Su.

"That came yesterday. I have sent the bearer of it back, and this gathering is to consider the reply," said he. Lu Su read the letter:

"When I, the Prime Minister, received the imperial command to punish a fault, my banners went south and Liu Zong became my prisoner, while the people of Jingzhou flocked to my side at the first rumor of my coming. Under my hand are one million strong and a thousand able leaders. My desire is, General, that we go on a great hunting expedition into Jiangxia and together attack Liu Bei. We will share his land between us, and we will swear perpetual amity. If happily you would not be a mere looker-on, I pray you reply quickly."

"What have you decided upon, my lord?" asked Lu Su as he finished the letter. "I have not yet decided." Then Zhang Zhao said, "It would be imprudent to withstand Cao Cao's hundred legions backed by the imperial authority. Moreover, your most important defense against him is the Great River; and since Cao Cao has gained possession of Jingzhou, the river is his ally against us. We cannot withstand him, and the only way to tranquillity, in my opinion, is submission."

"The words of the speaker accord with the manifest decree of providence," echoed all the assembly. Sun Quan remaining silent and thoughtful. Zhang Zhao again took up the argument, saying, "Do not hesitate, my lord. Submission to Cao Cao means tranquillity to the people of the South Land and safety for the inhabitants of the six territories."

Sun Quan still remained silent. His head bent in deep thought. Presently he arose and paced slowly out at the door, and Lu Su followed him. Outside he took Lu Su by the hand, saying, "What do you desire?"

"What they have all been saying is very derogatory to you. A common person might submit. You cannot."

"Why? How do you explain that?"

"If people like us servants submitted, we would just return to our village or continue holding our offices, and everything would go on as before. If you submit, whither will you go? You will be created a lord of some humble fief, perhaps. You will have one carriage, no more; one saddle horse, that is all. Your retinue will be some ten. Will you be able to sit facing the south and call yourself by the kingly title of 'The Solitary'? Each one in that crowd of hangers-on is thinking for himself, is purely selfish, and you should not listen to them, but take a line of your own and that quickly. Determine to play a bold game!"

Sun Quan sighed, "They all talk and talk: They miss my point of view. Now you have just spoken of a bold game, and your view is the same as mine. Surely God has expressly sent you to me. Still Cao Cao is now the stronger by all Yuan Shao's and Liu Biao's armies, and he has possession of Jingzhou. I fear he is almost too powerful to contend with."

"I have brought back with me Zhuge Liang, the younger brother of our Zhuge Jin. If you questioned him, he would explain clearly."

"Is Master Sleeping Dragon really here?"

"Really here, in the guest-house."

"It is too late to see him today. But tomorrow I will assemble my officials, and you will introduce him to all my best. After that we will debate the matter." With these instructions Lu Su retired.

Next day he went to the guest-house and conveyed Sun Quan's commands to the guest, particularly saying, "When you see my master, say nothing of the magnitude of Cao Cao's army."

Zhuge Liang smiled, saying, "I shall act as circumstances dictate. You may be sure I shall make no mistakes." Zhuge Liang was then conducted to where the high officers, civil and military to the number of forty and more, were assembled. They formed a dignified conclave as they sat in stately ranks with their tall headdresses and broad girdles. Zhang Zhao sat at the head, and Zhuge Liang first saluted him. Then, one by one, he exchange the formal courtesies with them all. This done he took his seat in the guest's chair. They, on their part, noted with interest Zhuge Liang's refined and elegant manner and his commanding figure, thinking within themselves, "Here is a persuader fitted for discourse."

Zhang Zhao led the way in trying to bait the visitor. He said, "You will pardon the most insignificant of our official circle, myself, if I mention that people say you compare yourself with those two famous men of talent, Guan Zhong and Yue Yi. Is there any truth in this?"

"To a trifling extent I have compared myself with them," replied Zhuge Liang.

"I have heard that Liu Bei made three journeys to visit you when you lived in retirement in your simple dwelling in the Sleeping Dragon Ridge, and that when you consented to serve him, he said he was as lucky as a fish in getting home to the ocean. Then he desired to possess the region about Jingzhou. Yet today all that country belongs to Cao Cao. I should like to hear your account of all that."

Zhuge Liang thought, "This Zhang Zhao is Sun Quan's first adviser. Unless I can nonplus him, I shall never have a chance with his master."

So he replied, "In my opinion the taking of the region around the Han River was as simple as turning over one's hand. But my master Liu Bei is both righteous and humane and would not stoop to filching the possession of a member of his own house. So he refused the offer of succession. But Liu Zong, a stupid lad, misled by specious words, submitted to Cao Cao and fell victim to his ferocity. My master is in camp at Jiangxia, but what his future plans may be cannot be divulged at present."

Zhang Zhao said, "Be it so; but your words and your deeds are something discordant. You say you are the equal of the two famous ones. Well, Guan Zhong, as minister of Prince Huan, put his master at the very head of the feudal nobles, making his master's will supreme in all the land. Under the able statesmanship of Yue Yi, the feeble state of Yan conquered Qi, reducing nearly seventy of its cities. These two were men of most commanding and conspicuous talent.

"When you lived in retirement, you smiled scornfully at ordinary people, passed your days in idleness, nursing your knees and posing in a superior manner, implying that if you had control of affairs, Liu Bei would be more than human; he should bring good to everybody and remove all evil; rebellion and robbery would be no more. Poor Liu Bei, before he obtained your help, was an outcast and a vagabond, stealing a city here and there where he could. With you to help him, he was to become the cynosure of every eye, and every lisping school child was to say that he was a tiger who had grown wings; the Hans were to be restored and Cao Cao and his faction exterminated; the good old days would be restored, and all the people who had been driven into retirement by the corruption of political life would wake up, rub the sleep out of their eyes, and be in readiness to lift the cloud of darkness that covered the sky and gaze up at the glorious brilliancy of the sun and moon, to pull the people out of fire and water and put all the world to rest on a couch of comfort. That was all supposed to happen forthwith.

"Why then, when you went to Xinye, did not Cao Cao's army throw aside their arms and armors and flee like rats? Why could you not have told Liu Biao how to give tranquillity to his people? Why could you not aid his orphan son to protect his frontiers? Instead you abandoned Xinye and fled to Fancheng; you were defeated at Dangyang and fled to Xiakou with no place to rest in. Thus, after you had joined Liu Bei, he was worse off than before. Was it thus with Guan Zhong and Yue Yi? I trust you do not mind my blunt speech."

Zhuge Liang waited till Zhang Zhao had closed his oration, then laughed and said, "How can the common birds understand the long flight of the cranes? Let me use an illustration. A man has fallen into a terrible malady. First the physician must administer hashish, then soothing drugs until his viscera shall be calmed into harmonious action. When the sick man's body shall have been reduced to quietude, then may he be given strong meats to strengthen him and powerful drugs to correct the disorder. Thus the disease will be quite expelled, and the man restored to health. If the physician does not wait till the humors

第四章 古典小说英译的母语译者和非母语译者的定量比较研究

and pulse are in harmony, but throws in his strong drugs too early, it will be difficult to restore the patient. "My master suffered defeat at Runan and went to Liu Biao. He had then less than one thousand soldiers and only three generals—Guan Yu, Zhang Fei, and Zhao Zilong. That was indeed a time of extreme weakness. Xinye was a secluded, rustic town with few inhabitants and scanty supplies, and my master only retired there as a temporary refuge. How could he even think of occupying and holding it? Yet, with insufficient force, in a weak city, with untrained men and inadequate supplies, we burned Xiahou Dun at Bowang Slope, drowned Cao Ren and Cao Hong and their army in the White River, and set them in terror as they fled. I doubt whether the two ancient heroes would have done any better. As to the surrender of Liu Zong, Liu Bei knew nothing of it. And he was too noble and too righteous to take advantage of a kinsman's straits to seize his inheritance. As for the defeat at Dangyang, it must be remembered that Liu Bei was hampered with a huge voluntary following of common people, with their aged relatives and their children, whom he was too humane to abandon. He never thought of taking Jiangling, but willingly suffered with his people. This is a striking instance of his magnanimity.

"Small forces are no match for large armies. Victory and defeat are common episodes in every campaign. The great Founder of the Hans suffered many defeats at the hands of Xiang Yu, but Liu Bang finally conquered at Gaixia, and that battle was decisive. Was not this due to the strategy of Han Xin who, though he had long served Liu Bang, had never won a victory. Indeed real statesmanship and the restoration of stable government is a master plan far removed from the vapid discourses and debates of a lot of bragging babblers and specious and deceitful talkers, who, as they themselves say, are immeasureably superior to the rest of humankind but who, when it comes to deeds and decisions to meet the infinite and constant vicissitudes of affairs, fail to throw up a single capable person. Truly such people are the laughing stock of all the world."

Zhang Zhao found no reply to this diatribe.（2028 词）

罗 译: Lu Su and Kongming Bade Xuande and Liu Qi good-bye and sailed for Chaisang. On board they reviewed the situation. "When you see General Sun, sir," Lu Su emphasized, "be sure to avoid mentioning how large and well-commanded Cao Cao's army is." "There is no need, Su, to keep reminding me of this," responded Kongming. "I will make my own replies to him." When their boat docked, Lu Su invited Kongming to rest at the guesthouse while he went ahead to see Sun Quan. Sun Quan was already in council with his officers and officials. Informed of Lu Su's return, Quan summoned him and asked, "What did you learn in Jiangxia about the state of Cao Cao's forces?" "I have a general idea," replied Su, "but I will need time to report in full, sire." Quan showed him Cao Cao's summons and said, "Cao Cao had this delivered yesterday. I have sent the envoy back while we debate our response." Cao's note said.

Under a recent imperial mandate, I have authority to act against state criminals. Our banners tilted southward; Liu Zong bound his hands in submission. The populace of Jingzhou, sensing the direction of events, has transferred its allegiance to us. We have one million hardy warriors and a thousand able generals. We propose that you join us, General, in a hunting expedition to Jiangxia in order to strike the decisive blow against Liu. Then, sharing the territory between us, we may seal an everlasting amity. Please do not hesitate but favor us with a speedy reply.

After he had read the document, Lu Su said to Sun Quan, "What is your most honored view, my lord?" "A decision has yet to be reached," he responded. The adviser Zhang Zhao joined the discussion, saying, "Commanding a host of one million, cloaked in the Emperor's authority, Cao Cao has campaigned the length and breadth of the land. To resist is to rebel. Moreover, your major advantage was the Great River—until Cao Cao took Jingzhou. Now we share the river's strategic benefits with him. Really, there is no opposing him, and in my poor estimation we would do better with the total security which submission will afford." "Zhang Zhao's views," the counselors declared in unison, "conform to the wishes of Heaven itself." But Sun Quan pondered in silence. "Have no doubts, my lord," Zhang Zhao continued. "If we submit to Cao, the people of the region will be protected and the six districts of the Southland preserved." Sun Quan lowered his head and said nothing. A moment later Sun Quan rose to go to the privy. Lu Su followed. Aware that Su did not share the views of Zhang Zhao, Quan turned to him and asked, "But what is your mind on this?" "The majority's view, General, will be your ruin," Su replied. "They can submit to Cao, but you cannot" "What are you saying?" Quan asked. "For someone like me," Su went on, "submission means being sent home to my clan, my village. Eventually I'll regain high office. But what have you to go home to? A minor estate? A single carriage? A single mount? A handful of followers? And what of your claim to royalty? Your advisers all consider only themselves. You must not heed them. It is time to make a master plan for yourself."

At these words Sun Quan sighed. "Their counsel fails my hopes," he said. "But the point you make—the master plan— accords well with my thinking. You come to me by Heaven's favor. Cao Cao, however, has Yuan Shao's legions as well as the troops of Jingzhou. He seems impossible to resist." "I have brought back with me," Su went on, "Zhuge Jin's younger brother, Liang. Put your questions to him, my lord, and he will explain how things stand." "Master Sleeping Dragon is here?" exclaimed Quan. "Resting in the guesthouse," answered Lu Su. "It's too late to see him today," Quan said. "Tomorrow I shall gather my civil and military officers so he can get acquainted with the eminent men of the south before we proceed to formal discussion." Lu Su went to arrange things accordingly.

The following day Lu Su came for Kongming. Again he warned the guest not to mention the size of Cao Cao's army. "Let me respond as I see fit," Kongming said with a smile. "Nothing shall go amiss, I assure you." Lu Su conducted Kongming to the headquarters of General Sun, where he was introduced to Zhang Zhao, Gu Yong, and some twenty other officials and officers of the first rank. As they sat erect in full dress, with their high formal caps and broad belts, Kongming was presented to each in turn. The formalities concluded, Kongming was shown to the guest's seat.

From Kongming's air of self-assurance and dignified, confident carriage, Zhang Zhao and the others understood that he had come to exert his powers of persuasion. Zhao initiated the discussion with a provocative comment: "I, the least of the Southland's scholars, have been hearing for some time how you, ensconced in Longzhong, have compared yourself to the great ministers of antiquity, Guan Zhong and Yue Yi. Have you actually made such claims?" "There could be some slight basis for the comparison," was Kongming's reply. "I have also heard that Liu Xuande, 3 protector of Yuzhou, solicited you three times at that thatched hut and, considering himself fortunate to get you—'a fish finding water' was how he put it—expected to roll up Jingzhou in the palm of his hand. Now that the province belongs to Cao Cao, we await your explanation."

Aware that Zhang Zhao was Sun Quan's foremost adviser—the man he had to confound or else lose all hope of convincing Quan himself—Kongming replied, "In my view that province on the River Han could have been taken as easily as one turns one's palm. But my master, Lord Liu, precisely because he conducts himself humanely and honorably, could never bear to steal a kinsman's estate and refused to do so. The adolescent Liu Zong, the victim of insidious counsel, secretly surrendered himself, giving Cao Cao a free hand in the region. My master, however, with forces stationed at Jiangxia, has promising prospects of his own, not to be lightly dismissed."

"Then your words and deeds do not agree," said Zhang Zhao. "For the men with whom you are wont to compare yourself helped their lords win fame and power. The patriarch Huan dominated the feudal lords and kept the realm together during Guan Zhong's tenure as minister; and Yue Yi helped the feeble state of Yan subdue the seventy cities of mighty Qi. Those two had the talent to set the empire to rights.

第四章　古典小说英译的母语译者和非母语译者的定量比较研究

But you, sir, have dwelled in a thatched hut, delighting yourself with the breeze and moon, profoundly absorbed in meditation. After you entered Lord Liu's service, we expected you to promote the welfare of the living souls of the realm and to root out and destroy treason and sedition. "Before Lord Liu obtained your services, he was already a force to be reckoned with wherever he went, seizing this or that walled town. Now that he has you, people are saying that the ferocious tiger has grown wings and that we will witness the restoration of the Han and the elimination of the Caos. Old servants of the court and recluses of the mountains and forests have begun rubbing their eyes in expectation, imagining that the sky will clear, that the sun and moon will shine again. They hope to see the salvation of the people and the deliverance of the empire in their time. "One can only wonder why, then, after you had committed yourself to him, Lord Liu scurried for safety the moment Cao Cao stepped into the field, abandoning his obligations to Liu Biao for the security of the people of Jingzhou, and failing to sustain Liu Zong in the defense of his land. And what followed? Lord Liu quit Xinye, fled Fan, lost Dangyang, and bolted to Xiakou for refuge. But no one will have him! The fact is that Lord Liu was better off before you came. How does that measure up to what Guan Zhong and Yue Yi did for their lords? Kindly forgive my simple frankness."

　　Kongming broke into laughter. "The great roc ranges thousands of miles," he said. " Can the common fowl appreciate its ambition? When a man is gravely ill, he must be fed weak gruel and medicated with mild tonics until his internal state is readjusted and balanced and his condition gradually stabilizes. Only then can meat be added to his diet and powerful drugs be used to cure him. Thus is the root of the disease eradicated and the man's health restored. If you do not wait until breath and pulse are calm and steady but precipitately use powerful drugs and rich food, the attempt to cure the patient is sure to fail.

　　"When Lord Liu suffered defeat at Runan, he threw himself on

Liu Biao's mercy. He had less than a thousand men and no generals at all, except for Lord Guan, Zhang Fei, and Zhao Zilong. He was like a man wasted by disease. Xinye, a small town off in the hills, with few people and scant grain, was no more than a temporary refuge, hardly a place to hold permanently. And yet, despite our poor weapons, weak city walls, untrained forces, and day-to-day shortages of grain, we burned Cao out at Bowang, flooded him out at the White River, and put his leading generals, Xiahou Dun and Cao Ren, in a state of panic and dismay. I am not sure that Guan Zhong and Yue Yi surpassed us in warfare.

"As for Liu Zong's surrender to Cao Cao, the truth is that Lord Liu knew nothing about it. Nor could he bear to exploit the treason of the Cais to steal a kinsman's estate—such is his great humanity and devotion to honor. In the case of the Dangyang defeat, Lord Liu had several hundred thousand subjects, including the elderly and many young people, who were determined to follow him. Could he leave them to their fate? He was moving a mere ten li each day but never thought of racing ahead to capture Jiangling. He was content to suffer defeat with his people if he had to—another instance of his profound humanity and sense of honor.

"The few cannot oppose the many, and a warrior learns to endure his reverses. The founder of the Han, Gao Zu, was defeated over and over by Xiang Yu, but the final victory at Gaixia was the result of Han Xin's good counsel, was it not? The same Han Xin who, in his long history of service to Gao Zu, had compiled no impressive record of victories! For the grand strategy of the dynasty, the security of our sacred altars, truly there is a master planner, one utterly different from the boasting rhetoricians whose empty reputations overawe people, who have no peer in armchair debate and standing discussions, of whom not even one in a hundred has any idea how to confront a crisis or cope with its rapid development.

"What a farce to amuse the world!" To this oration Zhang Zhao had no reply. （1894 词）

第四章 古典小说英译的母语译者和非母语译者的定量比较研究

杨译：HAVING left Liu Bei and Liu Qi, Lu Su and Zhuge Liang went by boat to Chaisang. Once aboard they took counsel together and Lu Su said, "When you see General Sun, don't tell him how powerful Cao Cao's army actually is."

"Don't worry," replied Zhuge Liang. "I know what to say." When the boat arrived, Lu Su asked Zhuge Liang to wait in the hostel while he went to see Sun Quan. Sun Quan was conferring in the audience chamber with his civil and military officers. As soon as he heard that Lu Su was back, he called him in and asked: "What did you find out on your trip to Jiangxia?"

"I know the general situation and shall report it to you later," replied Lu Su. Then Sun Quan showed him a letter from Cao Cao, saying, "This arrived yesterday. I have sent the messenger back, and we are meeting now to decide on a reply." Lu Su read the letter, the gist of which was as follows:

"At the emperor's command, I have led my army south to punish the guilty. Liu Cong has been captured, his people have surrendered, and I now command a force of a million picked men and a thousand able generals. I hope you will join me, general, in a hunting expedition at Jiangxia to attack Liu Bei, so that we can divide his territory between us and pledge everlasting friendship. Do not hesitate, but give me an early reply!"

"What have you decided?" asked Lu Su as he finished the letter.

"I have not made up my mind yet," answered Sun Quan.

Then Zhang Zhao said, "Cao Cao has a great army a million strong, and in the emperor's name he is conquering territory on every side. To resist him would be opposing the emperor. And the only natural barrier between us is the Yangzi, but now by conquering Jing-zhou he has taken part of the river out of our hands, making it difficult for us to withstand him. In my humble opinion, our safest plan is submission."

All the other advisers chimed in, "Zhang Zhao's proposal accords with the will of Heaven."

Sun Quan thought hard but said nothing. Then Zhang Zhao

continued, "Have no doubt about it, my lord. Submission to Cao Cao means peace for the people of Wu, and retaining the six provinces south of the Yangzi."

Sun Quan bowed his head and said nothing. Presently he went out and Lu Su followed him. Noting this, Sun Quan took his hand and asked, "What do you think?"

"Their advice is the worst possible thing you could do. They may surrender to Cao Cao, but not you." "Why do you say that?"

"If men like myself went over to Cao Cao, we should be sent home and keep our official posts in the provinces. But in your case, where could you go? At the most you would be made a baron with one carriage and no more, one horse and just a few retainers. That would be the end of your kingship. The others are thinking of themselves. Don't listen to them but make up your mind quickly—this is an important decision."

"They have certainly disappointed me." Sun Quan sighed. "Your view of this is exactly the same as mine. Heaven must have sent you to me! But Cao Cao has just taken over Yuan Shao's army and the troops of Jingzhou too. I fear he may prove too powerful to resist."

Lu Su said, "I have brought Zhuge Jin's brother Zhuge Liang back with me from Jiangxia. You can find out the situation from him."

"What, is the Sleeping Dragon here?" cried Sun Quan.

"Yes, he's resting now in the hostel."

"It's too late to see him today. But tomorrow I shall asssemble all my officials and introduce him to the bravest and the best of our men, after which we can discuss the matter." With these instructions Lu Su withdrew. The next day he called on Zhuge Liang at the hostel and urged him, "When you see my master today, don't tell him how powerful Cao Cao's army is."

Zhuge Liang replied with a smile, "I shall do as circumstances dictate. I can promise not to let you down." Then Lu Su took him to Sun Quan's headquarters where they found more than twenty civil and military officers, including Zhang Zhao and Gu Yong, seated in state with high headdresses and broad belts. Zhuge Liang was introduced to them one by one, and after an exchange of greetings he took the guest's seat. Mean while his air of refinement and commanding appearance had not been lost on Zhang Zhao and the others, who judged that he must have come to offer advice. Zhang Zhao led the way in trying to bait the visitor. "I am one of the most insignificant scholars of this district," he said. "But is it true, as I have long heard, that while living as a recluse in Longzhong you compared yourself to Guan Zhong and Yue Yi?"

"In some trifling respects I did," replied Zhuge Liang.

"I heard that Liu Bei called three times at your thatched hut and was as delighted to discover you as a fish getting back to the water, because he aspired to the conquest of Jingzhou and Xiangyang. But today those districts have fallen into Cao Cao's hands. What is the reason for that?" Zhuge Liang reflected, "This Zhang Zhao is Sun Quan's foremost adviser. Unless I defeat him in argument, what chance have I with his master?" So he answered, "In my opinion, to take the land round the Han River is as simple as turning over your hand. But my master Liu Bei has too much humanity and sense of justice to want to take the property of a kinsman. That accounts for his letting it go. Liu Cong is a fool who listened to bad advice and surrendered to Cao Cao without consulting others, enabling him to run wild. My master has stationed his troops at Jiangxia and has a good plan which I am not free to divulge."

Zhang Zhao said, "In that case, your deeds hardly match your words. You compare yourself to Guan Zhong and Yue Yi. But the one was a minister serving Duke Huan of Qi who became chief of all the barons and united the country. The other helped Yan, a weak state, to conquer more than seventy towns in Qi. These two men were truly great statesmen, whereas you in your thatched hut led a frivolous existence, sitting idle all day long clasping your knees. Now that you have taken service under Liu Bei, you should do good and rid the people of evils, destroying rebels and traitors. In fact, before Liu Bei had you as his adviser, he managed to conquer some territory and take some cities, so that once he had you men expected great things of him—the very children imagined that wings had been given to a tiger, that the Han Dynasty would rise once more and Cao Cao would be destroyed. All the old ministers of Han and the hermits in mountain glades wiped their eyes and waited, believing that the time had come when the clouds would be scattered from the sky enabling the sun and moon to shine forth in splendour, and that you would rescue the people from hardships worse than flood and fire, restoring peace to the empire. Yet since you joined Liu Bei, his men have been flying before Cao Cao, abandoning their armour and spears. Failing to serve Liu Biao well and relieve the people or to support his son and preserve his land, he has lost Xinye, escaped to Fancheng, been defeated at Dangyang and fled to Xiakou, unable to find a refuge anywhere. In short, since you became his adviser, Liu Bei has fared worse than before. Would this have been so with Guan Zhong and Yue Yi? I hope you won't take offence at my blunt, foolish talk."

After hearing him out, Zhuge Liang laughed and said, "A giant roc flies ten thousand lt, but can the com mon birds understand his ambition? When a man falls dangerously ill, you must give him gruel first, then some mild restorative. Once his system is well regulated and quiet, you can give him nourishing meat and powerful drugs to cure his illness and preserve his life. If instead of waiting till humours and pulse are in harmony you give him powerful drugs and rich nourishment first, it will be difficult to restore him to health. Liu Bei was defeated at Runan and had to seek protection from Liu Biao. He had then less than a thousand men and none but Guan Yu, Zhang Fei and Zhao Yun as his officers. He was like a man dangerously ill and very weak. Xinye is a small mountainous district, sparsely populated and short of supplies, and Liu Bei simply used it as a temporary refuge, never intending to make it a permanent base. Yet with our scanty equipment, flimsy fortifications, untrained men and supplies sufficient for one day only, we burned Cao Cao's camp at Bowang and flooded his positions at Baihe, frightening his generals Xiahou Dun and Cao Ren into running away. To my mind, not even Guan Zhong or Yue Yi could have employed their troops to any better purpose. As for Liu Cong's surrender, Liu Bei had no knowledge of it and would not take advantage of the general confusion to seize his kinsman's estate. This shows his great humanity and justice. When he withdrew from Dangyang, several hundred thousand civilians, old and young, had flocked to join his just cause, and he would not abandon them; hence his army could only travel ten li a day; so he gave up attacking Jiangling and let himself be worsted. This again shows his great humanity and justice. The defeat of a small force by a great multitude is common enough in war. The first emperor of Han was defeated time and again by Xiang Yu, but finally triumphed in the Battle of Gaixia, and this shows Han Xin's brilliant strategy. Han Xin had served his sovereign for a long time without winning many battles for him; for affairs of state require a master plan. It is different in the case of boastful orators who deceive men with empty words: when it comes to talking, no one can surpass them; but in times of crisis when decisions have to be made, not one in a hundred shows any ability. In fact they become the laughing-stock of the whole world!" Zhang Zhao had not a word to say after this（1794 词）

张译：Having taken leave of Liu Bei and Liu Qi, Lu Su and Zhuge Liang embarked on a boat for chai sang. The two men were discussing affairs together in the boat. Lu Su said to Zhuge Liang, "When you see General Sun, don't tell him frankly that Cao Cao has a great many soldiers and generals." "You need not bid me do so," replied Zhuge Liang. "I know what to say and reply."

When the boat arrived, Lu Su asked Zhuge Liang to take a rest in the guests' quarters while he went alone to see Sun Quan.

Sun Quan, assembling his civil and military officers in his audience chamber, was discussing affairs with them. Hearing that Lu Su was back, he quickly called him in and asked, "What did you discover on your trip to Jiangxia?" "I have known the general situation. Allow me to report it to you later", replied Lu Su. Then Sun Quan showed a despatch from Cao Cao to Lu Su and said, "Yesterday Cao Cao sent a messenger to bring the despatch here. I have sent the messenger back and this gathering is considering the reply."

Lu Su read the despatch, the gist of which said, "At the imperial command to punish the guilt, my banners went south. Then Liu Cong has been captured, his people flocked to my side at the first rumour of my coming. I now command a force of a million picked men and a thousand able generals hope you will join me, General, in a hunting expedition at Jiangxia and we together attack liu Bei, so that we can divide his territory between us and pledge everlasting friendship. Do not hesitate but give me an early reply."

"What have you decided, my Lord?" asked Lu Su as he finished the dispatch "I have not had any decision yet", answered Sun Quan. Then Zhang Zhao said, "Cao Cao has a great army of a million picked soldiers, and in the emperors name he is conquering territory on every side. To resist him would be opposing the emperor. Moreover my lord's most important defence against Cao Cao is the Yangtse River and since Cao Cao has gained possession of Jinzhou, he has taken part of the advantage of the river from our hands. We cannot withstand him. In my humble opinion, the safest plan is submission." All the other advisers said, "Zhang Zhao's proposal accords with the will of Heaven."

Sun Quan pondered and hesitated but said nothing. Then Zhang Zhao said again, "Do not hesitate, my lord. Submission to Cao means peace for the people of wu and safety for the six provinces south of the Yangtse river". Sun Quan bowed his head and said nothing. Presently he arose and went out and Lu Su followed him. Knowing Lu Su's idea, Sun Quan took his hand and asked, " What do you desire?" "What they have just said is very harmful to you. They may surrender to CaoCao, but not you." " Why do you say that?"

"If people like us surrendered to Cao Cao, we should be sent home and keep our official posts in the provinces or districts. But if you surrender to Cao Cao, where will you go? At the most you would be made a marquis with one carriage and no more one horse and just a few retainers. That would be the end of your kingship. The others are thinking for themselves. Don't listen to them, but quickly fix upon your important plan."

"Their arguments make me disappointed greatly." Sun Quan sighed. "You have just talked about the important plan and your view of this is exactly the same as mine. Heaven must have sent you to me. But Cao Cao has just taken over Yuan Shao's army and the troops of Jingzhou too. I fear he may prove too powerful to resist."

Lu Su said, "From Jiangxia I have brought Zhuge Jin's brother, Zhuge Liang, back with me. My lord may ask him. Then you may know the real Situation Is ' Master Sleeping Dragon' here?" said Sun Quan. "Yes, he is resting now in the guest-house." "It is too late to see him to-day. but tomorrow I will assemble my civil and military officers. First let him see my bravest and best men. After that we will discuss the matter."

With these instructions Lu Su withdrew. Next day he went to the guest-house to call on Zhuge Liang and earnestly said to him again, "when you see my master to-day, don't tell him that Cao Cao has a great many soldiers."

Zhuge Liang said with a smile, "I shall do as circumstances dictate. I must not make any mistakes." Then Lu Su led Zhuge Liang to Sun Quan's headquarters where they found more than twenty civil and military officers, including Zhang Zhao and Gu Yong, all seated in state with tall headdresses and broad belts. Zhuge Liang was introduced to them one by one, and after an exchange of greetings, he took the guests seat. Then Zhang Zhao and the others, noting Zhuge Liang's refined and elegant manner and commanding appearance, judged that he must have come to offer advice. Zhang Zhao led the way in trying to use some sentences to bait the visitor. "I am the most insignificant scholar in this district," he said, "But, as I have long heard, while living as a recluse in Long zhong, you compared yourself to Guan Zhong and Yue Yi. Is it true that you really said so?"

"In some trifling respects I did," replied Zhuge Liang.

"Recently I heard that Liu Bei called at your thatched hut three times. Liu Bei thought that it was fortunate for him to discover you and that he was as lucky as a fish getting back to the water. Then he desired to take possession of Jingzhou and Xiangyang. But to-day those two districts belong to Cao Cao, what is your account of that?" said Zhang Zhao.

Zhuge Liang thought to himself, "Zhang Zhao is Sun Quan's first adviser. If I do not defeat him in argument first, how can I persuade Sun Quan?" So he answered, "In my opinion, to take the land round the Han river is as simple as turning over one's hand. But as my master Liu Bei has humanity and sense of justice, he cannot bear to take the possession of a kinsman's basic property by force. So he strongly refused to take it. Liu Cong is a stupid lad who listened to bad advice and surrendered to CaoCao secretly, enabling Cao Cao to run wild. Now my master has stationed his troops at Jiangxia and has another good plan which cannot be easily known."

Zhang Zhou said, "In that case, your deeds hardly match your words. You compare yourself to Guan Zhong and Yue Yi. But Guan Zhong was a minister serving Duke Huan, put Duke Huan at the head of all the feudal princes and united the country. Yue Yi helped Yan, a weak state, to conquer more than seventy cities of Qi. These two men were truly great geniuses with the abilities of saving the world, whereas you in your thatched hut smiled scornfully at ordinary people, sitting idle all day long clasping your knees. Now that you have taken service under Liu Bei, you should do something good for the people, rid the people of evils and destroy rebels and traitors. Moreover, before Liu Bei obtained your help, he could still manage freely to conquer some territory here and take some cities there, so that once he got you, people all expected great things of him-even the three feet tall children said that the tiger had grown wings, that the Han dynasty would rise once more and that Cao Cao would soon be destroyed. All the old courtiers of Han and the hermits in mountain glades wiped their

第四章 古典小说英译的母语译者和非母语译者的定量比较研究

eyes and waited, thinking that the time had come when Li Bei would wipe away the clouds of darkness from the high sky, gaze up at the glorious brilliancy of the sun and moon, save the people out of fire and water and put the country to rest on a couch of comfort. Why is it that as you joined Liu Bei, his men abandon their armour, threw away their spears and fled like rats as soon as Cao Cao's army came out? On the one hand, failing to serve Liu Biao (Liu Bei's kinsman, who ruled over Jingzhou. After his death, his son Liu Cong succeeded him, but soon surrendered to Cao Cao.) well and relieve the people, and on the other hand, failing to support his son and preserve his land, Liu Bei had lost Xinye, escaped to Fancheng, been defeated at Dangyang and fled to Xiakou, unable to find a refuge anywhere.

Thus, after you had joined Liu Bei, he was worse off than before. Would this have been so with guan Zhong and Yue Yi? I trust you do not mind my blunt speech."

After hearing him out, Zhuge Liang laughed and said, " A roc flies ten thousand "li", but can the common birds understand his ambition? For example, when a man falls seriously ill, we should give him gruel first, then some mild restorative. Once his viscera are well regulated and his body is gradually getting quiet, we then can give him nourishing neat and powerful drugs to cure his illness until there is no illness at all. Then the man's life is preserved. If instead of waiting till breath and pulse are in harmony we just give him powerful drugs and rich nourishment first, it will be difficult to restore him to health. My master, Liu Bei was defeated at Runan and had to depend upon Liu Biao. At that time he had less than a thousand soldiers and only Guan Yu, Zhang Fei and Zhao Yun as his officers. Under such circumstance, he was just like a. man in a time of extreme illness and weakness. Xinye is a small mountainous and secluded district with few inhabitants and scanty food supplies, and Liu Bei simply used it as a temporary refuge. Will he really stay there permanently? Yet with our scanty equipment, a weakly built city, untrained soldiers, and food supplies insufficient for more than one day, we burned Cao Cao's camp at Bowang and flooded his positions at Baihe, frightening his generals such as Xiaho Dun and Cao Ren into a serious panic. To my mind, even Guan Zhong and Yue Yi could not necessarily have employed their troops more skillfully. As for Liu Cong's surrender to Cao Cao, Liu Bei. In fact, had no knowledge of it and could not bear to take advantage of the general confusion to seize his kinsman inherited territory. This is indeed great humanity and justice. As to the defeat at Dangyan, Liu Bei saw several hundred thousand civilians with feeling of justice, follow him with their aged relatives and children, So he could not bear to abandon them; hence his army could only travel ten li a day, so he gave up attacking Jiangling and willingly shared the suffering of defeat with his people. This is also great humanity and justice. As small army is no match for large one, victory and defeat are common episodes in war. The first emperor of Han was defeated time and again by Xiang Yu, but finally was successful in that single Battle of Gaixia. Was that not Han Xin's brilliant strategy? Han Xin had served the first emperor of Han for a long time without winning many battles or him; for affairs of a state and safety and danger of a country there must be a master plan. It is different in the case of boastful orators who deceive men with vain reputation: when it comes to talking no one can do as well as they but in time of crisis when decisions have to be made, not one in a hundred can show any ability. Truly such people are the laughing-stock of the whole world!" This diatribe kept Zhang Zhao silent（2027词）

例6：

原文：却说鲁肃领了周瑜言语，径来舟中相探孔明。孔明接入小舟对坐。肃曰："连日措办军务，有失听教。"孔明曰："便是亮亦未与都督贺喜。"肃曰："何喜？"孔明曰："公瑾使先生来探亮知也不知，便是这件事可贺喜耳。"諕得鲁肃失色，问曰："先生何由知之？"孔明曰："这条计只好弄蒋干。曹操虽被一时瞒过，必然便省悟，只是不肯认错耳。今蔡、张两人既死，江东无患矣，如何不贺喜？吾闻曹操换毛玠、于禁为水军都督，则这两个手里，好歹送了水军性命。"鲁肃听了，开口不得，把些言语支吾了半晌，别孔明而回。孔明嘱曰："望子敬在公瑾面前勿言亮先知此事，恐公瑾心怀妒忌，又要寻事害亮。"鲁肃应诺而去，回见周

第四章　古典小说英译的母语译者和非母语译者的定量比较研究

瑜,把上项事只得实说了。瑜大惊曰:"此人决不可留,吾决意斩之。"肃劝曰:"若杀孔明,却被曹操笑也。"瑜曰:"吾自有公道斩之,教他死而无怨。"肃曰:"何以公道斩之?"瑜曰:"子敬休问,来日便见。"

次日,聚众将于帐下,教请孔明议事。孔明欣然而至。坐定,瑜问孔明曰:"即日将与曹军交战,水路交兵,当以何兵器为先?"孔明曰:"大江之上,以弓箭为先。"瑜曰:"先生之言,甚合愚意。但今军中正缺箭用,敢烦先生监造十万枝箭,以为应敌之具。此系公事,先生幸勿推却。"孔明曰:"都督见委,自当效劳。敢问十万枝箭,何时要用?"瑜曰:"十日之内,可完办否?"孔明曰:"操军即日将至,若候十日,必误大事。"瑜曰:"先生料几日可完办?"孔明曰:"只消三日,便可拜纳十万枝箭。"瑜曰:"军中无戏言。"孔明曰:"怎敢戏都督?愿纳军令状:三日不办,甘当重罚。"瑜大喜,唤军政司当面取了文书,置酒相待曰:"待军事毕后,自有酬劳。"孔明曰:"今日已不及,来日造起。至第三日,可差五百小军到江边搬箭。"饮了数杯,辞去。鲁肃曰:"此人莫非诈乎?"瑜曰:"他自送死,非我逼他。今明白对众要了文书,他便两胁生翅,也飞不去。我只分付军匠人等,教他故意迟延,凡应用物件,都不与齐备。如此,必然误了日期。那时定罪,有何理说?公今可去探他虚实,却来回报。"

肃领命来见孔明,孔明曰:"吾曾告子敬,休对公瑾说,他必要害我。不想子敬不肯为我隐讳,今日果然又弄出事来。三日内如何造得十万箭?子敬只得救我。"肃曰:"公自取其祸,我如何救得你?"孔明曰:"望子敬借我二十只船,每船要军士三十人,船上皆用青布为幔,各束草千余个,分布两边,吾别有妙用。第三日,包管有十万枝箭。只不可又教公瑾得知,若彼知之,吾计败矣。"肃允诺,却不解其意,回报周瑜,果然不提起借船之事,只言:"孔明并不用箭竹、翎毛、胶漆等物,自有道理。"瑜大疑曰:"且看他三日后如何回复我。"

却说鲁肃私自拨轻快船二十只,各船三十余人,并布幔束草等物,尽皆齐备,候孔明调用。第一日,却不见孔明动静;第二日,亦只不动。至第三日四更时分,孔明密请鲁肃到船中。肃问曰:"公召我来何意?"孔明曰:"特请子敬同往取箭。"肃曰:"何处去取?"孔明曰:"子敬休问,前去便见。"遂命将二十只船,用长索相连,径望北岸进发。(1234字)

邓译:Lu Su departed on his mission and found Zhuge Liang seated in his little craft.

"There has been so much to do that I have not been able to come to listen to your instructions," said Lu Su.

"That is truly so," said Zhuge Liang, "and I have not yet congratulated the Commander-in-Chief."

"What have you wished to congratulate him upon?"

"Why Sir, the matter upon which he sent you to find out whether I knew about it or not. Indeed I can congratulate him on that."

Lu Su turned pale and gasped, saying, "But how did you know, Master?"

"The ruse succeeded well thus played off on Jiang Gan. Cao Cao has been taken in this once, but he will soon rise to it. Only he will not confess his mistake. However, the two men are gone, and the South Land is freed from a grave anxiety. Do you not think that is a matter for congratulation? I hear Mao Jie and Yu Jin are the new admirals, and in their hands lie both good and evil for the fate of the northern fleet."

Lu Su was quite dumbfounded. He stayed a little time longer passing the time in making empty remarks, and then took his leave. As he was going away, Zhuge Liang cautioned him, saying, "Do not let Zhou Yu know that I know his ruse. If you let him know, he will seek some chance to do me harm." Lu Su promised. Nevertheless he went straight to his chief and related the whole thing just as it happened. "Really he must be got rid of," said Zhou Yu. "I have quite decided to put the man out of the way." "If you slay him, will not Cao Cao laugh at you?"

"Oh, no! I will find a legitimate way of getting rid of him so that he shall go to his death without resentment."

"But how can you find a legitimate way of assassinating him?"

"Do not ask too much. You will see presently."

Soon after all the officers were summoned to the main tent, and Zhuge Liang's presence was desired. He went contentedly enough. When all were seated, Zhou Yu suddenly addressed Zhuge Liang, saying, "I am going to fight a battle with the enemy soon on the water. What weapons are the best?"

"On a great river arrows are the best," said Zhuge Liang.

"Your opinion and mine agree. But at the moment we are short of them. I wish you would undertake to supply about a hundred thousand arrows for the naval fight. As it is for the public service, you will not decline, I hope."

"Whatever task the Commander-in-Chief lays upon me, I must certainly try to perform," replied Zhuge Liang. "May I inquire by what date you require the hundred thousand arrows?"

"Could you have them ready in ten days?"

"The enemy will be here very soon. Ten days will be too late," said Zhuge Liang.

"In how many days do you estimate the arrows can be ready?"

"Let me have three days. Then you may send for your hundred thousand."

"No joking, remember!" said Zhou Yu. "There is no joking in war time."

"Dare I joke with the Commander-in-Chief? Give me a formal military order. If I have not completed the task in three days, I will take my punishment."

Zhou Yu, secretly delighted, sent for the secretaries and prepared the commission then and there. Then he drank to the success of the undertaking and said, "I shall have to congratulate you most heartily when this is accomplished."

"This day is too late to count," said Zhuge Liang. "On the third from tomorrow morning send five hundred soldiers to the river side to convey the arrows."

They drank a few more cups together, and then Zhuge Liang took his leave. After he had gone, Lu Su said, "Do you not think there is some deceit about this?"

"Clearly it is not I! It is he who has signed his own death warrant," said Zhou Yu. "Without being pressed in the least, he asked for a formal order in the face of the whole assembly. Even if he grew a pair of wings, he could not escape. Only I will just order the workers to delay him as much as they can, and not supply him with materials, so that he is sure to fail. And then, when the certain penalty is incurred, who can criticize? You can go and inquire about it all and keep me informed." So off went Lu Su to seek Zhuge Liang, who at once reproached him with having blabbed about the former business.

Zhuge Liang said, "He wants to hurt me, as you know, and I did not think you could not keep my secret. And now there is what you saw today, and how do you think I can get a hundred thousand arrows made in three days? You will simply have to rescue me."

"You brought the misfortune on yourself, and how can I rescue you?" said Lu Su.

"I look to you for the loan of twenty vessels, manned each by thirty people. I want blue cotton screens and bundles of straw lashed to the sides of the boats. I have good use for them. On the third day, I shall undertake to deliver the fixed number of arrows. But on no account must you let Zhou Yu know, or my scheme will be wrecked."

Lu Su consented, and this time he kept his word. He went to report to his chief as usual, but he said nothing about the boats. He only said, "Zhuge Liang is not using bamboo or feathers or glue or varnish, but has some other way of getting arrows."

"Let us await the three days' limit," said Zhou Yu, puzzled though confident. On his side Lu Su quietly prepared a score of light swift boats, each with its crew and the blue screens and bundles of grass complete and, when these were ready, he placed them at Zhuge Liang's disposal.

Zhuge Liang did nothing on the first day, nor on the second. On the third day at the middle of the fourth watch, Zhuge Liang sent a private message asking Lu Su to come to his boat.

"Why have you sent for me, Sir?" asked Lu Su.

"I want you to go with me to get those arrows."

"Whither are you going?"

"Do not ask. You will see."

Then the twenty boats were fastened together by long ropes and moved over to the north bank. (1098 词)

第四章　古典小说英译的母语译者和非母语译者的定量比较研究

罗译：ZHOU YU SENT LU SU to find out if Kongming had detected the subterfuge. Kongming welcomed Lu Su aboard his little boat, and the two men sat face-to-face. "Every day I am taken up with military concerns and miss your advice," Lu Su began. "Rather, I am the tardy one, having yet to convey my felicitations to the chief commander," answered Kongming. "What felicitations?" asked Lu Su. "Why," replied Kongming, "for that very matter about which he sent you here to see if I knew." The color left Lu Su's face. "But how did you know, master?" he asked. Kongming went on: "The trick was good enough to take in Jiang Gan.

Cao Cao, though hoodwinked for the present will realize what happened quickly enough—he just won't admit the mistake. But with those naval commanders dead, the Southland has no major worry, so congratulations are certainly in order. I hear that Cao Cao has replaced them with Mao Jie and Yu Jin.

One way or another, those two will do in their navy!" Lu Su, unable to respond sensibly, temporized as best he could before he rose to leave. "I trust you will say nothing about this in front of Zhou Yu," Kongming urged Lu Su, "lest he again be moved to do me harm." Lu Su agreed but finally divulged the truth when he saw the field marshal. Astounded, Zhou Yu said, "The man must die. I am determined." "If you kill him," Lu Su argued, "Cao Cao will have the last laugh." "I will have justification," answered Zhou Yu. "And he will not feel wronged." "How will you do it?" asked Lu Su. "No more questions now. You'll see soon enough," Zhou Yu replied. The next day Zhou Yu gathered his generals together and summoned Kongming, who came eagerly. At the assembly Zhou Yu asked him, "When we engage Cao Cao in battle on the river routes, what should be the weapon of choice?" "On the Great River, bow and arrow," Kongming replied. "My view precisely, sir," Zhou Yu said. "But we happen to be short of arrows. Dare I trouble you, sir, to undertake the production of one hundred thousand arrows to use against the enemy? Please favor us with your cooperation in this official matter." "Whatever task the chief commander assigns, I shall strive to complete," replied Kongming. "But may I ask by what time you will require them?" "Can you finish in ten days?" asked Zhou Yu. "Cao's army is due at any moment," said Kongming. "If we must wait ten days, it will spoil everything." "How many days do you estimate you need, sir?" said Zhou Yu. "With all respect, I will deliver the arrows in three days," Kongming answered. "There is no room for levity in the army," Zhou Yu snapped. "Dare I trifle with the chief commander?" countered Kongming. "I beg to submit my pledge under martial law: if I fail to finish in three days' time, I will gladly suffer the maximum punishment." Elated, Zhou Yu had his administrative officer publicly accept the document. He then offered Kongming wine, saying, "You will be well rewarded when your mission is accomplished." 1 "It's too late to begin today," said Kongming. "Production begins tomorrow. On the third day send five hundred men to the river for the arrows." After a few more cups, he left. Lu Su said to Zhou Yu, "This man has to be deceiving us." "He is delivering himself into our hands!" replied Zhou Yu. "We did not force him. Now that he has publicly undertaken this task in writing, he couldn't escape if he sprouted wings. Just have the artisans delay delivery of whatever he needs. He will miss the appointed time; and when we fix his punishment, what defense will he be able to make? Now go to him again and bring me back news."

Lu Su went to see Kongming. "Didn't I tell you not to say anything?" Kongming began. "He is determined to kill me. I never dreamed you would expose me. And now today he actually pulled this trick on me! How am I supposed to produce one hundred thousand arrows in three days? You have to save me!"

"You brought this on yourself," said Lu Su. "How can I save you?" "You must lend me twenty vessels," Kongming went on, "with a crew of thirty on each. Lined up on either side of each vessel I want a thousand bundles of straw wrapped in black cloth. I have good use for them. I'm sure we can have the arrows on the third day. But if you tell Zhou Yu this time, my plan will fail." Lu Su agreed, though he had no idea what Kongming was up to, and reported back to Zhou Yu without mentioning the boats: "Kongming doesn't seem to need bamboo, feathers, glue, or other materials. He seems to have something else in mind." Puzzled, Zhou Yu said, "Let's see what he has to say after three days have gone by." Lu Su quietly placed at Kongming's disposal all he had requested. But neither on the first day nor on the second did Kongming make any move. On the third day at the fourth watch he secretly sent for Lu Su.

"Why have you called me here?" Su asked. "Why else? To go with me to fetch the arrows," Kongming replied. "From where?" inquired Lu Su. "Ask no questions," said Kongming. "Let's go; you'll see." He ordered the boats linked by long ropes and set out for the north shore.（930 词）

杨译：Lu Su went as instructed to Zhuge Liang's boat. He was asked into the cabin and both men sat down.

"The fighting has kept us so busy these last few days that I haven't come to hear your instruction," said Lu Su.

Zhuge Liang replied, "It was most remiss of me not to have gone to congratulate your commander."

"Congratulate him for what?"

"The matter Zhou Yu has sent you to find out whether I knew about or not. That calls for congratulations."

Lu Su turned pale and asked, "But how did you know?"

"The trick was only good enough to fool Jiang Gan. Though Cao Cao was taken in at the time, he must have realized his mistake at once; only of course he won't admit it. Now that Cai Mao and Zhang Yun are dead, your troubles are over. This certainly is a case for congratulation. I hear that Cao Cao has appointed Mao Jie and Yu Jin as his new admirals—his fleet is as good as doomed."

Flabbergasted, Lu Su made small talk for a while before taking his leave.

"Please don't tell Zhou Yu that I knew this," said Zhuge Liang. "He would be jealous and find some excuse to kill me."

Although Lu Su agreed, he went straight to Zhou Yu and reported all that had happened. Staggered, Zhou Yu exclaimed, "Shall this man live? I am determined to get rid of him!"

"If you kill Zhuge Liang, Cao Cao will laugh."

"I shall find some plausible pretext so that he can't complain of any injustice."

"How will you do that?"

"Don't ask me. Just wait and see."

The next day Zhou Yu assembled his officers and summoned Zhuge Liang to a council. The latter went there cheerfully, and after they had taken seats Zhou Yu asked, "What arms are most important in naval fighting? We shall be engaging the forces of Cao Cao soon."

"On the river, arrows are best," said Zhuge Liang. "I agree with you. But we are rather short of arrows. Would you undertake to supply a hundred thousand for our next fight? Since this is for the common good, I am sure you won't refuse!"

"I shall certainly do my best to carry out your orders," said Zhuge Liang. "May I ask when you want the arrows?"

"Could you have them ready in ten days?"

"The enemy may be here any time. Ten days would be too late."

"In that case how long do you think you will need?" "In three days I can give you a hundred thousand arrows."

"We don't appreciate jokes in the army!" said Zhou Yu.

"How dare I joke with you, commander?" protested Zhuge Liang. "Give me a written order. If I haven't done the job in three days, I am willing to accept any punishment."

In high good humour Zhou Yu ordered his adjutant to draw up an order forthwith. Then he drank to Zhuge Liang's success and said, "When this task is completed, you will be rewarded."

"It is too late to start today. I will start tomorrow," said Zhuge Liang. "Three days from tomorrow you can send five hundred men to the river bank to fetch the arrows." After drinking a few more cups he took his leave.

第四章　古典小说英译的母语译者和非母语译者的定量比较研究

"Do you think he is up to some trick?" asked Lu Su. "I think he has signed his own death warrant," said Zhou Yu. "I didn't push him into this. He asked for that formal order before the whole council. Even if he sprouts wings he can hardly escape this time. I shall just tell the workmen to hold things up and not supply him with the material he needs, so that of course he can't produce the arrows. Then, when I condemn him, no one can protest. Go and see what he's doing now and keep me informed."

So off went Lu Su to see Zhuge Liang, who said, "I asked you not to let Zhou Yu know or he would kill me. But you couldn't hold your tongue, and now I'm in trouble. How am I to make a hundred thousand arrows in three days? You must come to my rescue."

"You brought this on yourself," replied Lu Su. "How can I help you?"

"I want the loan of twenty boats, each manned by thirty men. All the boats should have black cloth curtains and a thousand bundles of straw lashed to both sides. I shall make good use of them. On the third day I promise to deliver the arrows. But on no account tell Zhou Yu, or my plan will fall through." Although Lu Su was puzzled, when he went back to Zhou Yu he did not mention the boats. He said only that Zhuge Liang had not asked for bamboo, feathers, glue or varnish, but had some other way of producing arrows. Zhou Yu was puzzled too but simply said, "Well, we'll see what he has to say in three days' time."

Lu Su quietly prepared twenty fast ships each manned by more than thirty men, as well as the curtains and straw. The first and second days, Zhuge Liang made no move. Before dawn on the third day at about the fourth watch, he secretly invited Lu Su to his boat. When asked the reason he said, "I want you to come with me to fetch those arrows."

"Where from?"

"Don't ask that. You will see."

Then Zhuge Liang had the twenty ships fastened together with a long rope and made them row towards the north bank.（930 词）

张译: Lu Su went as instructed to Zhuge Liang's boat. He was asked into the cabin and both men sat down.

"The fighting has kept us so busy these few days that I haven't come to hear your instructions." said Lu Su.

Zhuge Liang replied, "It was most remiss of me not to have gone to congratulate your commander."

"Congratulate him for what?"

The matter Zhou Yu has sent you to find out whether I knew about or not. That calls for congratulations.

Lu Su turned pale and asked, "But how did you know?"

"The trick was only good enough to fool Jiang Gan. Though Cao Cao was taken in at the time, he must have realized his mistake at once; only of course he wont admit it. now that Cai Mao and Zhang Yun are dead, your troubles are over. This certainly is a case for congratulation. I hear that Cao Cao has appointed Mao Jie and Yu Jin as his new admirals. his fleet is as good as doomed."

Flabbergasted, Lu Su made small talk for a while before taking his leave. "Please don't tell Zhou Yu that I knew this," said Zhuge Liang. "He would be jealous and find some excuse to kill me."

Although Lu Su agreed, he went straight to Zhou Yu and reported all that had happened. Staggered, Zhou Yu exclaimed, "Shall this man live? I am determined to get rid of him!"

"If you kill Zhuge Liang, Cao Cao will laugh."

"I shall find some plausible pretext so that he can't complain of any injustice."

"How will you do that?"

"Don't ask me, Just wait and see."

The next day Zhou Yu assembled his officers and summoned Zhuge liang to a council. The latter went there cheerfully, and after they had taken seats zhou Yu asked," What arms are most important in naval fighting? We shall be engaging the forces of Cao Cao soon." "On the river, arrows are best," said Zhuge Liang.

"I agree with you. But we are rather short of arrows. Would you

第四章　古典小说英译的母语译者和非母语译者的定量比较研究

undertake to supply a hundred thousand for our next fight? Since this is for the common good, I am sure you won't refuse!"

"I shall certainly do my best to carry out your orders," said Zhuge Liang." May I ask when you want the arrows?" "

""Could you have them ready in ten days?" "

"The enemy may be here any time, Ten days would be too late."

"In that case how long do you think you will need?"

"In three days I can give you a hundred thousand arrows. We don't appreciate jokes in the army!" said Zhou Yu.

"How dare I joke with you, commander?" protested Zhuge Liang. "Give me a written order. If I haven't done the job in three days, I am willing to accept any punishment."

"In high good humour Zhou Yu ordered his adjutant to draw up an order forth with. Then he drank to Zhuge Liang's success and said, "When this task is completed, you will be rewarded."

"It is too late to start today. I will start tomorrow," said Zhuge Liang. "Three days from tomorrow you can send five hundred men to the river bank to fetch the arrows. After drinking a few more cups he took his leave.

"Do you think he is up to some trick?" asked Lu Su

"I think he has signed his own death warrant," said Zhou Yu. "I didn't push him into this. He asked for that formal order before the whole council. Even if he sprouts wings he can hardly escape this time. I shall just tell the workmen to hold things up and not supply him with the material he needs, so that of course he can't produce the arrows. Then, when I condemn him, no one can protest. Go and see what he's doing now and keep me informed."

So off went Lu Su to see Zhuge Liang, who said, "I asked you not to let Zhou Yu know or he would kill me. But you couldn't hold your tongue, and now I'm in trouble. How am I to make a hundred thousand arrows in three days? You must come to my rescue."

"You brought this on yourself," replied Lu Su. " How can I help you?"

"I want the loan of twenty boats, each manned by thirty men. All the boats should have green cloth curtains and a thousand bundles of straw lashed to both sides. I shall make good use of them. On the third day I promise to deliver the arrows. But on no account tell Zhou Yu, or my plan will fall through."

Although Lu Su was puzzled, when he went back to Zhou Yu he did not mention the boats. He said only that Zhuge Liang had not asked for bamboo

feathers, glue or varnish, but had some other way of producing arrows.

Zhou Yu was puzzled too but simply said, "Well, we'll see what he has to say in three days time."

Lu Su quietly prepared twenty fast ships each manned by more than thirty men, as well as the curtains and straw. The first and second days, Zhuge Liang made no move. Before dawn on the third day at about the fourth watch, he secretly invited Lu Su to his boat. when asked the reason he said, "I want you to come with me to fetch those arrows."

"Where from?"

"Don't ask that. You will see." Then Zhuge Liang had the twenty ships fastened together with a long rope and made them row towards the north bank. (933 词)

从以上例句来看,并不意味着母语译者的形符数一定大于非母语译者的形符数。形符数的多少受多种因素的影响和制约,母语译者思维模式的影响只是其中一个因素。

4.2.2 类符

类符数(types)是指特定文本中所使用单词的种类,反映了译文所使用单词的种类的多少。类符数的大小反映了译文所使用的单词的种类的多少,类符数越大,说明译文所使用的词汇越丰富,反之,则说明译文所使用的词汇相对越少。同一原文的不同译文的类符数,反映了译文词汇的丰富程度。词汇的丰富程度对于译文如何再现原文的精神内涵

第四章　古典小说英译的母语译者和非母语译者的定量比较研究

和风格上的细腻微妙之处具有重要影响。一般来说,译文的类符数越大,词汇越丰富,越有助于再现原文的精神内涵和风格上的细腻微妙之处;反之,类符数越小,词汇相对越少,则译文对于原文的精神内涵和风格的细腻微妙之处的再现越受影响和制约。基于此,类符数是反映译文风格的一个重要指标,其大小对于译文再现原文的风格具有重要影响,是反映译者受诸多因素,尤其是译者自身的翻译风格、翻译策略和文化倾向性的影响的重要指标。下面本研究将从类符数的视角来对母语译者和非母语译者的译文进行考察和比较分析。

从《三国演义》三个英文全译本的类符数的统计来看,我们可以发现邓译本的类符数为14209,罗译本的类符数为16163,虞译本的类符数为13785。三位译者在类符数方面的差异较为明显。类符数依次由大到小排列,罗译本最多,其次是邓译本,虞译本最少。其中,类符数最多的罗译本比类符数最少的虞译本多出2378个单词,比排第二位的邓译本多出1954个单词,排第二位的邓译本比类符数最少的虞译本多424个单词。罗译本与虞译本的差距最为明显,2378个单词相对于14209或13785的总单词量来说,所占比例是比较大的。两位母语译者的类符数要大于非母语译者的类符数。而且从罗译本的形符数相对于虞译本要小的情况来看,罗译本的词汇的丰富度更为有助于译文的创造性和灵活性,尤其是有助于译文再现原文的精神内涵和风格的细腻微妙之处。

从《三国演义》四个英文节译本的类符数的统计来看,我们可以发现邓译本(节译)的类符数为4233,罗译本(节译)的类符数为4790,杨译本(节译)的类符数为3212,张译本(节译)的类符数为3842。四位译者在类符数方面的差异比较显著。按照类符数的大小依次由大到小排列,罗译本(节译)最多,邓译本(节译)排第二位,第三位是张译本(节译),杨译本(节译)最小。其中,类符数最多的罗译本(节译)比类符数最小的杨译本(节译)多出1578个单词,比排第三位的张译本(节译)多出948个单词,差异非常显著。排第二位的邓译本(节译)比类符数最小的杨译本(节译)多出1021个单词,比排第三位的张译本(节译)多出391个单词,差异也比较明显。

从以上对于《三国演义》两位母语译者和一位非母语译者的类符数的统计,以及对于《三国演义》从第43回到第50回共8回的两位母语译者和两位非母语译者的类符数的统计来看,母语译者和非母语译者在类符数方面的差异比较显著,表现为对于同一原作,母语译者的类符数显著大于非母语译者的类符数。基于以上《三国演义》的全译本和节译本的母语译者和非母语译者形符数的统计和比较分析,我们可以认为特定文本的译文类符数的大小与译者的文化身份密切相关,表现为母语译者的类符数大于非母语译者的类符数。

  母语译者的类符数大于非母语译者的类符数,对于二者译文的风格特征具有重要的影响。如前文所述,文本的类符数是反映文本风格特征的重要指标之一,类符数的大小是影响译文创造性和灵活性以及再现原文精神风貌和风格的细腻微妙之处的重要因素。类符数越大,词汇种类越丰富,意味着译者对原文中同一词汇在不同上下文中使用语义内涵和感情色彩等层面具有细微差异的近义词或同义词进行处理;或者对于原文中的句子或语篇使用相对于原文更为丰富的词类进行再创造。对于同一原作的内容和风格来说,译文所使用的词汇越丰富,种类越多,越有助于充分和细腻入微地进行再创造,也越有助于原文的内容和风格以目的语的载体得到"重生",也越有助于译文接近或达到"神似"或"化境"。就词汇丰富度对于译文的影响来说,母语译者的类符数较高的特征对其译文的创造性和灵活性以及再现原文的精神风貌和风格的细腻微妙之处具有重要的作用。基于母语译者和非母语译者在类符数方面的差异,我们可以认为译文类符数较高是母语优势的一个重要特征。下面是《三国演义》英译的例子。

  例7:
  原文:曹操连饮数杯,不觉沉醉,唤左右捧过笔砚,亦欲作铜雀台诗。刚才下笔,"东吴使华歆表奏刘备为荆州牧,孙权以妹嫁刘备,汉上九郡大半已属备矣。"操闻之,手脚慌乱,投笔于地。程昱曰:"丞相在万军之中,矢石交攻之际,未尝动心;今闻刘备得了荆州,何故如此失惊?"操曰:"刘备,人中之龙也,生平未尝得水。今得荆州,是困龙入大海矣,孤安得不动心哉?"程昱曰:"丞相知华歆来意否?"操曰:"未知。"昱曰:"孙权本忌刘备,欲以兵攻之,但恐丞相乘虚而击,故令华歆为使,表荐刘备,乃安备之心,以塞丞相之望耳。"操点头曰:"是也。"昱曰:"某有一计,使孙、刘自相吞并,丞相乘间图之,一鼓而二敌俱破。"操大喜,遂问其计。程昱曰:"东吴所倚者,周瑜也。丞相今表奏周瑜为南郡太守,程普为江夏太守,留华歆在朝重用之,瑜必自与刘备为仇敌矣。我乘其相并而图之,不亦善乎?"操曰:"仲德之言,正合孤意。"遂

第四章 古典小说英译的母语译者和非母语译者的定量比较研究

召华歆上台,重加赏赐。当日筵散,操即引文武回许昌,表奏周瑜为总领南郡太守,程普为江夏太守。封华歆为大理少卿,留在许都。使命至东吴,周瑜、程普各受职讫。

周瑜既领南郡,愈思报仇,遂上书吴侯,乞令鲁肃去讨还荆州。孙权乃命肃曰:"汝昔保借荆州与刘备,今备迁延不还,等待何时?"肃曰:"文书上明白写着,得了西川便还。"权叱曰:"只说取西川,到今又不动兵,不等老了人?"肃曰:"某愿往言之。"遂乘船投荆州而来。(581字)

邓译:After this oration Cao Cao drank many cups of wine in quick succession till he became very intoxicated.He bade his servants bring him brush and inkstone so that he might compose a poem.But as he was beginning to write, they announced, "The Marquis of Wu has sent Hua Xin as an envoy and presented a memorial to appoint Liu Bei Imperial Protector of Jingzhou. Sun Quan's sister is now Liu Bei's wife, while on the River Han, the greater part of the nine territories is under Liu Bei's rule." Cao Cao was seized with quaking fear at the news and threw the pen on the floor. Cheng Yu said to him, "O Prime Minister, you have been among fighting soldiers by myriads and in danger from stones and arrows many a time and never quailed. Now the news that Liu Bei has got possession of a small tract of country throws you into a panic. Why is it thus?" Cao Cao replied, "Liu Bei is a dragon among humans. All his life hitherto he has never found his element, but now that he has obtained Jingzhou: It is as if the dragon, once captive, had escaped to the mighty deep. There is good reason for me to quake with fear."

"Do you know the reason of the coming of Hua Xin?" said Cheng Yu.

"No, I know not," said the Prime Minister.

"Liu Bei is Sun Quan's one terror, and Sun Quan would attack Liu Bei were it not for you, O Prime Minister. Sun Quan feels you would fall upon him while he was smiting his enemy. Wherefore he has taken this means of calming Liu Bei's suspicions and fears and at the same time directing your enmity toward Liu Bei and from himself." Had Duke Zhou, the virtuous, died, while foul-mouthed Slander was spreading vile rumors; Or Wang Mang, the treacherous, while he was noted for the deference paid to learned men; None would have known their real characters. Cao Cao nodded. "Yes," he said. Cheng Yu continued, "Now this is my plan to set Sun Quan and Liu Bei at one another and give you the opportunity to destroy both. It can be done easily."

"What is your plan?" asked Cao Cao.

"The one prop of the South Land is Zhou Yu. Remove it by memorializing that Zhou Yu be appointed Governor of Nanjun. Then get Cheng Pu made Governor of Jiangxia, and cause the Emperor to retain this Hua Xin in the capital to await some important post. Zhou Yu will assuredly attack Liu Bei, and that will be our chance. Is not the scheme good?"

"Friend Cheng Yu, you are a man after my own heart."

Wherefore Cao Cao summoned the emissary from the South Land and overwhelmed him with gifts. That day was the last of the feastings and merry-makings; and Cao Cao, with all the company, returned to the capital where he forthwith presented a memorial assigning Zhou Yu and Cheng Pu to the governorships of Nanjun and Jiangxia, and Hua Xin was retained at the capital with a post of ministry.

The messenger bearing the commissions for their new offices went down to the South Land, and both Zhou Yu and Cheng Pu accepted the appointments. Having taken over his command, the former thought all the more of the revenge he contemplated and, to bring matters to a head, he wrote to Sun Quan asking him to send Lu Su and renew the demand for the rendition of Jingzhou. Wherefore Lu Su was summoned, and his master said to him, "You are the guarantor in the loan of Jingzhou to Liu Bei. He still delays to return it, and how long am I to wait?" "The writing said plainly that the rendition would follow the occupation of Yizhou." Sun Quan shouted back, "Yes, it said so! But so far they have not moved a soldier to the attack. I will not wait till old age has come to us all." "I will go and inquire?" said Lu Su. So he went down into a ship and sailed to Jingzhou.（类符：307）

罗译：The wine had inspired Cao Cao. He called for writing brush

第四章　古典小说英译的母语译者和非母语译者的定量比较研究

and inkstone, intending to celebrate the Bronze Bird Tower in verse and was about to set pen to paper when someone announced: "Lord Sun Quan has sent Hua Xin with a petition recommending Liu Bei as protector of Jingzhou. Sun Quan's sister is now Liu Bei's wife, and most of the nine districts along the River Han already belong to Liu Bei." This report shattered Cao Cao's composure, and he threw the brush to the ground.

Cheng Yu said, "Your Excellency has led tens of thousands of men, faced slings and arrows in the heat of battle, and never once lost his nerve. Why does Liu Bei's capture of Jingzhou trouble you so?" "Liu Bei," Cao Cao replied, "is a veritable dragon among men, but he has never found his element. Now the dragon is confined no more; he has reached the open sea. Of course I am troubled." "Do you know what Hua Xin really wants?" Cheng Yu asked. "No," Cao replied. "Liu Bei worries Sun Quan," Cheng Yu explained. "Quan wants to attack him but fears that Your Excellency might attack the Southland while he is occupied with Liu Bei. That is why he has sent Hua Xin to recommend the appointment: to reassure Liu Bei and thus deter any move by Your Excellency against the south." "True enough," said Cao Cao, nodding. Cheng Yu continued: "I have a plan, however, for turning Sun and Liu against each other. It would allow Your Excellency to maneuver both enemies into ruining each other—two vanquished at one stroke!"

Cao was delighted and asked for details. "The pillar of the south," Cheng Yu went on, "is Zhou Yu, the chief commander. Your Excellency should petition the throne to appoint Zhou Yu governor of Nanjun and Cheng Pu governor of Jiangxia; 7and Hua Xin should be kept here at court and given an important position. Zhou Yu will then consider Liu Bei his mortal enemy, and we will profit from their conflict. Does this not seem apt?"

"My thought exactly," Cao Cao responded. He called Hua Xin to the dais and bestowed rich gifts on him. After the banquet Cao Cao led his officials and officers back to Xuchang, where he submitted the appointments for Zhou Yu and Cheng Pu to the Emperor. Hua Xin was made junior minister of justice and kept in the capital. The documents confirming the appointments were then sent to the south, and Zhou Yu and Cheng Pu accepted their new offices.

Now governor of Nanjun, Zhou Yu pondered his revenge against Xuande even more intently. His first step was to petition Lord Sun Quan to have Lu Su try again to reclaim Jingzhou. Accordingly, Sun Quan commanded Lu Su: "You served as guarantor when we loaned Jingzhou to Liu Bei. But he's dragging things out. How long must we wait to get it back?" "The document," Lu Su said, "provides for its return only after they acquire the Riverlands." This answer provoked Sun Quan to say, "That's all I hear, but so far they haven't sent one soldier west. I don't intend to wait for it until I've grown old." "Let me go and speak to them," responded Lu Su. And so he sailed to Jingzhou once more. （类符：278）

虞译：After this speech Cao Cao drank several cups of wine in quick succession and became quite intoxicated. He told his servants to bring him writing brush and inkstone so that he might also compose a poem. But as he was beginning to write there suddenly came reports of startling news. He was told that Sun Quan, ruler of Wu, had sent an envoy to present a petition that recommended Liu Bei to be appointed Governor of Jingzhou; that Sun Quan's sister was now Liu Bei's wife; and that along the River Han the greater part of the nine districts was under Liu Bei's rule. Cao Cao was seized with such a quaking fear at the news that he threw the brush on the floor. Cheng Yu was surprised and said to him, "You have been among fighting men for myriads, sir, and you have been in danger from stones and arrows many a time, but never have you betrayed any sign of agitation. Why are you then so affected at the news of Liu Bei's possession of Jingzhou?"

Cao Cao replied, "Liu Bei is a dragon among men. All his life so far he has never found his opportunities, but now that he has obtained Jingzhou it is as though the dragon, once a captive, has escaped to the mighty deep. There is good reason for me to tremble with fear."

"Do you know the reason of the coming of Hua Xin?" asked Cheng Yu. Cao Cao replied that he did not. "Sun Quan is apprehensive of Liu Bei and he would have attacked him were it not for you, sir. He fears that you might fall upon him while he is wrestling with Liu Bei. Therefore he has taken this measure to relieve Liu Bei of his suspicions and at the same time to keep you from invading him." Cao Cao nodded his agreement. Cheng Yu continued, "Now I have a plan to set Sun and Liu at one another and give you the opportunity to destroy them both."

"What is it?" asked Cao Cao.

"The mainstay of Wu is Zhou Yu. You can get Zhou Yu appointed prefect of Nanjun, Cheng Pu as prefect of Jiangxia, and retain the envoy Hua Xin in the capital for some important post. As both these cities have fallen into Liu Bei's hands, Zhou Yu will assuredly attack Liu Bei and that will be our chance. Isn't this a good scheme?"

"You are really a man after my own heart." So he summoned the emissary from Wu and overwhelmed him with gifts. That day was the last of the feasting and merry-making and Cao Cao, with all the company, returned to the capital, where he at once presented a memorial to the Emperor assigning Zhou Yu and Cheng Pu to the posts mentioned above, while retaining Hua Xin at the capital. A messenger bearing the commissions for their new offices was sent down to Wu and both Zhou Yu and Cheng Pu accepted the appointments. This move of Cao Cao's made Zhou Yu all the more anxious to have his revenge on Liu Bei. He wrote to Sun Quan, asking him to send Lu Su to Liu Bei to renew the demand for returning Jingzhou. So Lu Su was summoned and his master said to him, "You are the guarantor in the loan of Jingzhou to Liu Bei, but he still delays in returning it. How long am I to wait?"

"The writing said plainly that it would be handed over to us after his occupation of West Chuan."

"What is the use of such an empty promise?" Sun Quan retorted. "So far, they have not moved a single soldier to capture it. Am I supposed to wait until I grow old?"

"I will go and inquire," said Lu Su. So he took a boat and sailed to Jingzhou. （类符：272）

例 8：

原文：不说江中鏖兵。且说甘宁令蔡中引入曹寨深处，宁将蔡中一刀砍于马下，就草上放起火来。吕蒙遥望中军火起，也放十数处火，接应甘宁。潘璋、董袭分头放火呐喊，四下里鼓声大震。曹操与张辽引百馀骑，在火林内走，看前面无一处不着。正走之间，毛玠救得文聘，引十数骑到。操令军寻路。张辽指道："只有乌林地面空阔可走。"操径奔乌林。正走间，背后一军赶到，大叫："曹贼休走！"火光中现出吕蒙旗号。操催军马向前，留张辽断后，抵敌吕蒙。却见前面火把又起，从山谷中拥出一军，大叫："凌统在此！"曹操肝胆皆裂。忽斜刺里一彪军到，大叫："丞相休慌，徐晃在此！"彼此混战一场，夺路望北而走。

忽见一队军马屯在山坡前，徐晃出问，乃是袁绍手下降将马延、张顗，有三千北地军马，列寨在彼。当夜见满天火起，未敢转动，恰好接着曹操。操教二将引一千军马开路，其馀留着护身。操得这枝生力军马，心中稍安。马延、张顗二将飞骑前行。不到十里，喊声起处，一彪军出，为首一将大呼曰："吾乃东吴甘兴霸也！"马延正欲交锋，早被甘宁一刀斩于马下。张顗挺枪来迎，宁大喝一声，顗措手不及，被宁手起一刀，翻身落马。后军飞报曹操。操此时指望合淝有兵救应，不想孙权在合淝路口望见江中火光，知是我军得胜，便教陆逊举火为号。太史慈见了，与陆逊合兵一处，冲杀将来。操只得望彝陵而走，路上撞见张郃，操令断后。（559 词）

邓译：While fire was consuming the naval base of Cao Cao, Gan Ning made Cai Zhong guide him into the innermost recesses of Cao Cao's camp. Then Gan Ning slew Cai Zhong with one slash of his sword. After this Gan Ning set fire to the jungle; and at this signal, Lu Meng put fire to the grass in ten places near to each other. Then other fires were started, and the noise of battle was on all sides.

Cao Cao and Zhang Liao, with a small party of horsemen, fled through the burning forest. They could see no road in front; all seemed on fire. Presently Mao Jie and Wen Ping, with a few more horsemen, joined them. Cao Cao bade the soldiers seek a way through.

Zhang Liao pointed out, saying, "The only suitable road is

through the Black Forest." And they took it. They had gone but a short distance when they were overtaken by a small party of the enemy, and a voice cried, "Cao Cao, stop!"

It was Lu Meng, whose ensign soon appeared against the fiery background. Cao Cao urged his small party of fugitives forward, bidding Zhang Liao defend him from Lu Meng. Soon after Cao Cao saw the light of torches in front, and from a gorge there rushed out another force.

And the leader cried, "Ling Tong is here!"

Cao Cao was scared. His liver and gall both seemed torn from within. But just then on his half right, he saw another company approach and heard a cry, "Fear not, O Prime Minister, I am here to rescue you!"

The speaker was Xu Huang, and he attacked the pursuers and held them off. A move to the north seemed to promise escape, but soon they saw a camp on a hill top. Xu Huang went ahead to reconnoiter and found the officers in command were Cao Cao's Generals Ma Yan and Zhang Zi, who had once been in the service of Yuan Shao. They had three thousand of northern soldiers in camp. They had seen the sky redden with the flames, but knew not what was afoot so dared make no move.

This turned out lucky for Cao Cao who now found himself with a fresh force. He sent Ma Yan and Zhang Zi, with a thousand troops, to clear the road ahead while the others remained as guard. And he felt much more secure.

The two went forward, but before they had gone very far, they heard a shouting and a party of soldiers came out, the leader of them shouting, "I am Gan Ning of Wu!" Nothing daunted the two leaders, but the redoubtable Gan Ning cut down Ma Yan. And when his brother warrior Zhang Zi set his spear and dashed forward, he too fell beneath a stroke from the fearsome sword of Gan Ning. Both leaders dead, the soldiers fled to give Cao Cao the bad news.

At this time Cao Cao expected aid from Hefei, for he knew not that Sun Quan was barring the road. But when Sun Quan saw the fires and so knew that his soldiers had won the day, he ordered Lu Xun to give the answering signal. Taishi Ci seeing this came down and his force joined up with that of Lu Xun, and they went against Cao Cao. As for Cao Cao, he could only get away toward Yiling. On the road Cao Cao fell in with Zhang He and ordered him to protect the retreat. （类符：261）

罗译：While the sea war raged, on land Gan Ning ordered Cai Zhong to bring him deep into Cao's camp.Then he struck Zhong a single blow, and he fell dead from his horse. Gan Ning began setting fires at once. Southland commander Lü Meng, seeing flames above Cao Cao's central camp, set his fires in response. Pan Zhang and Dong Xi did the same, and their troops made a great uproar, pounding their drums on all sides.

Cao Cao and Zhang Liao had little more than one hundred horsemen. Fleeing through the burning wood, they could see no place free of fire. When Mao Jie rescued Wen Ping, another dozen riders caught up with them. Cao Cao demanded that they find an escape route. Pointing to the Black Forest, Zhang Liao said, "That's the only area that seems free and clear," so Cao Cao dashed straight for the Black Forest. A troop of soldiers overtook him as their leader shouted, "Cao Cao! Stand, traitor!" Lü Meng's ensign appeared in the fiery glare.

Letting Zhang Liao deal with Lü Meng, Cao pushed on, only to be confronted by a fresh company charging out of a valley, bearing torches. A shout: "Ling Tong is here!" Cao Cao felt his nerve fail, his courage crack. Suddenly a band of soldiers veered toward him. Again, a shout: "Your Excellency, fear not, it's Xu Huang!" A rough skirmish followed. Cao Cao managed to flee some distance north before he encountered another company stationed on a slope ahead. Xu Huang rode over and found Ma Yan and Zhang Kai, two of Cao's commanders, formerly under Yuan Shao, with their force of three thousand northerners arrayed on the hill. They had seen the night sky full of flames and had hesitated to move. Now they were perfectly positioned to receive Cao Cao. He sent the two commanders ahead with one thousand men to clear a path and reserved two thousand as his

第四章　古典小说英译的母语译者和非母语译者的定量比较研究

personal guard.

Fortified by this fresh body of men, Cao's mind was easier. Ma Yan and Zhang Kai rode swiftly on, but within ten li voices rent the air, and another band of soldiers materialized. Their commander cried, "Know me for Gan Ning of the Southland!" Ma Yan tried to engage him, but Ning cut him down with one stroke. Zhang Kai raised his spear and offered combat. Whooping, Ning struck again with his sword, and Zhang Kai fell dead. Soldiers in the rear raced to inform Cao Cao.

Cao had been counting on support from troops in Hefei, unaware that Sun Quan already controlled all routes to the east. Assured of victory by the conflagration on the river, Sun Quan had Lu Xun signal TaishiCi with fire. The moment he saw it, Taishi Ci joined Lu Xun and raced toward Cao, forcing him to flee toward Yiling; on the way Cao met up with Zhang He, whom he ordered to guard the rear.（类符：272）

杨译：Leaving the battle on the river, let us turn to the shore. Gan Ning made Cai Zhong lead him through the northern camp, then cut him down from his horse with one sweep of his sword and set fire to the grass. When Lii Meng, some way off, saw the flames in Cao Cao's headquarters, he followed Gan Ning's lead and set fire to a dozen more places. Pan Zhang and Dong Xi did the same elsewhere, raising a great din and thunder of drums all around.

Cao Cao and Zhang Liao with about a hundred horsemen galloped through the burning forest—everywhere was ablaze. Presently Mao Jie, who had rescued Wen Pin, joined them with a dozen more horsemen. Cao Cao ordered them to find a way out, and pointing ahead Zhang Liao said, "There is more open ground in Wulin. Let us go that way!"

As they headed for Wulin, a party of the enemy came after them, calling, "Halt, you traitor!" In the light of the flames, they saw Lii Meng's name on the flag. Cao Cao urged his men on, leaving Zhang Liao to hold Lii Meng off.

But presently more torches gleamed ahead and another force

charged out of the valley crying, "Here is Ling Tong!" Cao Cao was nearly paralysed with fright when a third party interposed itself from one side, and the newcomers cried, "All is well, Prime Minister! Xu Huang is here!" While Xu Huang battled with Ling Tong, Cao Cao fled to the north.

　　When more cavalry was sighted on the slope ahead, Xu Huang reconnoitred and found the officers in command were Ma Yan and Zhang Yi, who had served under Yuan Shao but come over to Cao Cao. They had three thousand men and horses encamped here; but the blazing fires all round had made them afraid to move. This was a stroke of luck for Cao Cao, who ordered a thousand men to clear the road while the rest remained as his guard. This reinforcement put fresh heart into him. Ma Yan and Zhang Yi galloped forward, but before they had gone ten li they heard battle cries and another force appeared, the leader of them shouting, "Here is Gan Ning!" Before Ma Yan could engage him, Gan Ning had felled him from his horse. Then, spear in hand, Zhang Yi charged; but Gan Ning raised a mighty cry and catching Zhang Yi off guard cut him down too. This was hastily reported by the others to Cao Cao, who hoped that his Hefei troops would come to his aid. But Sun Quan was barring the road to Hefei and when he saw the fire on the river and knew that his side was winning, he ordered Lu Xun to give the pre-arranged signal. At once Taishi Ci joined forces with Lu Xun to charge, and Cao Cao had to flee towards Yiling. On the road he met Zhang He and told him to cover the retreat. (类符: 248)

　　张译: Leaving the battle on the river, let us turn to the shore. Gan Ning made Cai Zhong lead him through the northern camp, then cut him down his horse with one sweep of his sword and set fire to the grass. When Lu Meng, some way off, saw the flames in Cao Cao's headquarters, he followed Gan Ning's lead and set fire to a dozen more places. Pan Zhang and Dong Xi did the same elsewhere, raising a great din and thunder of drums all around.

　　Cao Cao and Zhang Liao with about a hundred horsemen galloped through the burning forest, everywhere was ablaze. Presently Mao Jie, who had rescued Wen Pin, joined them with a dozen more horse men. Cao Cao ordered them to find a way out, and pointing ahead Zhang Liao said, "There is more open ground in Wulin. Let us go that way!"

As they headed for Wulin, a party of the enemy came after them, calling, "Halt, you traitor!" In the light of the flames, they saw Lu Meng's name on the flag. Cao Cao urged his men on, leaving Zhang Liao to hold Lu Meng off.

But presently more torches gleamed ahead and another force charged out of the valley crying, "Here's Ling Tong!" Cao Cao was nearly paralysed with fright when a third party interposed itself from one side, and the newcomers cried, "All is well, Prime Minister! Xu Huang is here!" While Xu Huang battled with Ling Tong, Cao Cao fled to the north.

When more cavalry was sighted on the slope ahead Xu Huang reconnoitred and found the officers in command were Ma Yan and Zhang Yi, who had served under Yuan shao but come over to Cao Cao. They had three thousand men and horses encamped here, but the blazing fires all round had made them afraid to move. This was a stroke of luck for Cao Cao, who ordered two generals to lead a thousand men to clear the road while the rest remained as his guard.

This reinforcement put fresh heart into him. Ma Yan and Zhang Yi galloped forward, but before they had gone ten "li", they heard battle cries and another force appeared, the leader of them shouting, " Here is Gan Ning!" Before Ma Yan could engage him, Gan Ning had felled him from his horse. Then, spear in hand, Zhang Yi charged; but Gan Ning raised a mighty cry and catching Zhang Yi off guard cut him down too.

This was hastily reported by the others to Cao Cao, who hoped that his Hefei troops would come to his aid. But Sun Quan was barring the road to Hefei and when he saw the fire on the river and knew that his side was winning, he ordered Lu Xun to give the prearranged signal. At once Taishi Ci joined forces with Lu Xun to charge, and Cao

Cao had to flee towards Yiling. On the road he met Zhang He and told him to cover the retreat.（类符：241）

例9：

原文：孤近承帝命，奉词伐罪。旌麾南指，刘琮束手，荆襄之民，望风归顺。今统雄兵百万，上将千员，欲与将军会猎于江夏，共伐刘备，同分土地，永结盟好。幸勿观望，速赐回音。

邓译："When I, the Prime Minister, received the imperial command to punish a fault, my banners went south and Liu Zong became my prisoner, while the people of Jingzhou flocked to my side at the first rumor of my coming. Under my hand are one million strong and a thousand able leaders. My desire is, General, that we go on a great hunting expedition into Jiangxia and together attack Liu Bei. We will share his land between us, and we will swear perpetual amity. If happily you would not be a mere looker-on, I pray you reply quickly."（类符：75）

罗译：Under a recent imperial mandate, I have authority to act against state criminals. Our banners tilted southward; Liu Zong bound his hands in submission. The populace of Jingzhou, sensing the direction of events, has transferred its allegiance to us. We have one million hardy warriors and a thousand able generals. We propose that you join us, General, in a hunting expedition to Jiangxia in order to strike the decisive blow against Liu. Then, sharing the territory between us, we may seal an everlasting amity. Please do not hesitate but favor us with a speedy reply.（类符：75）

杨译："At the emperor's command, I have led my army south to punish the guilty. Liu Cong has been captured, his people have surrendered, and I now command a force of a million picked men and a thousand able generals. I hope you will join me, general, in a hunting expedition at Jiangxia to attack Liu Bei, so that we can divide his territory between us and pledge everlasting friendship. Do not hesitate, but give me an early reply!"（类符：63）

张译："At the imperial command to punish the guilt, my banners went south. Then Liu Cong has been captured, his people flocked to

第四章　古典小说英译的母语译者和非母语译者的定量比较研究

my side at the first rumour of my coming. I now command a force of a million picked men and a thousand able generals hope you will join me, General, in a hunting expedition at Jiangxia and we together attack liu Bei, so that we can divide his territory between us and pledge everlasting friendship. Do not hesitate but give me an early reply."（类符：68）

《三国演义》英译的母语译者形符数相较于非母语译者较多的特征也可以从散文英译中得到佐证。笔者使用 Wconcord 对《匆匆》《背影》和《荷塘月色》的葛译和其他四位中国译者的英译本分别进行了统计。就类符数来看，葛译最多，与徐译、杨译和朱译相比，分别多出 46，133 和 40。徐译和朱译相差不大，杨译最少。类符数反映的是文本词汇的丰富程度，葛译明显比其他三位译者的词汇丰富。

葛浩文作为母语译者和其他三位作为非母语译者在形符数和类符数方面的差异还可以从我国的经典文学名著《红楼梦》的两个英译本得到佐证。霍克斯译本和杨宪益译本是迄今为止公认的成就最多，最有影响力的两个译本。笔者使用 PowerConc 对霍克斯译本和杨宪益译本分别进行统计发现，同样是母语译者和非母语译者，霍克斯译本的类符数为 23404，远多于杨宪益译本的 17146。这说明母语译者和非母语译者在类符数方面的差异并不是偶然现象。下面我们来探讨葛译与其他三位译者形符数和类符数存在较大差异的原因。

汉英两种语言的差异直接决定了汉英两种语言在翻译过程中进行转换的复杂性。汉语注重意合，句子的连接以及语义的组合多通过词意的内在关联来完成；英语注重形合，句子的连接和语义的组合多通过功能词来完成。这是造成汉语原文翻译成英语文本之后形符数一般比原文文本要多，译文一般要比原文文本要长的现象的一个重要原因。我们发现葛译符合这一汉译英的通常现象，而其他三位译者的译文与这一现象不同。从母语译者和非母语译者身份的角度来看，母语思维模式的影响是造成这一差异的重要原因。我们再结合具体例句来分析两者的差异以及背后的原因。下面是参照语料《红楼梦》英译的例子。

例 10：

原文（霍译蓝本）：士隐听了大叫："妙极！弟每谓兄必非久居人下者，今所吟之句，飞腾之兆已见，不日可接履于云霄之上了。可贺可贺！"乃亲斟一斗为贺。雨村饮干，忽叹道："非晚生酒后狂言，若论时尚之学,晚生也或可去充数挂名。只是如今行李路费一概无措,神京路远,非赖卖字撰文即能到得。"士隐不待说完,便道:"兄何不早言!弟已久有此意,但每遇兄时并未谈及,故未敢唐突。今既如此,弟虽不才,'义利'二字却还识得。且喜明岁正当大比,兄宜作速入都,春闱一捷,方不负兄之所学。其盘费馀事,弟自代为处置,亦不枉兄之谬识矣。"当下即命小童进去,速封五十两白银并两套冬衣。又云:"十九日乃黄道之期,兄可即买舟西上,待雄飞高举,明冬再晤,岂非大快之事!"雨村收了银衣,不过略谢一语,并不介意,仍是吃酒谈笑。那天已交三鼓,二人方散。(341字)

原文(杨译蓝本):士隐听了,大叫:"妙哉!吾每谓兄必非久居人下者,今所吟之句,飞腾之兆已见,不日可接履于云霓之上矣。可贺,可贺!"乃亲斟一斗为贺。雨村饮干酒,叹道:"非晚生酒后狂言,若论时尚之学,晚生也或可去充数沽名,只是目今行囊路费一概无措,神京路远,非赖卖字撰文即能到者。"士隐不待说完,便道:"兄何不早言。愚每有此心,但每遇兄时,兄并未谈及,愚故未敢唐突。今既及此,愚虽不才,'义利'二字却还识得。且喜明岁正当大比,兄宜作速入都,春闱一战,方不负兄之所学也。其盘费馀事,弟自代为处置,亦不枉兄之谬识矣!"当下即命小童进去,速封五十两白银,并两套冬衣。又云:"十九日乃黄道之期,兄可即买舟西上,待雄飞高举,明冬再晤,岂非大快之事耶!"雨村收了银衣,不过略谢一语,并不介意,仍是吃酒谈笑。那天已交了三更,二人方散。(349字)

霍译:"Bravo!" said Shi-yin loudly. "I have always insisted that you were a young fellow who would go up in the world, and now, in these verses you have just recited, I see an augury of your ascent. In no time at all we shall see you up among the clouds! This calls for a drink!" And, saying this, he poured Yu-cun a large cup of wine.

Yu-cun drained the cup, then, surprisingly, sighed:

"Don't imagine the drink is making me boastful, but I really do believe that if it were just a question of having the sort of qualifications now in demand, I should stand as good a chance as any of getting myself on to the list of candidates. The trouble is that I simply have no means of laying my hands on the money that would be needed for lodgings and travel expenses. The journey to the capital is a long one,

第四章 古典小说英译的母语译者和非母语译者的定量比较研究

and the sort of money I can earn from my copying is not enough—"

"Why ever didn't you say this before?" said Shi-yin interrupting him. "I have long wanted to do something about this, but on all the occasions I have met you previously, the conversation has never got round to this subject, and I haven't liked to broach it for fear of offending you. Well, now we know where we are. I am not a very clever man, but at least I know the right thing to do when I see it. Luckily, the next Triennial is only a few months ahead. You must go to the capital without delay. A spring examination triumph will make you feel that all your studying has been worth while. I shall take care of all your expenses. It is the least return I can make for your friendship." And there and then he instructed his boy to go with all speed and make up a parcel of fifty tales of the best refined silver and two suits of winter clothes.

"The almanac gives the nineteenth as a good day for travelling," he went on, addressing Yu-cun again. "You can set about hiring a boat for the journey straight away. How delightful it will be to meet again next winter when you have distinguished yourself by soaring to the top over all the other candidates!"

Yu-cun accepted the silver and the clothes with only the most perfunctory word of thanks and without, apparently, giving them a further moment's thought, for he continued to drink and laugh and talk as if nothing had happened. It was well after midnight before they broke up. (类符: 231)

杨译: "Excellent!" cried Shiyin. "I've always maintained that you were cut out for great things. These lines foretell rapid advancement. Very soon you will be treading upon the clouds. Let me congratulate you." He filled another large cup. Yucun tossed it off and then sighed.

"Don't think this is just drunken talk," he said. "I'm sure I could acquit myself quite creditably in the examinations; but I have no money in my wallet for travelling expenses and the capital is far away. I can't raise enough as a scrivener..."

"Why didn't you say so before?" interposed Shiyin. "I've often wondered about this, but since you never mentioned it I didn't like to broach the subject. If that's how things are, dull as I am at least I know what's due to a friend. Luckily the Metropolitan Examinations are coming up next year. You must go as fast as you can to the capital and prove your learning in the Spring Test. I shall count it a privilege to take care of the travelling expenses and other business for you."

He sent his boy in to fetch fifty taels of silver and two suits of winter clothes.

"The nineteenth is a good day for travelling," he continued. "You can hire a boat then and start your journey westward. How good it will be to meet again next winter after you have soared up to dizzy heights."

Yucun accepted the silver and clothes with no more than perfunctory thanks, then said no more of the matter but went on feasting and talking. They did not part until the third watch（类符：171）

例 11：

原文(霍译蓝本)：说着，引人进入房内。只见其中收拾的与别处不同，竟分不出间隔来。原来四面皆是雕空玲珑木板，或"流云百蝠"，或"岁寒三友"，或山水人物，或翎毛花卉，或集锦，或博古，或万福万寿，各种花样，皆是名手雕镂五彩，销金嵌玉的。一格一格，或贮书，或设鼎，或安置笔砚，或供设瓶花，或安放盆景。其格式样或圆或方，或葵花蕉叶，或连环半璧，真是花团锦簇，剔透玲珑。倏尔五色纱糊，竟系小窗；倏尔彩绫轻覆，竟系幽户。且满墙皆是随依古董玩器之形抠成的槽子，如琴、剑、悬瓶之类，俱悬于壁，却都是与壁相平的。众人都赞："好精致！难为怎么做的！"

原来贾政等走进来了，未到两层，便都迷了旧路，左瞧也有门可通，右瞧也有窗隔断，及到跟前，又被一架书挡住，回头又有窗纱明透门径。及至门前，忽见迎面也进来了一群人，与自己的形相一样，却是一架大玻璃镜。转过镜去，越发见门多了。贾珍笑道："老爷随我来，从这里出去就是后院，出了后院倒比先近了。"引着贾政及众人转了两层纱厨，果得一门出去，院中满架蔷薇。转过花障，只见青溪前阻。众人诧异："这水又从何而来？"贾珍遥指道："原从那闸起流至洞口，从东北山凹里引到那村庄里，又开一道岔口，引至西南上，共总流到这里，仍旧合在一处，从那墙下出去。"众人听了，都道："神妙之极！"说着，忽见大山

第四章　古典小说英译的母语译者和非母语译者的定量比较研究

阻路,众人都迷了路,贾珍笑道:""跟我来。"乃在前导引,众人随着,由山脚下一转,便是平坦大路,豁然大门现于面前,众人都道:"有趣,有趣!搜神夺巧,至于此极!"于是大家出来。(623字)

原文(杨译蓝本):说着,引人进入房内。只见这几间房内收拾的与别处不同,竟分不出间隔来的。原来四面皆是雕空玲珑木板,或"流云百蝠",或"岁寒三友",或山水人物,或翎毛花卉,或集锦,或博古,或万福万寿各种花样,皆是名手雕镂,五彩销金嵌宝的。一槅一槅,或有贮书处,或有设鼎处,或安置笔砚处,或供花设瓶,安放盆景处。其槅各式各样,或天圆地方,或葵花蕉叶,或连环半璧。真是花团锦簇,剔透玲珑。倏尔五色纱糊就,竟系小窗;倏尔彩绫轻覆,竟系幽户。且满墙满壁,皆系随依古董玩器之形抠成的槽子。诸如琴、剑、悬瓶、桌屏之类,虽悬于壁,却都是与壁相平的。众人都赞:"好精致想头!难为怎么想来!"

原来贾政等走了进来,未进两层,便都迷了旧路,左瞧也有门可通,右瞧又有窗暂隔,及到了跟前,又被一架书挡住。回头再走,又有窗纱明透,门径可行;及至门前,忽见迎面也进来了一群人,都与自己形相一样——却是一架玻璃大镜相照。及转过镜去,益发见门子多了。贾珍笑道:"老爷随我来。从这门出去,便是后院,从后院出去,倒比先近了。"说着,又转了两层纱橱锦槅,果得一门出去,院中满架蔷薇,宝相。转过花障,则见青溪前阻。众人诧异:"这股水又是从何而来?"贾珍遥指道:"原从那闸起流至那洞口,从东北山坳里引到那村庄里,又开一道岔口,引到西南上,共总流到这里,仍旧合在一处,从那墙下出去。"众人听了,都道:"神妙之极,"说着,忽见大山阻路。众人都道"迷了路了。"贾珍笑道:"随我来。"仍在前导引,众人随他,直由山脚边忽一转,便是平坦宽阔大路,豁然大门前见。众人都道:"有趣,有趣,真搜神夺巧之至!"于是大家出来。(670字)

霍译: He led them inside the building. Its interior turned out to be all corridors and alcoves and galleries, so that properly speaking it could hardly have been said to have rooms at all. The partition walls which made these divisions were of wooden panelling exquisitely carved in a wide variety of motifs: bats in clouds, the "three friends of winter"—pine, plum and bamboo, little figures in landscapes, birds and flowers, scrollwork, antique bronze shapes, "good luck" and "long life" characters, and many others. The carvings, all of them the work

· 117 ·

of master craftsmen, were beautified with in-lays of gold, mother-o'-pearl and semi-precious stones. In addition to being panelled, the partitions were pierced by numerous apertures, some round, some square, some sun-flower-shaped, some shaped like a fleur-de-lis, some cusped, me fan-shaped. Shelving was concealed in the double thickness of the partition at the base of these apertures, making it possible to use them for storing books and writing materials and for the display of antique bronzes, vases of flowers, miniature tray-gardens and the like. The overall effect was at once richly colourful and, because of the many apertures, airy and graceful.

The trompe-l'ail effect of these ingenious partitions had been further enhanced by inserting false windows and doors in them, the former covered in various pastel shades of gauze, the latter hung with richly-patterned damask portieres. The main walls were pierced with window-like perforations in the shape of zithers, swords, vases and other objects of virtù.

The literary gentlemen were rapturous:

"Exquisite!" they cried. "what marvellous workmanship!"

Jia Zheng, after taking no more than a couple of turns inside this confusing interior, was already lost. To the left of him was what appeared to be a door. To the right was a wall with a window in it. But on raising its portiere he discovered the door to be a bookcase; and when, looking back, he observed—what he had not noticed before—that the light coming in through the silk gauze of the window illuminated a passage-way leading to an open doorway, and began walking towards it, a party of gentlemen similar to his own came advancing to meet him, and he realized that he was walking towards a large mirror. They were able to circumvent the mirror, but only to find an even more bewildering choice of doorways on the other side.

"Come!" said Cousin Zhen with a laugh. "Let me show you the way! If we go out here we shall be in the back courtyard. We can reach the gate of the garden much more easily from the back courtyard than from the front."

第四章 古典小说英译的母语译者和非母语译者的定量比较研究

He led them round the gauze hangings of a summer-bed, then through a door into a garden full of rambler roses. Behind the rose-trellis was a stream running between green banks. The literary gentlemen were intrigued to know where the water came from. Cousin Zhen pointed in the direction of the weir they had visited earlier:

"The water comes in over that weir, then through the grotto, then under the lea of the north-east 'mountain' to the little farm. There a channel is led off it which runs into the south-east corner of the garden. Then it runs round and rejoins the main stream here. And from here the water flows out again underneath that wall."

"How very ingenious!"

They moved on again, but soon found themselves at the foot of a tall "mountain".

"Follow me!" said Cousin Zhen, amused at the bewilderment of the others, who were now completely at sea as to their whereabouts. He led them round the foot of the "mountain"—and there, miraculously, was a broad, flat path and the gate by which they had entered, rising majestically in front of them.

"Well!" exclaimed the literary gentlemen. "This beats everything! The skill with which this has all been designed is quite out of this world!"

Whereupon they all went out of the garden. （类符：338）

杨译：He led the way into the building. It was unusually set out with no clear-cut divisions between the different rooms. There were only partitions formed of shelves for books, bronze tripods, stationery, flower vases and miniature gardens, some round, some square, some shaped like sunflowers, plantain leaves or intersecting arcs. They were beautifully carved with the motifs "clouds and a hundred bats" of the "three companions of winter"—pine, plum and bamboo—as well as landscapes and figures, birds and flowers, scrollwork, imitation curios and symbols of good fortune or long life. All executed by the finest craftsmen, they were brilliantly coloured and inlaid with gold or precious stones. The effect was splendid, the workmanship exquisite.

Here a strip of coloured gauze concealed a small window, there a gorgeous curtain hid a door. There were also niches on the walls to fit antiques, lyres, swords, vases or other ornaments, which hung level with the surface of the wall. Their amazement and admiration for the craftsmen's ingenuity knew no bounds.

After passing two partitions Jia Zheng and his party lost their way. To their left they saw a door, to their right a window; but when they went forward their passage was blocked by a bookshelf. Turning back they glimpsed the way through another window; but on reaching the door they suddenly saw a party just like their own confronting them — they were looking at a big mirror. Passing round this they came to more doorways.

"Follow me, sir," urged Jia Zhen with a smile. "Let me take you to the back courtyard and show you a short cut."

He conducted them past two gauze screens out into a courtyard filled with rose trellises. Skirting round the fence, Baoyu saw a clear stream in front.

All exclaimed in astonishment, "Where does this water come from?" Jia Zhen pointed to a spot in the distance.

"It flows from that lock we saw through the ravine, then from the northeast valley to the little farm, where some is diverted southwest. Here both streams converge to flow out underneath the wall."

"Miraculous!" they marvelled.

Now another hill barred their way and they no longer had any sense of direction; but Jia Zhen laughingly made them follow him, and as soon as they rounded the foot of the hill they found themselves on a smooth highway not far from the main entrance.

"How diverting," they said. "Really most ingenious."

And so they left the garden.（类符：252）

4.2.3 高频词

高频词就是指在特定文本中使用频率特别高的词语。选作高频词

第四章 古典小说英译的母语译者和非母语译者的定量比较研究

的依据是该词语在整个文本中所占的百分比或者该词语在整个词频中所处的前后位置。高频词与形符数和类符数一样，也是反映文本特征的一个重要指标。高频词根据其定义，可以知道其在一个文本中的最显著的特征或者说其根本特征就是极高的使用频率。特定文本中的高频词以及其分布和使用频次受诸多因素的影响和制约，包括文本所属语言的特征、文本的文体、文本的体裁、文本的题材、文本的内容、作者或译者自身的因素。就译者自身来说，其所处的社会文化语境、翻译观、翻译倾向性、翻译策略、译者的语言使用偏好。译者的文化身份等因素对译文的风格具有决定性影响。就本研究来说，我们主要关注的是译者个人的因素对译文高频词及其分布和使用频次的影响。具体来说，就是译者的文化身份，母语译者或非母语译者的身份对其译文高频词的影响。

对于译者的文化身份对译文高频词的影响的研究，本研究依然采用对同一原作的多个母语译者和非母语译者的译本进行比较分析的方法进行考察研究。《三国演义》的母语译者和非母语译者的三个全译本的排前30的高频词的情况以及《三国演义》的母语译者和非母语译者的4个节译本的排前30的高频词的情况分别如表5.和表6.所示。

表5.《三国演义》三个英文全译本高频词

次序	邓译本 词	频次	罗译本 词	频次	虞译本 词	频次
1	the	36343	the	32750	the	34984
2	and	24012	and	18686	to	22824
3	to	19161	to	17991	and	20273
4	of	15664	of	11761	of	14421
5	he	9798	a	8601	he	11429
6	a	9483	his	8336	his	10996
7	his	8901	Cao	6892	a	9550
8	in	7399	he	6881	in	7917
9	was	6534	in	6724	was	6545
10	you	6389	I	4806	you	6380
11	I	6090	you	4558	I	6156
12	Cao	6072	with	3900	Cao	5733

续表

	邓译本		罗译本		虞译本	
13	is	4739	for	3750	him	4902
14	said	4113	was	3618	that	4389
15	that	4110	him	3481	with	4388
16	with	4046	is	3215	is	4302
17	him	3915	said	3164	for	3816
18	but	3843	that	3018	but	3708
19	they	3724	on	2878	at	3648
20	not	3438	had	2837	said	3524
21	for	3367	have	2569	as	3271
23	as	3323	at	2486	they	3239
24	at	3164	but	2481	will	3218
25	this	3034	your	2411	this	3199
26	be	2970	as	2394	be	3080
27	will	2961	Zhang	2381	had	3002
28	had	2914	will	2371	not	2996
29	it	2836	it	2248	on	2772
30	on	2755	from	2247	it	2752
31	then	2585	we	2128	men	2706
32	have	2579	my	2048	so	2556

表6.《三国演义》四个英文节译本高频词

	邓译本		罗译本		杨译本		张译本	
次序	词	频次	词	频次	词	频次	词	频次
1	the	2129	the	1911	the	1267	the	1358
2	and	1412	to	1115	to	1069	to	1123
3	to	1157	and	1088	and	966	and	1015
4	of	855	of	677	of	569	Cao	638
5	Cao	638	Cao	673	a	534	of	613
6	you	589	a	500	Cao	465	a	564
7	a	583	his	468	his	457	you	504

122

第四章 古典小说英译的母语译者和非母语译者的定量比较研究

续表

8	he	565	I	398	he	449	he	450
9	I	508	you	398	you	389	his	437
10	his	449	in	397	in	343	I	432
11	in	420	he	393	I	290	in	368
12	is	387	Yu	346	is	290	Yu	336
13	Yu	321	Zhou	341	with	252	is	308
14	was	298	for	264	Zhou	232	with	282
15	said	281	with	251	was	228	him	269
16	Zhou	273	is	249	that	227	that	265
17	that	272	said	247	Yu	225	said	256
18	not	261	Kongming	242	for	206	Zhou	253
19	with	253	on	226	have	202	was	235
20	but	238	have	208	on	173	for	220
21	have	232	that	202	had	169	have	210
22	him	232	was	191	this	163	Liang	201
23	as	224	your	182	but	158	this	193
24	they	222	him	173	they	152	on	184
25	be	221	at	166	him	151	Zhuge	174
26	for	219	we	166	Zhuge	148	but	168
27	on	212	but	164	at	146	had	168
28	will	204	be	160	as	144	they	162
29	Zhuge	198	will	152	are	138	at	160
30	are	196	it	148	we	136	are	158

从上表我们可以发现《三国演义》三个英文全译本排前10位的高频词基本一致。邓译本排前10位的高频词依次为 the,and,to,of,he,a,his,in,was,you;罗译本排前10位的高频词依次为 the,and,to,of,a,his,Cao,he,in,I;虞译本排前10位的高频词依次为 the,to,and,of,he,his,a,in,was,you。三位译者排前10位的高频词都以冠词 the 和 a,连接词 and,介词 of 和 in 以及 to,he,his 为主。我们再把三位译者排前10位的高频词与 BNC（英国国家语料库）排前10位的高频词来

进行比较。BNC排前10位的高频词依次为the、be、of、and、a、in、to、have、it、I。我们发现《三国演义》三个英文全译本排前10位的高频词与BNC排前10位的高频词也基本一致，BNC排前10位的高频词是以冠词the和a，连接词and，介词of和in以及to、I为主。但《三国演义》英文全译本的三位译者排前10位的高频词与BNC的还有一些差异，BNC排前10位的高频词中的be、have、it是《三国演义》三位译者前10位高频词所没有的，这是一个明显的差异。

从《三国演义》三位译者与BNC排前10位的高频词的比较来看，冠词the和a，连接词and，介词of和in以及to的高频率使用是其共性，这一共性应该是由英语语言特征在词汇使用方面的特征所决定的。三位译者与BNC相比，排前10位的高频词都缺少be、have、it，同时，三位译者的人称代词he、his、you以及was则是BNC所没有的。就造成这一现象的因素来说，原作《三国演义》本身的内容和语言风格应该是主要因素，因为三位译者，既包括母语译者也包括非母语译者，应该排除译者文化身份的因素，同时三位译者翻译时所处的时代跨度比较大，前后相距接近百年的时间，受时代的社会文化因素的影响也应该排除。

从母语译者和非母语译者的视角来考察，三位译者排前10位的高频词除了共性以外，还有一些细微的差异。两位母语译者的译本邓译本和罗译本排前5位的高频词当中and、to、a的排位与虞译本的排位存在差异。在邓译本和罗译本中，and和to分别排在第二和第三位；a在邓译本中排第六位，在罗译本中排第五位。虞译本中，and排在第三位，a排在第七位，to排在第二位。在排前10位的高频词当中，《三国演义》全译本的母语译者和非母语译者的差异主要表现为and、a、to的排序不同。

从《三国演义》四个英文节译本高频词中，我们可以发现四位译者的排前10位的高频词也基本一致。邓译本（节译）排前10位的高频词依次为the、and、to、of、Cao、you、a、he、I、his；罗译本（节译）排前10位的高频词依次为the、to、and、of、Cao、a、his、I、you、in；杨译本（节译）排前10位的高频词依次为the、to、and、of、a、Cao、his、he、you、in；张译本（节译）的高频词排前10位的依次为the、to、and、Cao、of、a、you、he、his、I。四位译者排前10位的高频词当中，都以冠词the和a，连接词and，介词of以及to、he、his、you、I、Cao为主。参照BNC排前10位的高频词进行比较，我们可以发现与BNC排前10位的高频词

第四章　古典小说英译的母语译者和非母语译者的定量比较研究

以冠词 the 和 a，连接词 and，介词 of 和 in 以及 to，I 为主的特征基本上是一致的。除此之外，《三国演义》节译本的四位译者排前 10 位的高频词中 he，his，you，Cao 则是 BNC 前 10 位的高频词所没有的，BNC 的 be，have，it 也是节译本的四位译者所没有的。四位译者与 BNC 在排前 10 位的高频词方面的共性应该是受英语语言在词汇使用方面的特征影响并决定的。同样排除掉译者文化身份的因素以及译者所处时代的社会文化因素的影响之后，四位译者与 BNC 在排前 10 位的高频词方面的差异应该是原作《三国演义》本身的内容和语言风格为主要因素影响并决定的。

《三国演义》节译本的四位译者除了以上共性以外，也存在一些细微差异。四位译者排前 10 位的高频词的排序大体一致，但有细微的差异。邓译本（节译）的 and 排第二位，to 排第三位，其他三位译者都是 and 排第三位，to 排第二位；杨译本（节译）排前 10 位的高频词中缺失 I，其他三位译者排前 10 位的高频词则包括 I；罗译本（节译）和杨译本（节译）排前 10 位的高频词包括 in，邓译本（节译）和张译本（节译）的则不包括。这些细微的差异是体现和反映了四位译者在翻译风格上的差异。

综合以上对于《三国演义》全译本的两位母语译者和一位非母语译者以及节译本的两位母语译者和两位非母语译者的排前 10 位的高频词的考察和比较分析，我们发现母语译者和非母语译者之间并不存在显著的差异。高频词更多反映和体现的是英语语言的某些词汇使用特征以及原作内容和语言风格的某些特征。

高频词是特定文本中使用频率特别高或其使用频率排序特别靠前的词汇，反映了文本在词汇使用方面的某些特征，只是文本词汇特征的某一侧面。多数情况下，高频词由于受所属的语言特征、文本内容、文本体裁、文本体裁以及特定社会文化的影响和制约更大一些，更大程度上反映的是上述因素的特征。译者自身的风格特征需要更为精细的词汇特征或对高频词进行更为精细的分类来考察分析。下面本研究将把高频词分为高频名词、高频动词、高频介词、高频形容词和高频副词来对研究语料进行进一步的考察分析。同时，将特别关注各高频词的使用频次，以此来探究母语译者和非母语译者各自在高频词方面的词汇使用特征，考察母语译者相较于非母语译者的区别性特征。

4.2.3.1 高频名词

《三国演义》的母语译者和非母语译者的三个全译本高频名词的情况以及《三国演义》的母语译者和非母语译者的四个节译本高频名词的情况分别如表 7. 和表 8. 所示：

表 7.《三国演义》三个英文全译本高频名词（去除人名称谓）（前 5 个）

次序	邓译本		罗译本		虞译本	
	词	频次	词	频次	词	频次
1	army	1719	men	1654	men	2706
2	soldiers	1134	troops	1259	army	1721
3	troops	1069	man	1107	city	1171
4	city	933	army	1039	man	1044
5	camp	924	commanders	832	officers	1002

表 8.《三国演义》四个英文节译本高频名词（去除人名称谓）（前 5 个）

次序	邓译本		罗译本		杨译本		张译本	
	词	频次	词	频次	词	频次	词	频次
1	soldiers	77	men	103	men	141	men	141
2	river	67	river	73	officers	71	time	71
3	ships	66	southland	63	time	63	officers	68
4	way	57	commanders	59	man	52	man	58
5	camp	55	man	59	troops	48	troops	49

《三国演义》三个英文全译本中，去除人名称谓以外，邓译本词频排前五位的名词是 army（1719 次），soldiers（1134 次），troops（1069 次），city（933 次），camp（924 次）；罗译本词频排前五位的名词是 men（1654 次），troops（1259 次），man（1107 次），army（1039 次），commanders（832 次）；虞译本词频排前五位的名词是 men（2706 次），army（1721 次），city（1171 次），man（1044 次），officers（1002 次）。《三国演义》四个英文节译本中，去除人名称谓以外，邓译本（节译）词频排前三位的名词是 soldiers（77 次），river（67 次），ships（66 次）；罗译本（节译）词频排前三位的名词是 men（103 次），river（73 次），southland（63 次）；杨译本（节译）词频排前三位的名词是 men（141 次），officers（71

第四章　古典小说英译的母语译者和非母语译者的定量比较研究

次),time(63次);张译本(节译)词频排前三位的名词是men(141次)、time(71次)、officers(68次)。

我们发现三个英文全译本中排前五位的名词以及三个英文节译本中,除了杨译(节译)time排第三位,和张译本(节译)time排第二位以外,排前三位的名词都是与小说原文题材相关的词汇,《三国演义》主要以政治和军事题材为主而展开故事情节的,小说中描写了大量的政治人物和军事战斗场面,因此译文中与政治和军事相关的词汇在名词中排位靠前应该是小说题材影响和决定的结果。同时,这一现象也说明原文小说对于政治和军事领域的描写远远超过对于社会其他领域的描写,这也是《三国演义》小说原文以及译文语言描写的一个重要特征。

《三国演义》三个英文全译本和四个英文节译本,词频排位靠前的名词当中,除了与小说原文题材相关的政治和军事的词汇之外,time是名词类里词频排第一的词语,其词频邓译本为772次,罗译本为813次,虞译本为921次,邓译本(节译)为30次,罗译本(节译)为34次,杨译本(节译)为48次,张译本(节译)为54次。根据笔者对《红楼梦》两个英译本霍克斯、闵福德译本和杨宪益、戴乃迭译本的统计,去除人名称谓以外,time也是这两个译本当中名词类里词频列第一的词语,其中霍译对time的使用频次为1641次,杨译对time的使用频次为1123次。根据BNC的词频统计,名词类中time也是排在第一位的词语。这说明,time在英语语言的使用当中,尤其是书面语的使用当中,在名词类中是使用频次最高的。《三国演义》的三个英文全译本和四个英文节译本以及《红楼梦》的两个英文全译本的time的词频在名词类中排第一位与BNC的词频统计当中time在名词类中列第一的情况相吻合。time在小说文本中的这一特征应该是由英语语言的使用特征决定的。

从母语译者和非母语译者的视角来考察,我们会发现,不论《三国演义》的三个英文全译本还是四个英文节译本,母语译者对于time的使用频次都要少于非母语译者对于time的使用频次。这是《三国演义》英译本中,母语译者和非母语译者对于英语语言使用频率最高的名词time的一个显著差异。比照《红楼梦》两个英文全译本的母语译者和非母语译者对于time的使用频率,我们发现《红楼梦》的母语译者相较于非母语译者,time的使用频率要高,而《三国演义》的母语译者和非母语译者对于time的使用频率与之相反,是非母语译者高于母语译者。不论是《三国演义》的英文全译本还是节译本,母语译者对于time的使用频次都少于非母语译者，而且差异比较明显。就全译本来看，邓译本为 772 次，罗译本为 813 次，虞译本为 921 次，非母语译者比母语译者分别高出 149 次和 108 次；就节译本来看，邓译本（节译）为 30 次，罗译本（节译）为 34 次，杨译本（节译）为 48 次，张译本（节译）为 54 次，非母语译者比母语译者分别高出 18 次、14 次以及 24 次和 20 次，差异比较显著。这一现象值得我们去关注研究以期发现其背后的原因。

例 12：

原文：周瑜谢出，暗忖曰："孔明早已料着吴侯之心，其计画又高我一头，久必为江东之患，不如杀之。"

邓译：Zhou Yu left. But in his innermost heart, he said to himself, "If that Zhuge Liang can gauge my master's thoughts so very accurately, he is too clever for me and will be a danger. He will have to be put out of the way."

罗译：Zhou Yu expressed his gratitude and left, observing inwardly, "Kongming divined my lord's state of mind before I did! In strategy, too, he excels me. In the long run such brilliance bodes danger to our land; we would be well rid of him now."

杨译：Having thanked Sun Quan and withdrawn, Zhou Yu reflected, "So Zhuge Liang guessed what was on my master's mind. He is a better tactician than I am. As time goes on he will become a serious rival. I had better kill him."

张译：Having thanked Sun Quan and withdrawn, Zhou Yu reflected, saying to himself. "So Zhuge Liang can gauge what is on my masters mind so quickly. He is cleverer than I and, as time goes on, he will be a danger to our kingdom. I had better kill him."

例 13：

原文：肃又将此言告孔明，孔明笑曰："公瑾令吾断粮者，实欲使曹操杀吾耳，吾故以片言戏之，公瑾便容纳不下。目今用人之际，只愿吴侯与刘使君同心，则功可成；

邓译：Lu Su went back and told this to Zhuge Liang, who smiled and said, "Zhou Yu only wanted me to go on this expedition because he wanted Cao Cao to kill me. And so I teased him a little. But he cannot bear that. Now is the critical moment, and Marquis Sun Quan and my master must act in harmony if we are to succeed.

罗译：Lu Su carried this new development back to Kongming, who smiled as he said, "All Zhou Yu really wanted was for Cao Cao to kill me. So I teased him with that remark. He is touchy, though. This is a critical moment. My only wish is for Lord Sun and Lord Liu to work together, for then we may succeed.

杨译：Lu Su told this to Zhuge Liang, who said with a laugh, "He asked me to cut their supply route in the hope that Cao Cao would kill me. That was why I provoked him with that remark which was more than he could stomach. But this is a time when every man counts. The Marquis of Wu must work in harmony with my master Liu Bei if we are to succeed.

张译：Lu Su told this to Zhuge Liang, who said with a laugh, "He asked me to cut their supply route in the hope that Cao Cao would kill me. That was why I provoked him with that remark which was more than he could stomach. But this is a time when every man counts. The Marquis of Wu must work in harmony with my master Liu Bei if we are to succeed.

通过以上译例的比较分析，我们可以发现，非母语译者多使用 time 来表达不同语境下的时间概念，用词缺少变化，多是依照原文词汇的意义进行翻译，对于意义相近的时间词汇的翻译较少依照上下文的语境使用不同的词汇进行表达和替换。母语译者对于原文中的时间概念会依据不同的上下文语境使用不同的词汇或是表达方式进行翻译，使其译文当中对于时间概念的表述较为多样化，对于原文时间概念在不同语境中的细腻的差异进行了再现。二者对于原文中的时间概念所采用的不同的翻译方法和策略是造成《三国演义》非母语译者的译文 time 的使用频次明显高于母语译者的使用频次的原因。母语译者和非母语译者对于 time 的不同频次的使用也印证了本研究前文对于《三国演义》三个英文全译本和四个英文节译本的类符数的统计结果，即母语译者的类符数大于非母语译者的类符数。二者在 time 的使用频次的不同也体现了母语译者和非母语译者在思维模式上的差异。

4.2.3.2 高频动词

《三国演义》的母语译者和非母语译者的 3 个全译本高频动词的情况以及《三国演义》的母语译者和非母语译者的 4 个节译本高频动词的情况分别如表 9. 和表 10. 所示。

表 9.《三国演义》三个英文全译本高频动词（前 5 个）

次序	邓译本 词	频次	罗译本 词	频次	虞译本 词	频次
1	was	6534	was	3618	was	6545
2	is	4739	is	3215	is	4302
3	said	4113	said	3164	said	3524
4	be	2970	had	2837	will	3218
5	will	2961	have	2569	be	3080

表 10.《三国演义》四个英文节译本高频动词（前 5 个）

次序	邓译本 词	频次	罗译本 词	频次	杨译本 词	频次	张译本 词	频次
1	is	387	is	249	is	290	is	308
2	was	298	said	247	was	228	said	256
3	said	281	have	208	have	202	was	235
4	have	232	was	191	had	169	have	210
5	be	221	be	160	are	138	had	168

《三国演义》英文全译本的高频动词排序如下：邓译本词频排前五位的动词依次为 was（6534 次），is（4739 次），said（4113 次），be（2970 次），will（2961 次）；罗译本词频排前五位的动词依次为 was（3618 次），is（3215 次），said（3164 次），had（2837 次），have（2569 次）；虞译本词频排前五位的动词依次为 was（6545 次），is（4302 次），said（3524 次），will（3218 次），be（3080 次）。

《三国演义》的全译本三位译者排前五位的高频动词大体一致。其中排前三位的都是 was, is, said, 这应该与小说原文的内容相关。was 和 is 是系动词，多用以陈述事物的性质和内容，这与原文对话或叙事中多陈述相关。said 是引导人物会话的报道动词，其排位高于原文中人

第四章　古典小说英译的母语译者和非母语译者的定量比较研究

物对话占据很大比例相关。邓译本和虞译本紧随其后的都是 will，be，只是排序不同，而罗译本中 will，be 分别排在第六和第七位，紧随 had，have 之后。罗译本与邓译本和虞译本相比，had，have 稍微靠前，反映了其在叙事方面所用时态与邓译本和虞译本的差异。

《三国演义》英文节译本的高频动词排序如下：杨译本（节译）词频排前五位的动词依次为 is(290 次)，was(228 次)，have(202 次)，had(169 次)，are（138 次）；张译本（节译）词频排前五位的动词依次为 is（308 次），said（256 次），was（235 次），have（210 次），had（168 次）；邓译本（节译）词频排前五位的动词依次为 is（387 次），was（298 次），said（281 次），have（232 次），be（221 次）；罗译本（节译）词频排前五位的动词依次为 is（249 次），said（247 次），have（208 次），was（191 次），be（160 次）。

《三国演义》的节译本四位译者排前五位的高频动词也大体一致。其中邓译本（节译）和罗译本（节译）的词类完全一致，只是词频排序略有差异，这反映了母语译者和非母语译者在动词使用方面存在一定的差异。is，was，have 是四位译者共有的，said 为邓译本（节译）、罗译本（节译）、张译本（节译）共有，said 在杨译本（节译）的动词类中排第九位，这反映了杨译本（节译）在人物会话引导词使用方面与其他三位译者的差异。杨译本（节译）在系动词方面比其他三位译者多了一个 are，had 为杨译本（节译）和张译本（节译）共有，这反映了杨译本（节译）在叙事和陈述方面的用词特征以及杨译本（节译）和张译本（节译）在处理动词时态方面的特征。四位译者除了上述词类之外，排位靠前的都是 will，其中邓译本（节译）will 排第六位，词频为 198 次，罗译本（节译）will 排第六位，词频为 152 次，杨译本（节译）will 排第八位，词频为 119 次，张译本（节译）will 排第八位，词频为 129 次。

根据 BNC 的词频统计，动词类词频排前五位的依次为 have，do，will，say，can。其中 have，will 的词频排序与《三国演义》三位全译本的译者以及四位节译本译者 have，will 的词频排序具有共性，排序都比较靠前。BNC have，will 在动词类中分别排第一和第三位。《三国演义》全译本中，邓译本 have，will 在动词类中分别排第七和第五位，词频分别为 2541 次和 2877 次；罗译本 have，will 在动词类中分别排第五和第六位，词频分别为 2572 次和 2294 次；虞译本 have，will 在动词类中分别排第七和第四位，词频分别为 2406 次和 3118 次。其中，就 have

的使用频次来看,三个全译本的母语译者比较接近,比非母语译者高115-125次,就词频排序来看,母语译者和非母语译者没有显著差异;四个节译本不论从使用频次还是词频排序来看,母语译者和非母语译者都没有明显差异。

　　下面,我们重点考察母语译者和非母语译者对于 will 的使用情况。就使用频次来看,三个全译本的母语译者对于 will 的使用频次要低于非母语译者,四个节译本的母语译者对于 will 的使用频次则要高于非母语译者;就词频排序来看,不论是三个全译本还是四个节译本其排序都比较靠前,其中四个节译本的母语译者的排序比非母语译者的排序略微靠前。我们再用同为我国古典名著的《红楼梦》两个英文全译本作为参照,对 will 的使用情况进行考察。

　　笔者使用语料库统计分析软件 Wconcord 和 PowerConc 对《红楼梦》的两个英文全译本霍译和杨译分别进行词频统计发现,《红楼梦》霍译本动词类词频排前五位的依次为 was, had, said, be, have, will 排在第十三位,词频为 1636 次;杨译本动词类词频排前五位的依次为 was, had, be, have, is, will 排在第三十一位,词频为 839 次。我们发现作为母语译者译文的《红楼梦》霍译本不仅 will 的使用频次高于作为非母语译者译文的杨译本,而且 will 的排序相较于杨译本较为靠前。

　　就《三国演义》的四个节译本来看,其母语译者和非母语译者对于 will 使用情况的差异与《红楼梦》母语译者和非母语译者对于 will 使用情况的差异相似。两者都表现为母语译者 will 的使用频次高于非母语译者,will 的排序比非母语译者要靠前。再结合 BNC 动词类排序中 will 的情况来看,will 应该是英语语言当中动词类使用频率较高的一个词,《三国演义》的四个英文节译本和《红楼梦》两个英文全译本的母语译者相较于非母语译者其对于 will 的使用频次比较高,词频排序也靠前的特征应该是母语译者在母语优势下的一个词语使用特征。《三国演义》英文全译本的非母语译者 will 的使用频次高于母语译者的使用频次应该与其翻译完成的年代有关,这与虞译本在形符数上和邓译本以及罗译本相差不大的特征应该是一致的。其原因在本研究的形符一节已有论述,此处不再赘述。

第四章 古典小说英译的母语译者和非母语译者的定量比较研究

表 11. 邓译本(节译)will 语境共现检索(前 5 个,共 198 个)

together attack Liu Bei. We	will	share his land between us,
land between us, and we	will	swear perpetual amity. If happily
. If you submit, whither	will	you go? You will be
whither will you go? You	will	be created a lord of some
humble fief, perhaps. You	will	have one carriage, no more

表 12. 罗译本(节译)will 语境共现检索(前 5 个,共 152 个)

of this," responded Kongming. "I	will	make my own replies to him."
idea," replied Su, "but I	will	need time to report in full
with the total security which submission	will	afford." "Zhang Zhao's views," the
, the people of the region	will	be protected and the six districts
majority's view, General,	will	be your ruin," Su replied.

表 13. 杨译本(节译)will 语境共现检索(前 5 个,共 119 个)

able generals. I hope you	will	join me, general, in
"Zhang Zhao's proposal accords with the	will	of Heaven." Sun Quan thought hard
and rich nourishment first, it	will	be difficult to restore him to
Your master, ignorant of Heaven's	will	, is still contending with him
personal matters. I hope you	will	excuse me." "After you have seen

表 14. 张译本(节译)will 语境共现检索(前 5 个,共 129 个)

a thousand able generals hope you	will	join me, General, in
Zhang Zhao's proposal accords with the	will	of Heaven." Sun Quan pondered and
for his questions first, then	will	try to goad him into action."
years. Then all my wishes	will	be satisfied." With that he laughed
me to the depths. I	will	sing a song, and you

4.2.3.3 高频介词和从属连词

《三国演义》的母语译者和非母语译者的三个全译本高频介词和从属连词的情况以及《三国演义》的母语译者和非母语译者的 4 个节译本

高频介词和从属连词的情况分别如表 15. 和表 16. 所示。

表 15.《三国演义》四个英文节译本介词和从属连词形符类符

	邓译本	罗译本	杨译本	张译本
介词和从属连词形符数	4534	4161	3834	4033
介词和从属连词类符数	63	66	59	61

表 16.《三国演义》三个英文全译本介词和从属连词形符类符

	邓译本	罗译本	虞译本
介词和从属连词形符数	152026	135742	162620
介词和从属连词类符数	82	85	79

　　从《三国演义》四个英文节译本的介词和从属连词总数以及总类的统计结果来考察，我们可以发现母语译者和非母语译者对于介词和从属连词的使用在总量和总类方面存在差异。鉴于 to 作为不定式符号也是英语语言在使用中区别于汉语的一个重要特征，以及使用语料库统计软件进行统计的方便，本小节对于介词的统计分析也把不定式符号 to 包括在内。统计结果显示，邓译本（节译）使用的介词和从属连词总数为 4534 次，使用的介词和从属连词总类为 63 种；罗译本（节译）使用的介词和从属连词总数为 4161 次，使用的介词和从属连词总类为 66 种；杨译本（节译）使用的介词和从属连词总数为 3834 次，使用的介词和从属连词总类为 59 种；张译本（节译）使用的介词和从属连词总数为 4033 次，使用的介词和从属连词总类为 61 种。从介词和从属连词的使用总量来看，母语译者显著大于非母语译者，从介词和从属连词的使用总类来看，母语译者也大于非母语译者，但差距并不显著。同时，统计结果也表明两位母语译者在介词和从属连词的使用总数和使用总类方面具有一致性，两位非母语译者具有一致性。

　　介词和从属连词在英语中是具有重要句法功能的词类，对于英语短语和句式的构造具有重要的作用。相比较而言，汉语当中，对于介词和从属连词的使用远没有英语对于介词和连词的使用范围广，其所起的句法功能作用也远比英语中介词和连词的句法功能要弱。基于汉语和英语中介词和连词使用范围大小和作用强弱的差异，对于介词和从属连词的使用数量以及种类便成为考察汉译英作品译者译文风格特征的一个重要指标。

第四章 古典小说英译的母语译者和非母语译者的定量比较研究

《三国演义》英文全译本的高频介词排序如下：邓译本词频排前五位的介词依次为 to(19161 次)，of(15664 次)，in(7399 次)，with(4046次)，for(3367 次)；罗译本词频排前五位的介词依次为 to(17991 次)，of(11761 次)，in(6724 次)，with(3900 次)，for(3750 次)；虞译本词频排前五位的介词依次为 to(22824 次)，of(14421 次)，in(7917 次)，with(4388 次)，for(3816 次)。

《三国演义》英文节译本的高频动词排序如下：杨译本(节译)词频排前五位的介词依次为 to(1069 次)，of(569 次)，in(343 次)，with(252次)，for(206 次)；张译本(节译)词频排前五位的介词依次为 to(1123次)，of(613 次)，in(368 次)，with(282 次)，for(220 次)；邓译本(节译)词频排前五位的介词依次为 to(1157 次)，of(855 次)，in(420 次)，with(253 次)，for(219 次)；罗译本(节译)词频排前五位的介词依次为 to(1115 次)，of(677 次)，in(397 次)，for(264 次)，with(251 次)。

从《三国演义》三个英文全译本和四个英文节译本对于各自词频排前五位的介词统计来看，不论是全译本还是节译本其词类和词频排序几乎一致。词频排前五位的介词依次为 to, of, in, with, for；根据 BNC 的统计，其词频排前五位的介词依次为 of, in, to, for, with。参照 BNC 的介词统计，我们发现《三国演义》三个英文全译本和四个英文节译本的词频排前五位的介词词类和 BNC 的词频排前五位的介词词类完全一致，只是排位顺序略有差异。这反映了《三国演义》三个英文全译本和四个英文节译本在高频介词的使用方面与 BNC 的使用特征接近，同时也体现了英语语言尤其是英语书面语在介词使用方面的一定特征。《三国演义》全译本和节译本共五位译者在词频排前五位的高频介词的词类上与 BNC 的一致性很大程度上是受英语语言对于介词使用特征影响和决定的；在排位顺序上与 BNC 的差异很大程度上应该是受小说原文影响和制约的结果。

从词频排前五位的介词的使用频次来看，《三国演义》全译本的母语译者和非母语译者在 to, in, with 的使用频次上存在一定差异。作为母语译者译文的邓译本和罗译本的 to, in, with 的词频与作为非母语译者译文的虞译本相比较其结果为：to(19161, 17991-22824)，in(7399, 6724-7917)，with(4046, 3900-4388)。从以上结果中，我们可以发现邓译本和罗译本对于 to, in, with 三个介词的使用频次要少于虞译本的使用频次。to 的使用频次差异介于 3663～4833 次之间，in 的使用频次差异介于 518 ~ 1193 次之间,with 的使用频次差异介于 342 ~ 488 次之间,相比较而言,to 的使用频次的差异最为明显。《三国演义》节译本的母语译者和非母语译者在 in 的使用频次上存在一定差异。作为母语译者译文的邓译本和罗译本的 in 的使用频次分别为 420 次和 397 次,作为非母语译者译文的杨译本和张译本的 in 使用频次分别为 343 次和 368 次,差异在 77,52-54,29 次之间。

4.2.4 特色词

特色词是指在特定文本中词频比较高而另一个类似文本或其他多个类似文本词频比较低的词汇。特色词直观反映了译者相较于其他译者的语言特色和风格,同时也直观地体现了译者相较于其他译者的差异。

4.2.4.1 特色动词

《三国演义》的母语译者和非母语译者的 3 个全译本动词的情况以及《三国演义》的母语译者和非母语译者的 4 个节译本动词的情况分别如表 17. 和表 18. 所示。

表 17.《三国演义》三个英文全译本动词形符类符

	邓译本	罗译本	虞译本
动词形符数	128108	113678	127709
动词类符数	5312	6366	5302

《三国演义》三个英文全译本的母语译者(参照非母语译者)的特色动词包括:conquers(30,24-5);played(20,18-6);settle(31,36-18);volunteer(8,25-4);begun(20,28-9);awaiting(20,27-9);backed(8,16-4);revived(8,16-3);signaled(8,15-4);examine(7,15-3);swallowed(9,12-4);involved(8,12-4);feasted(12,30-6);resolved(19,20-12);looks(21,17-9);acknowledged(10,25-5);exploit(16,14-7);serves(7,10-2);afford(5,10-2);heeded(5,11-1)共 20 个。

《三国演义》三个英文全译本的非母语译者(参照母语译者)的特色动词包括:challenge(65-26,32);stir(23-8,7);launch(22-3,8);

第四章 古典小说英译的母语译者和非母语译者的定量比较研究

revealed（11-1,3）共 4 个。

表 18.《三国演义》四个英文节译本动词形符类符

	邓译本	罗译本	杨译本	张译本
动词形符数	8065	7333	6914	7180
动词类符数	1586	1841	1464	1469

《三国演义》四个英文节译本的母语译者（参照非母语译者）的特色动词包括：began（15,26-3,3）；stood（13,20-5,7）；reached（13,17-6,6）；does（12,15-5,7）；bring（10,13-3,4）；spoke（9,12-5,4）；continued（7,13-3,1）；destroy（9,9-2,3）；received（10,10-1,2）；held（6,14-1,1）共 10 个。

《三国演义》四个英文节译本的非母语译者（参照母语译者）的特色动词包括：kill（31,33-5,12）；surrender（19,24-6,6）；dare（18,20-8,7）；defeat（20,21-4,4）；hope（17,18-7,6）；killed（10,10-2,3）共 6 个。

从表 19.《三国演义》三个英文全译本动词总数及总类和表 20.《三国演义》四个英文节译本动词总数及总类的统计结果来看，不论是全译本还是节译本，除了虞译本与邓译本的动词类符数相接近（5302-5312）以外，母语译者的动词类符数都明显大于非母语译者的动词类符数。就全译本来看，罗译本的动词类符数比虞译本多 1064 个词类，邓译本也比虞译本多 10 个词类；就节译本来看，邓译本（节译）的动词类符数比杨译本（节译）和张译本（节译）分别多出 122 个词类和 117 个词类，罗译本（节译）的动词类符数比杨译本（节译）和张译本（节译）分别多出 377 个词类和 372 个词类。除了全译本中的邓译本的虞译本的差异较小以外，其余的母语译者和非母语译者的动词类符数的差异比较显著。同时，我们可以发现三个全译本和四个节译本的动词类符数在各自整个译本的类符数中占有很大比重，这说明动词在整个译本中的重要地位和作用。动词所占类符数比重较高的原因在于《三国演义》小说原作是一部以政治和军事斗争为主轴的历史小说，小说多以政治和军事斗争场面的描写为主，所以关于战争场面和人物心理活动以及动作描写的动词在整个小说的描写中便占有很大比重。所以，译文对于小说原作中的动词的翻译对整部小说的翻译就具有重要意义。

类符数是反映特定文本所使用单词种类的指标，对于特定的原文来说,其译文的类符数越大,则说明译文的此类越丰富,对于原文的再现则越精确、细腻。就《三国演义》动词占有整个类符数很大比重以及动词占有描写很大比重的小说来说,译文动词的类符数越大,说明译文对于原作动词描写的再现越精确、细腻。从以上对于《三国演义》三个英文全译本和四个英文节译本的母语译者和非母语译者动词类符的统计分析来看,我们发现动词类符数较高是《三国演义》英译文本的母语译者相较于非母语译者的一个重要的区别性特征。关于非母语译者译文虞译本的动词类符数与母语译者的译文邓译本相接近的原因与其译文的总类符数与邓译本相接近的原因一致,具体分析在本章的形符一节已经有详细论述,此处不再赘述。

下面本研究将从特色词的角度来比较分析《三国演义》的母语译者和非母语译者在动词使用方面的差异。从上述对于《三国演义》全译本和节译本的母语译者和非母语译者的特色动词的统计来看,不论是全译本还是节译本母语译者的特色动词数都大于非母语译者的特色动词数。《三国演义》全译本的母语译者的特色动词数为 20 个,非母语译者的特色动词数为 4 个;《三国演义》节译本的母语译者的特色动词数为 10 个,非母语译者的特色动词数为 6 个。全译本的母语译者和非母语译者的特色动词数差异比较显著,达 16 个,节译本的母语译者和非母语译者的特色动词数差异为 4 个。母语译者在动词类符数大于非母语译者的情况下,其特色动词数大于非母语译者,说明其译文不仅动词词类丰富,而且动词使用的特色也非常明显,尤其是全译本的母语译者的动词使用特色更为明显。但节译本的母语译者和非母语译者的动词类符数的差异比较明显,其母语译者在动词类符数显著大于非母语译者的情况下,特色动词数依然大于非母语译者,也反映了其母语译者动词使用具有较为显著的特色。

《三国演义》全译本母语译者的特色动词排位最靠前的是 conquers(30,24-5),差异比较显著。邓译本、罗译本和虞译本对于 conquers 的使用如表 19. 至表 21. 所示。

表 19.《三国演义》邓译本 conquers 的语境共现检索(前 5 次,共 30 次)

conferring the ranks of Commander Who	Conquers	the West on Ma Teng and
Li Yue was made General Who	Conquers	the North, and Han Xian

第四章 古典小说英译的母语译者和非母语译者的定量比较研究

续表

Han Xian was appointed General Who	Conquers	the East. The flight continued
Liu Bei was created General Who	Conquers	the East, Lord of Yicheng
; Huang Zhong, General Who	Conquers	the West; Wei Yan,

表20.《三国演义》罗译本conquers的语境共现检索（前5次，共24次）

Lord Cao, Han General Who	Conquers	the West,' my lifelong
not make Ma Teng General Who	Conquers	the South on the pretext of
Pang De to Vanguard Leader Who	Conquers	the West. They brought seven
Minister Musters a Massive Force and	Conquers	the Southern Rebels; The Man
the title of Field Marshal Who	Conquers	the West, in which capacity

表21.《三国演义》虞译本conquers的语境共现检索（共5次）

Cao Cao	Conquers	Hanzhong Zhang Liao Spreads
Capture of Dui Hill Zhao Yun	Conquers	a Host on the Han Waters
Zhuge Liang	Conquers	Hanzhong by Strategy Cao Cao
from three sides, and whoever	conquers	the enemy will be head of
strength, mightier than all,	conquers	every city, and from whose

　　从以上邓译本、罗译本和虞译本conquers的使用例句中，我们可以发现邓译本和罗译本的conquers多用于"Marshal/General Who Conquers…"当中，用来翻译原文中的"征……元帅/将军"，虞译本则多略去不译。

　　全译本特色动词排位仅次于conquers的是played（20, 18-6），差异比较显著。邓译本、罗译本和虞译本对于played的使用如表22.至表24.所示。

表22.《三国演义》邓译本played的语境共现检索（前5次，共20次）

As a child, Liu Bei	played	with the other village children beneath
in a tiger's lair, He	played	a waiting part, But when
. The drums were to be	played	, and the old drummers were
part of the game had been	played	, Xiahou Dun led forward five
a stunning blow, still he	played	his part; Partitioning his dwelling

表 23.《三国演义》罗译本 played 的语境共现检索（前 5 次，共 18 次）

Li Yue controlled the court and	played	the tyrant, beating the courtiers
through the trick Chen Deng had	played	. Finally, he met up
our own fate. Your skill	played	no part. My heart remains
ever and burning incense as he	played	. To his left, a
Southland, your contribution will have	played	no small part. Some contend

表 24.《三国演义》虞译本 played 的语境共现检索（前 5 次，共 6 次）

and the other village boys often	played	beneath this tree and he would
in a tiger's lair. He	played	a waiting part. But when
part of the game had been	played	, Xiahou Dun led 5,000 men
the melodious sound of a lute	played	most skillfully and the music was
and while they feasted the musicians	played	songs of victory and wine was

从以上邓译本、罗译本和虞译本对于 played 的使用例句中，我们可以发现，邓译本和罗译本对于 play 的使用频次要远高于虞译本的使用频次，同时邓译本和罗译本对于 play 的使用方式也比较多样，包括 play...role，play...part，play...trick，play...game 等固定搭配。其中，邓译本 play...part 5 次，play...trick 2 次，play...game 4 次，play into one's hands 2 次，play off 1 次，play with 1 次；罗译本 play...role 2 次，play...part 4 次，play...trick 1 次，play...game 1 次，play into one's hands 1 次，played havoc with 1 次；虞译本 play...game 1 次，play...part 2 次。

play 相关的固定搭配：邓译本共计 15 次，罗译本共计 10 次，虞译本共计 3 次。虞译本对于 play 相关的固定搭配的使用，不论是种类还是次数都明显少于邓译本和罗译本。

begin（全译本为 begun，节译本为 began）不论在全译本还是在节译本都是母语译者排位靠前的特色动词，其在母语译者的特色动词中占有重要位置。邓译本、罗译本和虞译本对于 begin 使用情况的统计如表 25. 至表 27. 所示。

第四章 古典小说英译的母语译者和非母语译者的定量比较研究

表 25.《三国演义》邓译本 begun 的使用频次(前 5 次,共 20 次)

engaged. The combat had hardly	begun	when Li Ru with a cohort
? "Wang Yun has already	begun	the construction of the Terrace of
"The rupture of the empire has	begun	, and warlords are seizing what
Zu on account of a quarrel	begun	over the wine cups. Both
being worse for liquor they had	begun	to discuss the worth of people

表 26.《三国演义》罗译本 begun 的使用频次(前 5 次,共 28 次)

scattered forces had barely reorganized and	begun	digging holes in the ground to
Jue and Guo Si had already	begun	to attack the city. They
the campaign against Chengdu had hardly	begun	when an urgent message came:
wine. Before the banquet had	begun	, Zhao Zilong presented the heads
. Soon all the commanders had	begun	to do the same. During

表 27.《三国演义》虞译本 begun 的使用频次(前 5 次,共 9 次)

this?" "He has already	begun	the construction of an altar for
"The disruption of the empire has	begun	and warriors are seizing what they
worse for liquor, they had	begun	to discuss the worth of people
taken possession. Then he had	begun	to recruit men, buy horses
recently surrendered to him had suddenly	begun	plundering the people in Jiangxia and

从以上邓译本、罗译本和虞译本对于 begun 的使用例句中,我们可以发现,邓译本和罗译本对于 begun 的使用不仅频次要远高于虞译本,同时邓译本和罗译本对于 begun 的特色搭配的使用频次也高于虞译本,其中邓译本 begun *ing 1 次,begun to 6 次,had hardly begun when 2 次;罗译本 begun *ing 11 次,begun to 6 次,had hardly begun when 2 次;虞译本 begun *ing 1 次,begun to 3 次,had hardly begun when 1 次。此外邓译本和罗译本 beginning,begin,began 的使用频次也高于虞译本,为(26,12-8)和(34,41-32),两者的特色搭配的频次也高于虞译本,其中邓译本 beginning to 8 次,罗译本 beginning to 8 次,虞译本

beginning to 6 次；邓译本 begin to 10 次，罗译本 begin to 7 次，虞译本 begin to 6 次；邓译本 began *ing 6 次，罗译本 began *ing 65 次，虞译本 began *ing 7 次；邓译本 begin *ing 0 次，罗译本 begin *ing 7 次，虞译本 begin *ing 1 次；邓译本 began to 101 次，罗译本 began to 53 次，虞译本 began to 103 次。

begin/began/begun *ing：邓译本共 8 次，罗译本共 78 次，虞译本共 9 次。

begin/began/begun to：邓译本共 127 次，罗译本共 73 次，虞译本共 119 次。

had hardly begun when：邓译本共 2 次，罗译本共 2 次，虞译本共 1 次。

begin 相关的固定搭配及常用句式：邓译本共计 137 次，罗译本共计 153 次，虞译本共计 129 次。

《三国演义》节译本母语译者和非母语译者对于 begin 相关的固定搭配及常用句式的使用情况如下：

begin/began/begun *ing：邓译本共 1 次，罗译本共 5 次，杨译本共 0 次，张译本共 0 次。

begin/began/begun to：邓译本共 12 次，罗译本共 5 次，杨译本共 3 次，张译本共 3 次。

begin 相关的固定搭配及常用句式：邓译本共计 13 次，罗译本共计 10 次，杨译本共计 3 次，张译本共计 3 次。

我们再以古典名著《红楼梦》的霍译和杨译为参照来比较分析母语译者相较于非母语译者对于 begin，began，begun，beginning 的使用特色。根据笔者对《红楼梦》两个英文全译本霍译和杨译的统计，霍译的特色动词首推 began（613-53）、begin（127-12）、beginning（131-21）、begun（41-2）。其中，begin/began/begun *ing：霍译共 242 次，杨译共 5 次；begin/began/begun to：霍译共 334 次，杨译共 36 次。以上结果表明《红楼梦》的母语译者对 begin，began，begun，beginning 的使用特色与《三国演义》的母语译者的使用特色相比，更为突出和显著。

我们再以英文原著小说为参照，来看英文原创小说对于 begin，began，begun，beginning 的使用特色。笔者使用语料库统计分析软件对参照语料库的英文 10 部原创小说的 begin，began，begun，beginning 的使用情况进行统计，其结果如下：

第四章 古典小说英译的母语译者和非母语译者的定量比较研究

begin/began/begun *ing：参照语料库共计 47 次，平均每部小说 4.7 次。

begin/began/begun to：参照语料库共计 740 次，平均每部小说 74 次。

begin 相关的固定搭配及常用句式：参照语料库共计 787 次，平均每部小说 78.7 次。

通过以上对于《三国演义》母语译者的特色动词 begun，began 及其各种形式的相关的固定搭配和常用句式的统计分析，并参照语料库《红楼梦》的霍译和杨译以及英文 10 部原创小说的 begin 的各种形式及其相关的固定搭配和常用句式的统计结果，我们发现不论是《三国演义》还是《红楼梦》的英译文本，对于 begin 的各种形式高频率使用及其固定搭配的一定频次的使用是母语译者相较于非母语译者的区别性特征。《三国演义》三个全译本的母语译者其他特色动词搭配的使用情况如下。

volunteer to：邓译本 6 次，罗译本 13 次，虞译本 2 次。

to volunteer：邓译本 6 次，罗译本 8 次，虞译本 2 次。

volunteer for：邓译本 1 次，罗译本 3 次，虞译本 0 次。

volunteer 相关的固定搭配：邓译本共计 13 次，罗译本共计 24 次，虞译本共计 4 次。

backed by：邓译本 6 次，罗译本 5 次，虞译本 3 次。

backed off：邓译本 0 次，罗译本 4 次，虞译本 0 次。

backed against：邓译本 0 次，罗译本 3 次，虞译本 0 次。

back 相关的固定搭配：邓译本共计 6 次，罗译本共计 12 次，虞译本共计 3 次。

be resolved：邓译本 0 次，罗译本 11 次，虞译本 0 次。

resolved to：邓译本 13 次，罗译本 7 次，虞译本 9 次。

resolved 的相关搭配：邓译本共计 13 次，罗译本共计 18 次，虞译本共计 9 次。

afford to：邓译本 1 次，罗译本 6 次，虞译本 1 次。

to afford：邓译本 3 次，罗译本 1 次，虞译本 0 次。

afford 的相关搭配：邓译本共计 4 次，罗译本共计 7 次，虞译本共计 1 次。

通过以上对《三国演义》全译本的母语译者的特色动词及其相关搭配的统计分析，我们发现不论在《三国演义》还是《红楼梦》的英译中，begin（began 或 begun）都是母语译者排位靠前的特色动词，同时与其相关的搭配的使用频率也译较大幅度高于非母语译者。母语译者对于 begin（began 或 begun）的这一使用特征得到了参照语料库 10 部英文小说的有力支撑。这说明对于 begin（began 或 begun）及其相关搭配的高频使用较少受小说题材的约束和影响，是母语译者在母语思维模式下对于动词使用的一个区别于非母语译者的重要特征。

　　除了 begin（began 或 begun）以及上文所统计的特色动词的相关搭配之外，母语译者的其他特色动词绝大多数都是与《三国演义》小说原作题材相关的动词。小说原作是以政治军事斗争为主题的历史小说，小说描写大多以政治军事场面和人物对话为主，因此小说中与政治军事场面以及人物动作相关的词汇占有较大比例。所以，母语译者的特色动词除 begin（began 或 begun）以外，如全译本的 conquers, played, settle, volunteer, awaiting, backed, revived, signaled, examine, swallowed, involved, feasted, resolved, looks, acknowledged, exploit, serves, afford 以及节译本的 stood, reached, bring, spoke, continued, destroy, received, held 大多与政治军事场面描写相关。不论是全译本还是节译本，母语译者的动词类符数都要大于非母语译者，尤其是节译本的母语译者的动词类符数更是以较大幅度大于非母语译者的动词类符数。母语译者在动词类符数多于非母语译者所使用的的情况下，其特色动词的数量以及一些特色动词相关的搭配数量和类型也多于非母语译者所使用的，说明母语译者在对于原文当中的政治军事场面相关的动作描写的再现更为精确和细腻。《三国演义》全译本和节译本的母语译者的这些特色动词除了反映并受小说原作政治军事场面描写的动作内容约束之外，某种程度上也反映了母语译者在母语思维模式下描写同样题材时动词的使用特色。

　　此外，节译本母语译者的特色动词中，除了 begin（began 或 begun）以外，值得特别关注的是 does，其具体使用情况如表 30. 所示。

　　does 在英语语言的使用当中，除了实义动词的用法之外，主要是作为助动词使用的，用以构成句式的疑问、否定和强调的语气。从节译本四位译者对于 does 的使用统计结果来看，母语译者对于 does 的使用有两个明显特征：一是母语译者 does 的使用排频次显著高于非母语译者，二是母语译者 does 多作为助动词使用。具体统计结果如下：

　　邓译本：does 用于否定句 5 次，用于疑问句 5 次，用于加强语气 1 次，用于常用句式 1 次。

第四章　古典小说英译的母语译者和非母语译者的定量比较研究

罗译本：does 用于否定句 3 次，用于疑问句 10 次，作为实义动词使用 2 次。

杨译本：does 用于否定句 2 次，用于疑问句 1 次，用于加强语气 1 次，作为实义动词使用 1 次。

张译本：does 用于否定句 1 次，用于疑问句 4 次，用于加强语气 1 次，作为实义动词使用 1 次。

例 14：

原文：若不待气脉和缓，便投以猛药厚味，欲求安保，诚为难矣。

邓译：If the physician does not wait till the humors and pulse are in harmony, but throws in his strong drugs too early, it will be difficult to restore the patient.

罗译：If you do not wait until breath and pulse are calm and steady but precipitately use powerful drugs and rich food, the attempt to cure the patient is sure to fail.

杨译：If instead of waiting till humours and pulse are in harmony you give him powerful drugs and rich nourishment first, it will be difficult to restore him to health.

张译：If instead of waiting till breath and pulse are in harmony, we just give him powerful drugs and rich nourishment first, it will be difficult to restore him to health.

表 28. 邓译本（节译）does 语境共现检索（前 5 次，共 12 次）

to health. If the physician	does	not wait till the humors and
to the destruction of anyone who	does	not follow the canon of a
upon his lord. Not only	does	he forgets his prince, but
collected a fleet. If he	does	not intend to invade the South
represents the actual conditions, why	does	not Liu Bei yield? "

表 29. 罗译本（节译）does 语境共现检索（前 5 次，共 15 次）

off before you came. How	does	that measure up to what Guan
rhapsody every day. What value	does	it have?" Cheng Deshu
supplies." "But how large a force	does	Cao have?" Sun Quan
Su said pointedly, "What chance	does	this mission has, good sir
. What I say, he	does	. What I propose, he

母语优势下的翻译策略研究

表 30. 杨译本（节译）does 语境共现检索（共 5 次）

knees, entreating, "Huang Gai	does	indeed, deserve death, but his
given nothing to do! What	does	this mean?" Zhuge Liang
for overcoming Cao Cao, but	does	not mean to disclose it too
on every side, and he	does	everything in the name of the
fearful of Cao Cao's numbers and	does	not believe our small force can

表 31. 张译本（节译）does 语境共现检索（前 5 次，共 7 次）

and preparing warships. If he	does	not intend to conquer your territory
your territory, what other territory	does	he intends to take? "
other than Lu Su, who	does	not know the real situation of
only exception is Liu Bei who	does	not know the real situation of
on all sides, and he	does	everything in the name of the

此外，全译本母语译者的特色动词中，除了 begin（began 或 begun）以外，值得特别关注的是 swallowed，其具体使用情况如下表所示。

表 32. 邓译本 swallowed 语境共现检索（前 5 次，共 9 次）

upon the maid, while he	swallowed	cup after cup of wine.
it was too coarse to be	swallowed	. Next day the Emperor conferred
guests on every hand and so	swallowed	a huge quantity of liquor.
of colored silk. Lu Bu	swallowed	the bait and ordered Gao Shun
the eye into his mouth and	swallowed	it. Then resuming his firm

表 33. 罗译本 swallowed 语境共现检索（前 5 次，共 12 次）

together and started to sob but	swallowed	their cries for fear of discovery
us; but if Yuan Shu	swallowed	him up and then allied with
was moved to write: Wei	swallowed	Han, and then Jin swallowed
swallowed Han, and then Jin	swallowed	Wei; From Heaven 's turning
, " he cried, and	swallowed	the eye. Then he went

表 34. 虞译本 swallowed 语境共现检索（共 4 次）

drink huge goblets, and so	swallowed	an enormous quantity of liquor.
the eye into his mouth and	swallowed	it. Then, resuming a
, only to find it also	swallowed	up by flames that seemed to
occupied Jingzhou, and Lu Bu	swallowed	up Xuzhou. Brigands rose like

第四章　古典小说英译的母语译者和非母语译者的定量比较研究

4.2.4.2 特色副词

副词在小说描写中也占有重要地位,多用于描写行为或动作的时间、地点、频率、方式、程度等。就翻译来说,译文对于副词的使用方式、使用数量的多少对其再现原文的风格具有重要影响。下面本研究将通过对《三国演义》三个英文全译本和四个英文节译本副词使用情况的定量比较分析,来考察母语译者和非母语译者在副词使用方面各自的特征。《三国演义》的母语译者和非母语译者3个全译本副词的情况如表35. 所示。

表35.《三国演义》三个英文全译本副词形符类符

	罗译本	虞译本	邓译本
副词形符数	30854	43642	42335
副词类符数	954	781	816

《三国演义》三个英文全译本的母语译者(参照非母语译者)的特色副词包括：west（29,36-9）; mightily（11,10-2）共2个。

《三国演义》三个英文全译本的非母语译者(参照母语译者)的特色副词包括：besides（54-2,5）; extremely（34-9,4）; deliberately（16-3,3）; secondly（15-4,3）共4个。

besides 是虞译本排首位的特色副词,其使用频次与邓译本和罗译本的差异最为显著,分别达49次和52次。从其使用频次的差异幅度来看,besides 是虞译本最具代表性的特色副词。两位母语译者对于besides 的使用频次非常低,邓译本为2次,罗译本为5次。笔者使用语料库统计软件对参照语料库10部英文小说的副词进行了统计,besides 的使用频次排在所有副词中的第216位,使用频次为45次,平均每部小说为4.5次,接近邓译本和罗译本的平均使用频次3.5次。其部分使用例句如表36. 至表40. 所示。

表36. 邓译本 besides 语境共现检索（共2次）

but a waste of words.	Besides	, we have no one to
, and 40,000 civil employees.	Besides	, there were granaries with 4,000,000

表37. 罗译本 besides 语境共现检索（共5次）

assignment once it's made.	Besides	, I need Zhao Lei to
always march down that route.	Besides	, with the River Wei ahead
I were you, General.	Besides	, in Yuan Shu you will
two months, had stalled.	Besides	, he had news requiring his
harmonious for you to undermine.	Besides	, the north is your main

表38. 虞译本 besides 语境共现检索（前5次，共54次）

a son and a daughter.	Besides	, he had adopted a son
to ask for his sake.	Besides	, I would like to see
a post in his army.	Besides	, he also gave him his
to write and exhort me.	Besides	, he even uses an ironic
temper and flog the soldiers.	Besides	, you're rash and will not

表39. 10部英文小说副词 besides 的语境共现检索（共45次）

苔丝.	do anything, my dear.	Besides	, perhaps there's more in it
苔丝.	about it than any 'prentice.	Besides	, that's only just a show
苔丝.	don't care if 'tis dozens.	Besides	, the cart is behind.' 'You
苔丝.	see which be their fancy-men.	Besides	, the house sometimes shuts up
苔丝.	and become a new one.	Besides	, another dairy-girl was as good
苔丝.	you ask me fifty times.	Besides	, you must bear in mind
苔丝.	off then as my property.	Besides	, if you were not the
苔丝.	it might be different…	Besides	, that's not all the difficulty
鲁宾逊.	Fruitless Wishes of being there.	Besides	, after some Pause upon this
鲁宾逊.	eager to be upon them.	Besides	, I fancied myself able
双城记.	of what I now say.	Besides	that I should know it to
双城记.	his last chance of life.	Besides	that all secret men are men
傲慢偏见.	let Mr. Darcy contradict it.	Besides	, there was truth in his

第四章　古典小说英译的母语译者和非母语译者的定量比较研究

续表

嘉莉妹妹.	and she had a few days.	Besides	, she was not sure that
嘉莉妹妹.	be up betimes and searching.	Besides	, many things might happen
嘉莉妹妹.	she would not endure long.	Besides	, she had discovered no resource
嘉莉妹妹.	the last to close.	Besides	, other things will happen." At
嘉莉妹妹.	was used to in business.	Besides	, the business varied. It
嘉莉妹妹.	, and day after day.	Besides	, he had the disagreeable fear
嘉莉妹妹.	or too wretched for him.	Besides	, winter was coming, the
大卫科波.	Larkins, what of that?	Besides	, I shall be one-and-twenty in
大卫科波.	night I must come out.	Besides	, it's the brightest time
傲慢偏见.	it will be very tolerable.	Besides	, it will not much signify
大卫科波.	be so unkind to Jip!	Besides	, I couldn't be such
大卫科波.	if you don't go.	Besides	, ' said Dora, putting
大卫科波.	you more so, too.	Besides	, you are very clever,
汤姆历险.	lifts things when he snores.	Besides	, I reckon he can't
简爱.	to emulation as I listened.	Besides	, school would be a complete
简爱.	a terror and an abyss.	Besides	, with this creed, I
简爱.	for their temporary suppression.	Besides	, Jane' - she paused. 'Well
简爱.	with comparative liberality.	Besides	, there were fewer to feed
简爱.	, gave me the advantage.	Besides	, the eccentricity of the

续表

简爱.	, cursed as I am?	Besides	, since happiness is irrevocably
简爱.	be the recipient of secrets.	Besides	, I know what sort of
简爱.	, and people bustling about.	Besides	, she added, a message
简爱.	when you go near her.	Besides	, you might have waited till
简爱.	the true, eternal Paradise.	Besides	, he could not bind all
简爱.	mute books and empty rooms.	Besides	, since yesterday I have
简爱.	bliss with a solemn brow.	Besides	, the words Legacy, Bequest
简爱.	is worn by continual dropping.	Besides	, you must know some day,
简爱.	unjust, or fiendishly ungrateful.	Besides	, I am resolved I will
简爱.	is contrary to all custom.	Besides	, the entire fortune is your
简爱.	what I had already hazarded.	Besides	, I was out of practice
简爱.	'I should never dream that.	Besides	, there is that peculiar voice
简爱.	enter into particulars that night.	Besides	, I wished to touch no

  extremely 是虞译本排第二位的特色副词，其使用频次与邓译本和罗译本的差异比较显著，分别达 25 次和 30 次。从其使用频次的差异幅度来看，besides 是虞译本具有代表性的特色副词。两位母语译者对于 extremely 的使用频次非常低，邓译本为 9 次，罗译本为 4 次。笔者使用语料库统计软件对参照语料库 10 部英文小说的副词进行了统计，extremely 的使用频次排在所有副词中的第 163 位，使用频次为 73 次，平均每部小说为 6.3 次，接近邓译本和罗译本的平均使用频次 6.5 次。虞译本对于 extremely 的使用频次较高的原因是其对原文中的词汇意义或其意义相近的表达方式使用同一词汇进行重复再现的结果，而两位母语译者较低频次的使用则说明其对在不同的上下文中使用了不同的词汇或表达方式进行了处理。虞译本、邓译本以及罗译本的 extremely 的语境共现检索如表 40. 至表 42. 所示。

第四章 古典小说英译的母语译者和非母语译者的定量比较研究

表 40. 邓译本 extremely 语境共现检索（前 5 次，共 9 次）

you can do, and an	extremely	easy one to perform; but
the crowd. He is so	extremely	rude that I feel sure he
wish." Cao Cao heard of this	extremely	correct behavior and thought all the
skillfully played and the air was	extremely	beautiful. He stopped his guide
Luocheng, and the situation is	extremely	dangerous. When the lips are

表 41. 罗译本 extremely 语境共现检索（共 4 次）

Cao. "He must be	extremely	powerful. "Once he
fiery temper. He was also	extremely	stingy. As a young boy
neighboring district. Our relations are	extremely	close, "Cui Liang responded
. Lu Su's family is	extremely	wealthy, and he is known

表 42. 虞译本 extremely 语境共现检索（前 5 次，共 34 次）

it." Hearing this Cao Cao was	extremely	pleased. At twenty he was
his household, followed by an	extremely	long procession of thousands of carts
Dian Wei from Chenliu, an	extremely	brave and strong warrior. He
in the tent, he was	extremely	surprised and at once turned to
to Huainan and you must be	extremely	careful not to allow any breach

deliberately 是虞译本四个特色副词中排第三位的特色副词，其使用频次与邓译本和罗译本的差异比较显著，分别达 13 次和 13 次。从其使用频次的差异幅度来看，deliberately 是虞译本具有代表性的特色副词。两位母语译者对于 deliberately 的使用频次非常低，邓译本为 3 次，罗译本为 3 次。笔者使用语料库统计软件对参照语料库 10 部英文小说的副词进行了统计，deliberately 的使用频次排在所有副词中的第 462 位，使用频次为 14 次，平均每部小说为 1.4 次，还要少于邓译本和罗译本的平均使用频次 3 次，虞译本对于 deliberately 的使用频次较高的原因是其对原文中的词汇意义或其意义相近的表达方式使用同一词汇进行重复再现的结果，而两位母语译者较低频次的使用则说明其在不同的上下文中使用了不同的词汇或表达方式进行了处理。虞译本、邓译本以及罗译本 deliberately 的语境共现检索如表 43. 至表 46. 所示。

表 43. 邓译本 deliberately 语境共现检索（共 3 次）

should have been killed." "To kill	deliberately	is very wrong," said Chen Gong
. Ma Teng very slowly and	deliberately	spoke his name. To a
had hurled at you had been	deliberately	arranged and intrigued by Kong Rong

表 44. 罗译本 deliberately 语境共现检索（共 3 次）

Bazhou unobserved. " Zhang Fei	deliberately	shouted loudly enough to be heard
him a good while before saying	deliberately	, " Are things well with
group asked who. Calmly and	deliberately	, Ma Teng spoke the name

表 45. 虞译本 deliberately 语境共现检索（前 10 次，共 16 次）

certainly, be in danger." "To kill	deliberately	is very wrong," said Chen Gong
some slanderous tongues around you,	deliberately	withheld the supplies of grain,
was being followed and he had	deliberately	slowed down, waiting for his
ask for more?" He	deliberately	sent them putrid meat and rotten
. Ma Teng very slowly and	deliberately	spoke his name. To a

表 46. 10 部英文小说副词 deliberately 的语境共现检索（共 14 次）

傲慢偏见.	did not suppose Lydia to be	deliberately	engaging in an elopement,
傲慢偏见.	after their father, who was	deliberately	pursuing his way towards a
双城记.	dress, such as it was—quite	deliberately	, as having dirtied the hand
双城记.	. ' As the ancient clerk	deliberately	folded and superscribed the
双城记.	me, Mr. Lorry. You	deliberately	advise me not to go up
双城记.	the money for them, and	deliberately	left the shop. 'There
大卫科波.	her breakfast, my aunt very	deliberately	leaned back in her chair,

· 152 ·

第四章 古典小说英译的母语译者和非母语译者的定量比较研究

续表

大卫科波.	, on a side-saddle, ride	deliberately	over the sacred piece of green
简爱.	your faces up to mine.' He	deliberately	scrutinised each sketch and
简爱.	to draw you into a snare	deliberately	laid, and strip you of
简爱.	white.' And the pocket-book	deliberately	produced, opened, sought
红字.	said Roger Chillingworth	deliberately	, and fixing an eye,
苔丝.	young man should have chosen	deliberately	to be a farmer, and
苔丝.	, as she would never have	deliberately	volunteered for. Towards the

secondly 是虞译本四个特色副词中排第一位的特色副词,其使用频次与邓译本和罗译本的差异比较显著,分别达 11 次和 12 次。从其使用频次的差异幅度来看,secondly 是虞译本具有代表性的特色副词。两位母语译者对于 secondly 的使用频次非常低,邓译本为 4 次,罗译本为 3 次。笔者使用语料库统计软件对参照语料库 10 部英文小说的副词进行了统计,secondly 的使用频次排在所有副词中的第 462 位,使用频次为 16 次,平均每部小说为 1.6 次,还要少于邓译本和罗译本的平均使用频次 3.5 次。虞译本、邓译本以及罗译本的 secondly 的语境共现检索如表 47. 至表 50. 所示。

表 47. 邓译本 secondly 语境共现检索(共 4 次)

betraying the Peach Garden Oath?	Secondly	, you are in charge of
literary grace and warlike exploits,	secondly	, handsome and highly esteemed and
Liaoxi to attack Xiping Pass.	Secondly	, the king of the Mang
short of food, and,	secondly	, they have sent an army

表 48. 罗译本 secondly 语境共现检索（共 3 次）

down in the northwest? And	secondly	, what lies beyond the lighter
wheat is used up, and	secondly	, because they have sent troops
's sister-in-law would provoke contempt.	Secondly	, it is her second marriage

表 49. 虞译本 secondly 语境共现检索（前 5 次，共 15 次）

is to be replaced by 'earth.'	Secondly	, there is an oracle which
restore peace in the country.	Secondly	, as Yuan Shao is very
of the Peach Garden oath.	Secondly	, your brother left his family
persists in his southern expeditions.	Secondly	, the northern men are unused
literary grace and martial arts;	secondly	, handsome and highly dignified;

表 50. 10 部英文小说副词 secondly 的语境共现检索（共 16 次）

傲慢偏见.	of matrimony in his parish.	Secondly	, that I am convinced it
傲慢偏见.	on the present occasion; and	secondly	, of my room. I
傲慢偏见.	the whole of the matter;	secondly	, she was very sure that
双城记.	with the Doctor and Lucie;	secondly	, because, on unfavourable
大卫科波.	be unlucky in life; and	secondly	, that I was privileged to
大卫科波.	had grown more shabby, and	secondly	, that I was now relieved
大卫科波.	never having seen it; and	secondly	, on account of the great
大卫科波.	them wholly from each other;	secondly	, that Mr. Wickfield seemed to
大卫科波.	much into the parks, and	secondly	, if I went much into
大卫科波.	treated with peppermint;	secondly	, that something peculiar in the
大卫科波.	was not my name; and	secondly	, I am inclined to think
简爱.	it was masculine; and,	secondly	, because it was dark,

第四章　古典小说英译的母语译者和非母语译者的定量比较研究

续表

简爱.	with Mrs. Fairfax's description；	secondly	, whether it at all resembled
鲁宾逊.	Time for thrice every Day.	Secondly	, The going Abroad with my
鲁宾逊.	Shore anywhere there about.	Secondly	, When I came to measure
鲁宾逊.	Moidores in my Favour.	Secondly	, There was the Account of

从以上对于虞译本的特色副词的统计分析及其与参照语料库的比较分析中，我们发现虞译本的四个特色副词 besides，extremely，deliberately，secondly 的使用频次不仅以较大幅度高于母语译者邓译本和罗译本的使用频次，而且也以较大幅度高于参照语料库 10 部英文小说的使用频次，母语译者对于这四个副词的使用频次与参照语料库的相接近。这从侧面佐证了《三国演义》全译本母语译者副词使用的特色，但这并不意味着不论是任何英文原创小说或英语母语译者译入语文学作品，besides，extremely，deliberately，secondly 四个副词的使用频次就一定很低。笔者推测母语译者以及参照语料库这四个副词使用频次较低的原因在于译者和原创小说的作者为了避免特定词语的重复使用，而会以其他词汇或表达方式进行替代，同时这些副词的使用还受到其他诸多因素尤其是作品内容的影响和制约。但母语译者以及参照语料库对其较低频率的使用说明母语译者在母语思维模式下在避免某一特定词语的重复使用方面是比较成功的。

《三国演义》英文全译本的母语译者的特色副词共 2 个，分别为 west（29,36-9）和 mightily（11,10-2），其中，west 最具代表性，与非母语译者的频次差距幅度分别为 20 次和 27 次，差异较为明显。West 是一个方向词，其母语译者的使用频次明显高于非母语译者主要反映了两位母语译者在处理原文方向词时，母语译者的文化视角。母语译者和非母语译者除了思维模式方面的差异之外，两者的母语文化以及在此基础上的文化观也截然不同，两者在翻译时所针对的潜在读者群和文化目的也不尽相同的，有时甚至是截然相反的。原文中有些具体的内容或词汇由于母语文化、翻译文化观、针对的潜在读者群、翻译目的的不同，母语译者和非母语译者会采取完全不同的翻译策略和处理方式。两位母语译者 mightily 的使用频次与非母语译者的使用频次分别以 9 次和 8 次的幅度高于非母语译者，其具体使用情况如下表所示。

从表中邓译本、罗译本、虞译本对于 mightily 的使用情况来看，我们发现邓译本中，mightily 多与 please 搭配，其中，please...mightily 5 次，be mightily pleased 1 次，其他搭配包括 waxed mightily 2 次，felt mightily 1 次，be mightily fond 1 次，gratified...mightily 1 次。罗译本中，mightily 多与 shouting 和 fought 搭配，其中，shouting mightily 4 次，fought mightily 4 次，其他搭配包括 swept mightily 1 次，striving mightily 1 次。虞译本中 please...mightily 2 次。

表 51. 邓译本 mightily 语境共现检索（前 5 次，共 11 次）

and the words pleased Dong Zhuo	mightily	. So, the next day Dong
his ability." This gratified Lu Bu	mightily	, and his host continued to
outer world. Every soldier felt	mightily	afraid. Liu Bei returned to
very prosperous, and he waxed	mightily	in influence and won the love
, suddenly shouted, "You are	mightily	fond of big words, Sir

表 52. 罗译本 mightily 语境共现检索（前 5 次，共 10 次）

. Zhong fought the two commanders	mightily	, joining with each in ten
Zhang Nan and Feng Xi fought	mightily	, only to fall in the
Huo took the lead, shouting	mightily	to hearten them. But as
themselves around Deng Ai and shouting	mightily	. Deng Ai did not recognize
Acceptance of the Abdication, shouting	mightily	, " Long live the new

表 53. 虞译本 mightily 语境共现检索（共 2 次）

| said seemed to please Zhuge Liang | mightily | , and he was sent on |
| of their leader's pleased them all | mightily | . In the meantime, Meng Huo |

《三国演义》的母语译者和非母语译者 4 个节译本副词的情况如表 54. 所示：

表 54.《三国演义》四个英文节译本副词形符类符

	邓译本	罗译本	杨译本	张译本
副词总形符数	2685	1938	2025	2231
副词总类符类	303	323	268	277

第四章　古典小说英译的母语译者和非母语译者的定量比较研究

《三国演义》四个英文节译本的母语译者(参照非母语译者)的特色副词包括：indeed（12,11-5,5）。

《三国演义》四个英文节译本的非母语译者(参照母语译者)的特色副词包括：无。

表 55. 邓译本(节译) indeed 语境共现检索(前 5 次,共 12 次)

and Zhao Zilong. That was	indeed	a time of extreme weakness.
had never won a victory.	Indeed	real statesmanship and the restoration of
on these river fogs: Mighty	indeed	is the Great River! Rising
, then the South Land would	indeed	be happy." "Kill me. I
for Huang Gai. "He is	indeed	most worthy of death, but

表 56. 罗译本(节译) indeed 语境共现检索(共 13 次)

Yu Fan. "Cao Cao did	indeed	bring into his fold the swarming
way to make Kongming give in."	Indeed	: When wits are matched,
! "Master, you are	indeed	supernatural," Lu Su said. "How
Eagerly, Kan Ze accepted.	Indeed	: A brave general requites his
a well-meaning friend, that is	indeed	the height of ignorance." On

表 57. 杨译本(节译) indeed 语境共现检索(共 5 次)

on his side. You are	indeed	a man who respects neither father
Cheng Deshu could not answer.	Indeed	all the scholars were put out
, entreating, "Huang Gai does	indeed	deserve death, but his loss
asked Zhuge Liang."It is	indeed	! "You must take a
It was a mighty battle	indeed	that day at the Red Cliff

表 58. 张译本(节译) indeed 语境共现检索(共 5 次)

entreating, " Huang Gai does	indeed	deserve death, but his loss
kinsman inherited territory. This is	indeed	great humanity and justice. As
asked Zhuge liang." It is	indeed	! "You must take a
.It was a mighty battle	indeed	that day at the Red Cliff
rebuke you to your face.	Indeed	your speech was most insulting to

4.2.4.3 特色形容词

《三国演义》的母语译者和非母语译者的三个全译本形容词的情况如表 59. 所示。

表 59.《三国演义》三个英文全译本形容词形符类符

	邓译本	罗译本	虞译本
形容词形符数	27062	26601	27779
形容词类符数	2093	2376	2031

《三国演义》三个英文全译本的母语译者（参照非母语译者）的特色形容词包括：correct（19,19-6）; confident（11,19-2）; dynastic（14,16-2）共 3 个。

《三国演义》三个英文全译本的非母语译者（参照母语译者）的特色形容词包括：neighboring（17-3,5）; deceased（13-1,1）共 2 个。

《三国演义》全译本的母语译者的特色形容词共 5 个，非母语译者的特色形容词共 2 个。就非母语译者的特色形容词来看，neighboring 和 deceased 在其译文中的使用频次都不高，分别为 17 次和 13 次，其中 neighboring 的使用频次与两位母语译者使用频次的差异幅度分别为 14 次和 12 次，deceased 的使用频次与两位母语译者的差异幅度分别为 12 次和 12 次，差异比较明显。neighboring 和 deceased 的使用情况如表 60. 至表 62. 所示。

Neighboring 在邓译本、罗译本、虞译本中的搭配如下。
neighboring towns：邓译本 0 次，罗译本 0 次，虞译本 5 次。
neighboring districts：邓译本 0 次，罗译 2 本，虞译本 6 次。
neighboring kingdoms：邓译本 0 次，罗译本 1 次，虞译本 0 次。
neighboring country/countries：邓译本 1 次，罗译本 0 次，虞译本 1 次。
neighboring counties：邓译本 1 次，罗译本 0 次，虞译本 0 次。
neighboring region/regions：邓译本 1 次，罗译本 1 次，虞译本 0 次。
neighboring points：邓译本 1 次，罗译本 1 次，虞译本 0 次。
neighboring cities：邓译本 0 次，罗译本 0 次，虞译本 1 次。
neighboring prefecture：邓译本 0 次，罗译本 0 次，虞译本 1 次。
neighboring lords：邓译本 0 次，罗译本 0 次，虞译本 1 次。
neighboring chieftain：邓译本 0 次，罗译本 0 次，虞译本 1 次。

第四章 古典小说英译的母语译者和非母语译者的定量比较研究

neighboring Xiangcheng：邓译本 0 次，罗译本 0 次，虞译本 1 次。

从以上对于 neighboring 的搭配统计中，我们发现虞译本的搭配种类和使用频次都远高于两位母语译者，同时通过比较虞译本和两位母语译者的译文以及原文，我们发现虞译本将原文字面所没有的两个地点之间的位置信息进行了补充翻译，以便目的语读者更好地理解原文中的内容。虞译本的 neighboring 大多都是对于原文两个地点位置关系的补充翻译，这是虞译本作为非母语译者在母语文化以及基于此的翻译文化观和翻译策略所影响的结果。母语译者和非母语译者除了从理解原文到翻译的过程中存在思维模式的差异之外，两者母语文化的不同，决定了两者的翻译文化观的不同。同时，两者翻译时所处的时空的差异导致两者所针对的潜在的读者群和翻译目的也存在差异。虞译本使用 neighboring 进行地点信息补充翻译与两位母语译者的对比，如下例所示。

例 15：

原文：河内太守张杨献米肉，河东太守王邑献绢帛，帝稍得宁。

邓译：But food and clothing were sent to the Emperor from the Governor of Henei, Zhang Yang, and the Governor of Hedong, Wang Yi, and the court began to enjoy a little repose.

罗译：Zhang Yang, governor of Henei, presented grain and meat to the Emperor. Wang Yi, governor of Hedong, submitted silk and cloth. As a result, the Emperor's distress was eased.

虞译：Then two prefects from the neighboring districts sent the Emperor some food and clothing and he began to enjoy a little repose.

例 16：

原文：策乃迎母、叔、诸弟俱归曲阿，使弟孙权与周泰守宣城，策领兵南取吴郡。

邓译：Sun Ce then settled his mother and the remainder of the family in Que, setting his brother, Sun Quan, and Zhou Tai over the city of Xuancheng. Then he headed an expedition to the south to reduce Wujun.

罗译：Sun Ce settled his uncle and cousins in Qu'e, leaving his younger brother Sun Quan and Zhou Tai guarding the walled town of Xuan. Next, Sun Ce led his troops south to capture Wujun.

虞译：He settled his mother and the rest of his family in Qua and appointed his brother, Sun Quan, to guard the city of Xuan together with Zhou Tai. And he himself headed for another expedition to the south to conquer Wujun and its neighboring districts.

例 17：

原文：诩劝表回荆州，绣守襄城，以为唇齿。两军各散。

邓译：On the advice of Jia Xu then Liu Biao returned to Jingzhou, while Zhang Xiu took up his position at Xiangyang so that each strengthened the other as the lips protect the teeth from cold.

罗译：Jia Xu persuaded Liu Biao to return to Jingzhou and Xiu to defend Xiangyang, so that the two could reinforce each other. Thus, the two armies parted.

虞译：On the advice of Jia Xu, Liu Biao returned to Jingzhou, while Zhang Xiu took up his position at the neighboring Xiangcheng, so that each strengthened the other as the lips protect the teeth.

例 18：

原文："不若分兵屯小沛，守邳城，为掎角之势，以防曹操。"玄德用其言，令云长守下邳，甘、糜二夫人亦于下邳安置。

邓译："We should send part of our forces to Xiaopei and guard Xiapi as a corner stone of our position." Liu Bei agreed and told off Guan Yu to guard Xiapi whither he also sent his two wives, Lady Gan and Lady Mi.

罗译："We'd better fortify Xiaopei and the town of Xiapi, giving us a two-pronged deployment against Cao Cao." Xuande approved the suggestion. He sent Lord Guan to Xiapi and placed his wives, Lady Gan and Lady Mi, in his care.

虞译："We should send part of our forces to the two neighboring towns of Xiaopei and Xiapi. The three places can assist each other against Cao Cao." Liu Bei agreed and told Guan Yu to guard Xiapi, to which he also sent his two wives, the ladies Gan and Mi.

表 60. 邓译本 neighboring 语境共现检索（共 3 次）

to coerce the chief of a	neighboring	region?" "You have concealed
cousin of Yang Fu. Being	neighboring	counties, we are very good
cause, and it behooves the	neighboring	countries to punish such a crime

第四章　古典小说英译的母语译者和非母语译者的定量比较研究

表 61. 罗译本 neighboring 语境共现检索（共 5 次）

won, Zhu Jun pacified several	neighboring	districts and reported to the throne
Ren to defend Nanjun and other	neighboring	points. He is sure to
. The governor is from the	neighboring	district. Our relations are extremely
in control of Yongzhou 7 and	neighboring	regions. He is a kinsman
for no good reason. Even	neighboring	kingdoms must call him to account

表 62. 虞译本 neighboring 语境共现检索（前 5 次，共 17 次）

and Liu Bei in the two	neighboring	towns. Liu Bei discussed the
content. Then conquer the four	neighboring	towns of Wuling, Changsha,
at Jiangling while also defending the	neighboring	town of Gongan. For the
His strength and valor frightened the	neighboring	lords, who dared not encroach
with the intention of subduing the	neighboring	districts. Meng Da arrived,

虞译本的另一个特色形容词 deceased 的具体使用情况如表 65. 所示，其使用频次明显高于邓译本和罗译本。但虞译本 deceased 使用频次较高更多是基于其翻译文化、翻译目的等因素方面的策略选择，而非其思维模式影响的结果，两位母语译者对于同样的原文所采取的翻译也是其翻译文化观以及翻译策略影响的结果。原文以及邓译本、罗译本、虞译本 deceased 的相关例句如例 19 所示，邓译本、罗译本、虞译本 deceased 的语境共现检索如表 63. 至表 65. 所示。

例 19：

原文："若奉孝在，决不使吾有此大失也。"遂捶胸大哭曰："哀哉奉孝！痛哉奉孝！惜哉奉孝！"

邓译："Had he been alive, he would not have let me suffer this loss." He beat his breast and wept, saying, "Alas for Guo Jia! I grieve for Guo Jia! I sorrow for Guo Jia!"

罗译："He could have prevented this dreadful defeat," Cao said. He beat his breast and howled: "I grieve for you, Guo Jia. Oh, what a loss, what a loss!"

虞译："Had he been alive he would not have let me suffer this loss." He beat his breast and, calling his deceased advisor by name, wept passionately.

表63. 邓译本 deceased 语境共现检索(共1次)

| .Sun Jian, the | deceased | father of the new Emperor, |

表64. 罗译本 deceased 语境共现检索(共1次)

| set up the tablets of the | deceased | emperors and to perform the grand |

表65. 虞译本 deceased 语境共现检索(前5次,共13次)

that he offered sacrifices to his	deceased	nephew and his eldest son,
vent to their anguish for their	deceased	prime minister. The soldiers struck
his voice and cried for his	deceased	minister, and with him cried
sacrifices at the tomb of the	deceased	minister. The two envoys took
who conferred high honors upon the	deceased	minister and advanced his sons to

就全译本的母语译者的特色形容词来看,共有correct(19,19-6), confident(11,19-2), dynastic(14,16-2)3个词,其具体使用情况如表66.至表68.所示,其搭配情况如下。

be correct:邓译本10次,罗译本11次,虞译本4次。
confident that:邓译本2次,罗译本5次,虞译本0次。
confident of:邓译本2次,罗译本4次,虞译本0次。
confident in:邓译本2次,罗译本3次,虞译本0次。
be/seem/feel confident:邓译本5次,罗译本7次,虞译本1次。
confident 的相关搭配:邓译本共计11次,罗译本共计19次,虞译本共计1次。
Dynastic Temple:邓译本5次,罗译本0次,虞译本0次。
dynastic family:邓译本4次,罗译本0次,虞译本0次。
dynastic shrines:邓译本0次,罗译本6次,虞译本0次。
dynastic altars:邓译本0次,罗译本2次,虞译本0次。
Dynastic Authority:邓译本0次,罗译本2次,虞译本0次。
dynastic rolls:邓译本1次,罗译本0次,虞译本1次。
dynastic title:邓译本0次,罗译本0次,虞译本1次。

第四章 古典小说英译的母语译者和非母语译者的定量比较研究

dynastic 的相关搭配：邓译本共计 10 次，罗译本共计 10 次，虞译本共计 2 次。

表 66. 邓译本 confident 语境共现检索（前 5 次，共 11 次）

ill, and he summoned his	confident	, Mi Zhu, to his
Hou Yi, proud of and	confident	in his archer's skill, gave
his merit. In feeling over	confident	, that's where one's weakness lay
said Zhou Yu, puzzled though	confident	. On his side Lu Su
truth is Zhou Yu is over	confident	, and he reckons us as

表 67. 罗译本 confident 语境共现检索（前 5 次，共 19 次）

, " Cao Cao is too	confident	of his power to agree to
Sun Qian stayed in Xiaopei.	Confident	of his plan, Zhang Fei
no obeisance? " With a	confident	air Deng Zhi responded, "
invincible, Meng Huo felt fully	confident	. Meanwhile, Kongming had advanced
you say, but I feel	confident	you are not deceiving us.

表 68. 虞译本 confident 语境共现检索（共 2 次）

| counsel. The son, quite | confident | , said, "Have no anxiety |
| his men are very keen and | confident | . Our best policy is to |

《三国演义》《三国演义》的母语译者和非母语译者的四个节译本形容词的情况如表 69. 所示。

表 69.《三国演义》四个英文节译本形容词形符类符

	邓译本	罗译本	杨译本	张译本
形容词形符数	1962	1770	1527	1634
形容词类符数	784	687	627	652

《三国演义》四个英文节译本的母语译者（参照非母语译者）的特色形容词包括 own（24,38-14,14）; southern（12,23-4,4）; last（12,11-4,3）; little（12,12-2,2）。

《三国演义》四个英文节译本的非母语译者（参照母语译者）的特色形容词包括：more（45,42-24,21）; green（8,9-1,3）。

163

《三国演义》四个英文节译本的母语译者的特色形容词排第一位的是 own，邓译本和罗译本的使用频次分别为 24 次和 38 次，杨译本和张译本的使用频次分别为 14 次和 14 次。邓译本与杨译本和张译本的使用频次的差异幅度都为 10 次，罗译本与杨译本和张译本的差异幅度都为 24 次。与邓译本相比，罗译本与两位非母语译者的差异更为显著。笔者使用语料库统计软件对参照语料库 10 部英文小说的词汇使用情况进行了统计，own 的使用频次在所有形容词中排第四位，10 部小说共用 1610 次，平均每部小说使用 161 次，使用频率比较高。笔者同样使用语料库统计软件对《红楼梦》的霍译本和杨译本进行了统计，结果显示 own 霍译 1142 次，在霍译所有形容词中排第四位，杨译 565 次，在杨译所有形容词中排第五位。《三国演义》三个全译本 own 的使用情况为：own 在三个全译本中共使用 1498 次，在所有形容词中排第三位；邓译本 own 共使用 512 次，在所有形容词中排第三位；罗译本 own 共使用 427 次，在所有形容词中排第二位；虞译本 own 共使用 559 次，在所有形容词中排第三位；罗译本 own 的使用频次虽然低于邓译本和虞译本，但其排位顺序要比邓译本和虞译本靠前，邓译本的使用频次略低于虞译本，但差异不大。

从以上对于《红楼梦》的霍译和杨译、《三国演义》的三个全译本和四个节译本、参照语料库的 10 部英文小说当中作为形容词的 own 使用情况的统计来看，形容词 own 的使用具有以下三个特征：一是 own 在参照语料库、《红楼梦》的英译、《三国演义》的全译本、《三国演义》的节译本中的使用频次普遍较高；二是 own 的使用频次在参照语料库、《红楼梦》的英译、《三国演义》的全译本、《三国演义》的节译本中所有形容词的排序中普遍靠前；三是参照语料库、《红楼梦》的英译、《三国演义》的全译本、《三国演义》的节译本的母语译者对于 own 的使用频次普遍高于的非母语译者（除了《三国演义》全译本的邓译本与虞译本相接近，罗译本略低于虞译本，但罗译本 own 的排序要比虞译本的靠前），以及母语译者的使用频次在所有形容词中的排序中普遍比非母语译者靠前。

节译本特色形容词中，另外一个值得关注的是 little。两位母语译者 little 的使用频次都为 12 次，两位非母语译者的使用频次都为 2 次，两者相差 10 次，差异较为显著。笔者使用语料库统计软件对参照语料库和《红楼梦》的霍译和杨译分别进行了统计，结果显示：在参照语料库的 10 部英文小说中作为形容词的 little 使用总频次为 2510 次，在所

第四章　古典小说英译的母语译者和非母语译者的定量比较研究

有形容词中排第一位,平均每部小说的使用频次为 251 次;《红楼梦》霍译作为形容词的 little 使用频次为 1240 次,在所有形容词中排第三位,《红楼梦》杨译作为形容词的 little 使用频次为 278 次,在所有形容词中排第十五位;《三国演义》全译本中,作为形容词的 little,邓译本的使用频次为 127 次,在所有形容词中排第三十五位,罗译本的使用频次为 112 次,在所有形容名词中排第三十一位,虞译本的使用频次为 91 次,在所有形容词中排第九十位。

从以上对于《红楼梦》的霍译和杨译、《三国演义》的三个全译本和四个节译本、参照语料库的 10 部英文小说当中作为形容词的 little 使用情况的统计来看,形容词 little 的使用具有以下三个特征:一是参照语料库和母语译者 little 的使用频次都比较高,在所有形容词中的排序也比较靠前;二是《红楼梦》的全译本、《三国演义》的全译本、《三国演义》的节译本中,母语译者 little 的使用频次都高于非母语译者;三是《红楼梦》的全译本、《三国演义》的全译本、《三国演义》的节译本中,母语译者 little 的使用频次在所有形容词中的排序都较非母语译者靠前。《三国演义》四个节译本 little 的具体使用情况如表 70. 至表 73. 所示。

除了从使用频次和其使用频次在所有形容词中的排序之外,我们再从 little 的相关搭配来考察母语译者相较于非母语译者的区别性特征,其相关搭配如下:

little use:邓译本(节译)0 次,罗译本(节译)0 次,杨译本(节译)2 次,张译本(节译)2 次。

little time/while:邓译本(节译)3 次,罗译本(节译)1 次,杨译本(节译)0 次,张译本(节译)0 次。

little boat/craft/fleet/convoy:邓译本(节译)4 次,罗译本(节译)3 次,杨译本(节译)0 次,张译本(节译 0)次。

little tongue:邓译本(节译)1 次,罗译本(节译)1 次,杨译本(节译)0 次,张译本(节译)0 次;

little trust/commitment/visit/ hope/mud/service/slip:邓译本(节译)2 次,罗译本(节译)5 次,杨译本(节译)0 次,张译本(节译)0 次;

little 的相关搭配:邓译本(节译)10 次,罗译本(节译)11 次,杨译本(节译)2 次,张译本(节译)2 次。

表 70. 邓译本（节译）little 语境共现检索（前 5 次，共 12 次）

outline, but I want a	little	time to prepare my report," replied
is a simple messenger and a	little	boat to ferry a couple of
,"I am ashamed of the	little	service I have rendered since I
And so, I teased him a	little	. But he cannot bear that
linen robe and seated in his	little	craft, the messenger reached Zhou

表 71. 罗译本（节译）little 语境共现检索（前 5 次，共 12 次）

. Kongming betook himself to a	little	boat of his own. His
Kongming welcomed Lu Su aboard his	little	boat, and the two men
By the fifth watch Kongming's	little	convoy was nearing Cao Cao's
for the Southland, there is	little	hope of defeating them in a
to entertain him. In a	little	while someone entered the tent and

表 72. 杨译本（节译）little 语境共现检索（共 2 次）

| ashamed to have been of so | little | use since coming to this land," |
| twenty men. They would be | little | use in a fight." "It would |

表 73. 张译本（节译）little 语境共现检索（共 2 次）

| ashamed to have been of so | little | use since coming to this land |
| twenty men. They would be | little | use in a fight." Said Cao |

　　除了特色形容词的视角之外，我们再从形容词类符数的视角来考察母语译者相较于非母语译者的区别性特征。从《三国演义》全译本和节译本的形容词形符类符的统计中，我们可发现《三国演义》全译本中，邓译本形容词的类符数为 2463 个单词，罗译本形容词的类符数为 2650 个单词，虞译本形容词的类符数为 2157 个单词；《三国演义》节译本中，邓译本（节译）形容词的类符数为 784 个单词，罗译本（节译）形容词的类符数为 687 个单词，杨译本（节译）形容词的类符数为 627 个单词，张译本（节译）形容词的类符数为 652 个单词。不论是全译本还是节译本，母语译者形容词的类符数都大于非母语译者形容词的类符数，全译本中，邓译本和罗译本的形容词类符数分别比虞译本多 306 个单词和 493 个单词，差异幅度比较明显；节译本中，邓译本（节译）的形容词类符数比杨译本（节译）和张译本（节译）分别高 157 个单词和 132 个单词，罗

第四章 古典小说英译的母语译者和非母语译者的定量比较研究

译本(节译)的形容词类符数比杨译本(节译)和张译本(节译)分别多60个单词和35个单词,差异幅度也比较明显。

形容词的类符数反映了特定文本中形容词种类的数量,形容词的类符数越大,则说明特定文本所使用的形容词种类越多;反之,则说明特定文本所使用的形容词种类越少。在文学作品,尤其是小说中,形容词具有非常重要的作用。在文学作品中常见的记叙、说明、议论、描写、抒情等写作方法当中,形容词对人物外貌、形象、性格、心理以及事件和事物的状态、性质、相互关系等的描写具有重要作用。特定文本当中,形容词的种类越多,则文本对于人物的外貌、形象、性格、心理以及事件和事物的状态、性质、相互关系等的描写越精确和细腻,文本的表达效果相对来说也更为生动活泼,富于表现力。从这一意义上来说,《三国演义》全译本以及节译本的母语译者相较于非母语译者,其形容词种类的丰富性使其在译文在人物外貌、形象、性格心理以及事件和事物的状态、性质、相互关系等方面的描写更有优势,更为精确和细腻。

4.2.4.4 特色名词

名词是文学作品中最重要的词类之一,用来指称人物、时间、地点、方位、物质、事物、抽象概念等。名词是小说信息的重要载体,其使用情况反映了小说人物、政治背景、时代风貌、自然环境等重要信息。下面本研究将从特色名词的角度来考察《三国演义》母语译者和非母语译者各自在名词使用方面的特征。《三国演义》的母语译者和非母语译者的三个全译本名词的情况以及《三国演义》的母语译者和非母语译者的四个节译本名词的情况分别如表 74. 和表 75. 所示。

表 74.《三国演义》全译本名词形符类符

	邓译本	罗译本	虞译本
名词总形符数	96373	99018	99766
名词总类符数	5923	6825	5874

《三国演义》三个英文全译本的母语译者(参照非母语译者)的特色名词包括:troops(1056,1244-249);generals(437,244-70);armies(277,247-146);governor(216,294-85)共 4 个。

《三国演义》三个英文全译本的非母语译者(参照母语译者)的特色名词包括:无。

表 75.《三国演义》四个英文节译本名词形符类符表

	邓译本	罗译本	杨译本	张译本
名词总形符数	7549	7728	6526	6752
名词总类符数	1911	2152	1623	1638

  《三国演义》四个英文节译本的母语译者（参照非母语译者）的特色名词包括：general（22,34-7,9）；guest（22,16-6,7）；moment（16,27-2,4）；sir（17,16-6,6）；reply（13,17-5,4）；point（12,18-3,2）；spear（9,10-2,2）共 7 个。

  《三国演义》四个英文节译本的非母语译者（参照母语译者）的特色名词包括：vessels（12,13-2,3）；adviser（11,9-4,4）共 2 个。

  从以上《三国演义》的全译本以及节译本的母语译者和非母语译者的特色名词的统计中，我们可以发现全译本中，母语译者的特色名词共 4 个，非母语译者的特色名词数为零；节译本中，母语译者的特色名词数共 7 个，非母语译者的特色名词数共 2 个，不论是全译本还是节译本，母语译者的特色名词数都大于非母语译者的特色名词数。这些特色名词反映了母语译者在名词使用方面相较于非母语译者的显著特色。

  《三国演义》全译本母语译者的特色名词共 4 个，分别为 troops，generals，armies，governor。troops 邓译本的使用频次为 1056 次，罗译本的使用频次为 1244 次，虞译本的使用频次为 249 次，邓译本和罗译本与虞译本的差异分别为 807 次和 995 次；generals 邓译本的使用频次为 437 次，罗译本的使用频次为 244 次，虞译本的使用频次为 70 次，邓译本和罗译本与虞译本的差异分别为 367 次和 174 次；armies 邓译本的使用频次为 277 次，罗译本的使用频次为 247 次，虞译本的使用频次为 146 次，邓译本和罗译本与虞译本的差异分别为 131 次和 101 次；governor 邓译本的使用频次为 216 次，罗译本的使用频次为 294 次，虞译本的使用频次为 85 次，邓译本、罗译本与虞译本的差异分别为 131 次和 209 次。从以上对于全译本母语译者特色名词的统计中，我们发现其特色名词具有以下两个特征：一是母语译者特色名词的使用频次远高于非母语译者的使用频次，差异非常显著；二是这些特色名词都是与小说原文题材相关的常见的政治军事名词。这说明在与小说题材相关的政治军事名词的使用方面，母语译者的译文对于小说原文题材的凸显更为明显。文化背景决定文化观念与语言思维方式，进而决定翻译策

第四章 古典小说英译的母语译者和非母语译者的定量比较研究

略,全译本两位母语译者以英语母语文化为背景,站在以英语为母语的读者群的立场并以其母语读者的角度来审视和考察小说原文中与文化和小说题材相关的词汇,在此基础上决定所采取的翻译策略。《三国演义》全译本的母语译者的特色名词体现了其母语译者在母语文化影响下的翻译特征和策略。

《三国演义》节译本母语译者的特色名词共7个,分别为general, guest, moment, sir, reply, point, spear。其中general, spear 是明显与小说原文题材相关的政治军事词汇,其与非母语译者使用频次的具体比较如下:general 邓译本(节译)的使用频次为22次,罗译本(节译)的使用频次为34次,杨译本(节译)的使用频次为7次,张译本(节译)的使用频次为9次,邓译本(节译)与杨译本(节译)和张译本(节译)的差异幅度分别为15次和13次,罗译本(节译)与杨译本(节译)和张译本(节译)的差异幅度分别为27次和25次,母语译者和非母语译者的差异比较显著;spear 邓译本(节译)的使用频次为9次,罗译本(节译)的使用频次为10次,杨译本(节译)的使用频次为2次,张译本(节译)的使用频次为2次,邓译本(节译)与杨译本(节译)和张译本(节译)的差异幅度分别为7次和7次,罗译本(节译)与杨译本(节译)和张译本(节译)的差异幅度分别为8次和8次,母语译者和非母语译者的差异也比较显著。这与全译本母语译者的特色名词全是与小说原文题材相关的政治军事词汇具有某种一致性。这种一致性从反面说明了全译本和节译本的三位非母语译者在使用与小说原文题材相关的政治军事词汇方面的一致性。这种母语译者之间的一致性和非母语译者之间的一致性同样基于其各自母语文化的影响。

节译本母语译者的特色名词中,另外两个值得关注的词是 moment 和 point,其与非母语译者使用频次的具体比较如下:moment 邓译本(节译)的使用频次为16次,罗译本(节译)的使用频次为27次,杨译本(节译)的使用频次为2次,张译本(节译)的使用频次为4次,邓译本(节译)与杨译本(节译)和张译本(节译)的差异幅度分别为14次和12次,罗译本(节译)与杨译本(节译)和张译本(节译)的差异幅度分别为25次和23次,母语译者和非母语译者的差异比较显著。两位母语译者对于 moment 的使用频次都显著高于两位非母语译者,这反映了《三国演义》节译本的母语译者在母语思维模式下,对于 moment 的使用特征。节译本 moment 的具体使用情况如表76.至表79.所示,搭配情况如下。

at...moment：邓译本 6 次，罗译本 11 次，杨译本 0 次，张译本 0 次。
for...moment：邓译本 4 次，罗译本 1 次，杨译本 0 次，张译本 1 次。
the moment...：邓译本 1 次，罗译本 8 次，杨译本 1 次，张译本 0 次。
during...moment：邓译本 0 次，罗译本 0 次，杨译本 1 次，张译本 1 次。
moment 的相关搭配：邓译本 11 次，罗译本 20 次，杨译本 2 次，张译本 2 次。

笔者使用语料库统计分析软件对参照语料库 10 部英文小说 moment 的使用情况进行了统计，结果显示：参照语料库 10 部英文小说 moment 的使用总频次为 759 次，平均每部小说 75.9 次，其相关的搭配情况如下：

at...moment：153 次；for...moment：168 次；the moment...：46 次；during...moment：0 次。

从以上节译本以及参照语料库 10 部英文小说 moment 的使用情况的统计中，我们发现节译本母语译者和参照语料库 moment 的使用频都比较高，而且参照语料库的使用频次相对更高；母语译者和参照语料库 moment 的搭配种类相对都比较多；其中值得注意的是，对于 during...moment 的使用，节译本母语译者和参照语料库的都为 0 次，而非母语译者，杨译本（节译）和张译本（节译）各为 1 次。节译本母语译者 moment 的使用特征得到了参照语料库的有力支撑。

表 76. 邓译本（节译）moment 语境共现检索（前 5 次，共 16 次）

master has not recognized the fateful	moment	, and to contend with a
I did despise him for a	moment	, and it has very nearly
that. Now is the critical	moment	, and Marquis Sun Quan and
Lu Su, "This is the	moment	to use people. You must
cannot get away even for a	moment	. If your master would only

表 77. 罗译本（节译）moment 语境共现检索（前 5 次，共 27 次）

cowards now, at the very	moment	we must rely on you—as if
be defeated. This is the	moment	to make Cao Cao your captive
though. This is a critical	moment	. My only wish is for
Guan had inspired. At that	moment	an emissary from Cao Cao arrived
I can defeat Cao." At that	moment	Cao Cao was informed of the

第四章 古典小说英译的母语译者和非母语译者的定量比较研究

表 78. 杨译本(节译)moment 语境共现检索(共 2 次)

| ants in my eyes. The | moment | I raise my hand they will |
| starts to revive. During the | moment | of change, there may naturally |

表 79. 张译本(节译)moment 语境共现检索(共 4 次)

took their leave. Just a	moment	later it was again announced that
smiled coldly for quite a long	moment	That evening it was reported
to give it up in a	moment	?" "If that is the
starts to revive. During the	moment	of change, there may naturally

　　point 邓译本(节译)的使用频次为 12 次,罗译本(节译)的使用频次为 17 次,杨译本(节译)的使用频次为 2 次,张译本(节译)的使用频次为 2 次,邓译本(节译)与杨译本(节译)和张译本(节译)的差异幅度分别为 10 次和 10 次,罗译本(节译)与杨译本(节译)和张译本(节译)的差异幅度分别为 15 次和 15 次,母语译者和非母语译者的差异也比较显著。相较于非母语译者,两位母语译者对于 point 的高频次使用反映了其母语思维模式下对 point 的使用特征。节译本 point 的具体使用情况如表 80. 至表 83. 所示,搭配情况如下。

　　point of:邓译本 2 次,罗译本 5 次,杨译本 0 次,张译本 0 次。
　　point by point:邓译本 0 次,罗译本 1 次,杨译本 0 次,张译本 0 次。
　　at…point:邓译本 3 次,罗译本 3 次,杨译本 0 次,张译本 0 次。
　　to the point:邓译本 2 次,罗译本 1 次,杨译本 0 次,张译本 0 次。
　　key/ critical/ important point:邓译本 0 次,罗译本 2 次,杨译本 1 次,张译本 1 次。
　　point against:邓译本 4 次,罗译本 0 次,杨译本 0 次,张译本 0 次。
　　on…point:邓译本 1 次,罗译本 1 次,杨译本 0 次,张译本 0 次。
　　point 的相关搭配:邓译本共计 12 次,罗译本共计 13 次,杨译本共计 1 次,张译本共计 1 次。
　　笔者使用语料库统计分析软件对参照语料库 10 部英文小说 point 的使用情况进行了统计,结果显示:参照语料库 10 部英文小说 point 的使用总频次为 280 次,平均每部小说 28 次,其相关的搭配情况如下。
　　point of:90 次;point by point:0 次;at…point:21 次;to the point:19 次;key/critical/important point:0 次;point against:0 次;on…point:51 次。

从以上节译本以及参照语料库 10 部英文小说 point 使用情况的统计中,我们发现节译本母语译者和参照语料库 point 的使用频都比较高,而且参照语料库的使用频次相对更高;母语译者和参照语料库 point 的搭配种类相对都比较多。节译本母语译者 point 的使用特征也得到了参照语料库的有力支撑。

表 80. 邓译本(节译) point 语境共现检索(前 5 次,共 12 次)

and talk: They miss my	point	of view. Now you have
march. This is the first	point	against Cao Cao. The northern
ships. That is the second	point	against him. Again, we
horses. That is the third	point	against. Soldiers from the central
malaria. That is the fourth	point	against. Now when Cao Cao's

表 81. 罗译本(节译) point 语境共现检索(前 5 次,共 18 次)

His power has grown to the	point	where it would be futile to
mind at ease on precisely this	point	, my lord. Your fears
produced the stolen letter and related	point	by point all that had happened
stolen letter and related point by	point	all that had happened in the
with their clubs. At this	point	the entire assembly got on their

表 82. 杨译本(节译) point 语境共现检索(共 2 次)

Qi, "Wuchang is a strategic	point	. Go back there and station
you to guard a most important	point	, but I have some scruples

表 83. 张译本(节译) point 语境共现检索(共 2 次)

Liu Qi "Wuchang is a strategic	point	. Go back there and station
you to guard a most important	point	, but I have some scruples

节译本母语译者的另外两个与其母语文化背景相关性较为明显的特色名词为 guest 和 sir。guest 邓译本(节译)的使用频次为 22 次,罗译本(节译)的使用频次为 16 次,杨译本(节译)的使用频次为 6 次,张译本(节译)的使用频次为 7 次,邓译本(节译)与杨译本(节译)和张译本(节译)的差异幅度分别为 16 次和 15 次,罗译本(节译)与杨译本(节译)和张译本(节译)的差异幅度分别为 10 次和 9 次,母语译者和非母语译者的差异也比较显著;sir 邓译本(节译)的使用频次为 17 次,罗译

第四章 古典小说英译的母语译者和非母语译者的定量比较研究

本(节译)的使用频次为 16 次,杨译本(节译)的使用频次为 6 次,张译本(节译)的使用频次为 6 次,邓译本(节译)与杨译本(节译)和张译本(节译)的差异幅度分别为 11 次和 11 次,罗译本(节译)与杨译本(节译)和张译本(节译)的差异幅度分别为 10 次和 10 次,母语译者和非母语译者的差异也比较显著。

4.2.4.5 特色介词和从属连词

《三国演义》的母语译者和非母语译者的 3 个全译本高频介词和从属连词的情况以及《三国演义》的母语译者和非母语译者的 4 个节译本高频介词和从属连词的情况分别如表 84. 和表 85. 所示。

表 84.《三国演义》三个英文全译本介词和从属连词形符类符

	邓译本	罗译本	虞译本
介词从属连词形符数	76013	67871	81310
介词从属连词类符数	82	85	79

《三国演义》三个英文全译本的母语译者(参照非母语译者)的特色介词从属连词包括:though(109,136-76);beyond(63,83-49)共 2 个。

《三国演义》三个英文全译本的非母语译者(参照母语译者)的特色介词从属连词包括:besides(15-2,1)共 1 个。

表 85.《三国演义》四个英文节译本介词和从属连词形符类符

	邓译本	罗译本	杨译本	张译本
介词从属连词总数	4534	4161	3834	4033
介词从属连词总类	63	66	59	61

《三国演义》四个英文节译本的母语译者(参照非母语译者)的特色介词从属连词包括:upon(34,9-2,5);though(11,14-6,8);along(15,11-5,6);between(11,11-4,5)共 4 个。

《三国演义》四个英文节译本的非母语译者(参照母语译者)的特色介词从属连词包括:once(9,8-1,2)共 1 个。

从以上《三国演义》的全译本以及节译本的母语译者和非母语译者的特色介词和从属连词的统计中,我们可以发现全译本中,母语译者的特色介词和从属连词共 2 个,非母语译者的特色介词和从属连词共 1 个;节译本中,母语译者的特色介词和从属连词共 4 个,非母语译者的特色介词和从属连词共 1 个,不论是全译本还是节译本,母语译者的特色介词数和从属连词数都大于非母语译者的特色介词数和从属连词数。这些特色介词和从属连词反映了母语译者在介词和从属连词使用方面相较于非母语译者一定的特色。

《三国演义》全译本母语译者的特色介词和从属连词共 2 个,分别为 though、beyond。though 邓译本的使用频次为 109 次,罗译本的使用频次为 136 次,虞译本的使用频次为 76 次,邓译本和罗译本与虞译本的差异分别为 33 次和 60 次;beyond 邓译本的使用频次为 63 次,罗译本的使用频次为 83 次,虞译本的使用频次为 49 次,邓译本和罗译本与虞译本的差异分别为 14 次和 34 次。全译本母语译者的特色介词和从属连词的使用频次与非母语译者的差异幅度不如其特色名词、特色动词、特色副词以及特色形容词与非母语译者的差异幅度那样显著。但笔者把它们归于特色词,主要出于两方面的考虑:一是介词和从属连词的种类数量相较于名词、动词、副词和形容词要少得多,不论是母语译者还是非母语译者对于有限数量的介词和从属连词中的某个词的使用频次以较大幅度的差异高于另一方的概率比较低;二是两位母语译者对于某一介词或从属连词的使用频次都在以一定幅度高于非母语译者,在某种程度上体现了母语译者与非母语译者的差异。而 though 作为全译本的特色介词或连词也得到了节译本的佐证,节译本母语译者的特色介词和连词中,两位母语译者对于 though 的使用频次也以一定幅度高于两位非母语译者。upon 和 beyond 作为《三国演义》全译本母语译者的特色介词也得到了《红楼梦》霍译特色介词的佐证。根据笔者的统计,《红楼梦》霍译的 3 个特色介词中就包含 upon 和 beyond,其中 upon 霍译的使用频次为 203 次,杨译的使用频次为 63 次,差异幅度为 140 次。beyond 霍译的使用频次为 66 次,杨译的使用频次为 25 次,差异幅度为 41 次。though 和 beyond 的具体使用情况如表 86. 至表 91. 所示。

表 86. 邓译本 though 语境共现检索(前 5 次,共 109 次)

in the left arm. Wounded	though	he was, Zhang Ba got
Shao rode out in advance.	Though	the emperor doesn't rule, though
Though the emperor doesn't rule,	though	the prince no office fills,
quarrel was made up. But	though	Lu Bu's body was with his
of Dong Zhuo's aggressions. Now	though	a general amnesty were proclaimed,

第四章　古典小说英译的母语译者和非母语译者的定量比较研究

表87. 罗译本 though 语境共现检索（前5次，共136次）

no match for Cao Cao.	Though	defeated, he would make sure
intelligence, and Xiang Yu,	though	the stronger, was eventually hunted
," said Xun Wenruo. "	Though	Yuan Shao has many troops,
battled hotly. Lü Bu,	though	a warrior of boundless courage,
mistreating them will die. "	Though	he heard Cao Cao, Chen

表88. 虞译本 though 语境共现检索（前5次，共76次）

"Do you feel vexed, as	though	troubles were piling up in your
my master is his brother.	Though	Liu Biao is dead, his
go and she'll surely agree." "Even	though	the Dowager permits I'm sure your
has obtained Jingzhou it is as	though	the dragon, once a captive
Cliff, he made his name;	Though	young in years a veteran's renown

表89. 邓译本 beyond 语境共现检索（前5次，共63次）

they left the farm. Not	beyond	one mile from the farm,
I look upon all the lords	beyond	the Pass as so much stubble
to leave his body and fly	beyond	the confines of heaven. His
my thanks to the noble supporters	beyond	the Pass for their efforts,
lay beneath the table. Scared	beyond	measure, his fellow-guest Zhang Ji

表90. 罗译本 beyond 语境共现检索（前5次，共83次）

away with his prize steed.	Beyond	the wall Cao's soldiers saw
to the wayside pavilion ten li	beyond	the city to see him off
, taking a toll in lives	beyond	numbering. The booty in weapons
Shao and Cao Cao stood barred	beyond	the outer gate as He Jin
Lady Mi added, " was	beyond	his control. "Be

表91. 虞译本 beyond 语境共现检索（前5次，共49次）

. "His power is incalculable,	beyond	the ken of gods or spirits
. He is such a wreck	beyond	cure that I will not give
him, "Life and death are	beyond	our control, so do not
ruses—do you think he can get	beyond	me? I only must
? "Because the task is	beyond	an old man's strength," said Wei

· 175 ·

节译本的特色介词和连词共 4 个,分别为:upon(34,9-2,5);though(11,14-6,8);along(15,11-5,6);between(11,11-4,5); 四个特色介词和从属连词当中,upon 是母语译者最具代表性的特色介词。其中,邓译本(节译)的使用频次为 34 次,罗译本(节译)的使用频次为 9 次,杨译本(节译)的使用频次为 2 次,张译本(节译)的使用频次为 5 次,邓译本(节译)与杨译本(节译)和张译本(节译)的差异分别为 32 次和 29 次,差异非常显著,罗译本(节译)与杨译本(节译)和张译本(节译)的差异分别为 7 次和 4 次,差异也比较明显。upon 作为《三国演义》节译本母语译者的特色介词也得到了《红楼梦》霍译特色介词的有力佐证。根据笔者的统计,《红楼梦》霍译的 3 个特色介词中就包含 upon,其使用频次为 204 次,杨译的使用频次为 62 次,差异幅度为 142 次。

4.2.5 独特词

就特定文本的译文来说,高频词反映了译文中使用频率特别高的具体词汇组成,译文高频词的具体构成受包括原文文体、原文题材、原文内容、译者的风格以及目的语等多种因素的制约和影响。如果同一原作的几个不同译文的高频词的具体构成比较接近,而且得到目的语语料库的有力支撑,则说明译文高频词受原文文体、原文题材、原文内容,尤其是目的语的影响和制约的程度更大一些。译文的特色词反映的是译文译者相较于其他译者对于某些特定词汇的使用倾向性和偏好,对于母语译者和非母语译者来说,各自的特色词反映了各自对相同词汇的使用倾向性和偏好。而母语译者和非母语译者由于受各自思维模式和母语文化的影响,其特色词反映的是各自思维模式下对相同词汇的使用倾向性和偏好,这种思维模式下的特色词汇进一步反映了其背后语言的某种习惯或特征。独特词考察的则是特定原作的某一或某些译者相较于其他译者所使用的完全不同词汇的情况,其具体的构成和数量的多少直接反映了某一或某些译者相较于其他译者不同用词特征的具体情况。就母语译者和非母语译者来说,其独特词的构成和数量反映了各自在母语思维模式下的不同用词特征,进一步反映了各自思维模式背后的语言使用习惯或特征。

第四章 古典小说英译的母语译者和非母语译者的定量比较研究

4.2.5.1 独特名词

《三国演义》三个英文全译本的母语译者(参照非母语译者)的独特名词包括：good-bye（2,38-0）; county（41,57-0）; saber（59,35-0）; scarves（38,46-0）; secretariat（26,34-0）; humans（48,1-0）; instructor（44,2-0）; formalities（2,38-0）; patriarch（16,22-0）; bureau（4,27-0）; era（17,12-0）; calendar（7,21-0）; contingents（1,27-0）; commoners（1,26-0）; courier（1,26-0）; deputy（13,9-0）; inner（4,16-0）; sack（1,19-0）; sedition（3,16-0）; patrimony（1,17-0）; dignities（7,10-0）; elder（2,15-0）; cauldron（6,9-0）; kingship（5,10-0）; senior（1,14-0）; boon（1,13-0）; bases（1,12-0）; mat（3,10-0）; coin（1,11-0）; protectorship（8,4-0）; science（1,11-0）; sphere（2,10-0）; administrator（10,1-0）; antiquity（4,7-0）; bamboos（10,1-0）; greeting（3,8-0）; stages（2,9-0）; workers（8,3-0）; complex（5,5-0）; controls（1,9-0）; delivery（1,9-0）; devices（3,7-0）; hostilities（2,8-0）; in-law（1,9-0）; park（4,6-0）; activity（3,6-0）; basis（1,8-0）; breadth（1,8-0）; circuit（7,2-0）; comparison（3,6-0）; notables（6,3-0）; roadway（1,8-0）; stability（4,5-0）; watches（5,4-0）; battle-axes（2,6-0）; blockade（1,7-0）; boast（2,6-0）; braves（5,3-0）; brigade（1,7-0）; code（2,6-0）; coins（4,4-0）; comment（2,6-0）; deities（4,4-0）; delegation（1,7-0）; engagements（4,4-0）; farms（3,5-0）; fore（2,6-0）; ingrate（2,6-0）; legion（7,1-0）; maze（3,5-0）; precipice（1,7-0）; sire（3,5-0）; slander（2,6-0）; torso（1,7-0）; townsmen（1,7-0）; tripod（5,3-0）; altars（2,5-0）; authorities（1,6-0）; expectation（2,5-0）; extremity（1,6-0）; fates（2,5-0）; inauguration（5,2-0）; jars（2,5-0）; khan（4,3-0）; kin（1,6-0）; lineage（2,5-0）; moats（4,3-0）; pheasant（4,3-0）; recommendations（1,6-0）; register（3,4-0）; salvation（2,5-0）; scale（2,5-0）; stratagems（1,6-0）; sunset（4,3-0）; underling（1,6-0）; writ（1,6-0）; activities（1,5-0）; anticipation（1,5-0）; belief（2,4-0）; breastplates（5,1-0）; clansman（1,5-0）; conclusions（5,1-0）; disaffection（3,3-0）; dwellers（2,4-0）; endeavor（2,4-0）; excellence（2,4-0）; flares（2,4-0）; gems（3,3-0）; hardships（1,5-0）;

· 177 ·

harem(2,4-0); ministry(2,4-0); missive(5,1-0); neighbor(3,3-0); officialdom(1,5-0); oration(5,1-0); paragons(1,5-0); parasol(4,2-0); planner(1,5-0); protectors(4,2-0); refugees(1,5-0); slack(2,4-0); stint(2,4-0); surprises(2,4-0); treasurer(1,5-0); vexation(1,5-0); whiskers(1,5-0)共126个。

《三国演义》三个英文全译本的非母语译者(参照母语译者)的独特名词包括:advisor(222-0,0); advisors(112-0,0); cicada(22-0,0); turbans(20-0,0); byroad(16-0,0); prefecture(13-0,0); tigertrap(9-0,0); sable(7,-0,0); caldron(6-0,0)共9个。

名词在一部小说的各种词类当中占有重要地位,名词是用来指称人物、事物、抽象概念等的实词,小说中的名词是构成小说当中人物、事物、社会环境、自然环境、文化背景等基本信息的最基本、最主要的载体。对于《三国演义》这样一部结构宏大,以政治军事斗争为主的涵盖生活、文化、人文、习俗等多方面内容,浓缩了我国古代政治军事斗争艺术精华的历史小说来说,基于汉英两种语言的文化背景的巨大差异,其诸多涉及名词或其相关信息的翻译,也更为复杂,对于译者的两种语言和文化熟悉程度以及翻译时对于两种文化的协调能力的要求也更高。《三国演义》以政治军事为主的题材决定了其所涉及的与我国古代封建政治军事方面相关的名词在其整体名词中占有很大比例,其翻译对于整部小说翻译的重要性不言而喻。

我们首先从独特名词数量的角度来考察全译本母语译者和非母语译者各自的特征以及两者的差异。从以上《三国演义》全译本的母语译者和非母语译者的独特名词的统计中,我们可以发现,母语译者的独特名词数量都远大于非母语译者的独特名词数量。全译本两位母语译者总计使用频次超过6次的独特名词总数为126个单词,非母语译者的总计使用频次超过6次的独特名词总数为9个单词,两者相差117个单词,差异非常显著。这说明两位母语译者在母语思维模式和母语文化背景的影响下,其对于小说原作当中诸多涉及名词或其相关信息的翻译在译文名词词汇的种类上要远多于非母语译者。如本研究在形符类符一节所论述的,一般来说,特定文本,其译文的类符数越多,则译文对于原文信息的处理就越精确和细腻。从这一意义上来说,《三国演义》全译本两位母语译者对于原作当中的名词及其相关信息的处理比非母语译者更为精确和细腻。母语译者独特名词数远多于非母语译者可以归因于

第四章　古典小说英译的母语译者和非母语译者的定量比较研究

其母语优势下的母语思维和母语文化背景的影响。

除了从独特名词数量的视角进行分析研究之外,我们再从特色名词的具体使用情况来分析母语译者和非母语译者各自特色名词的特征。母语译者特色名词除与小说题材相关的政治军事词汇之外,排首位的是 good-bye,邓译本和罗译本两者合计使用 40 次,其具体使用情况如表 92. 和表 93. 所示。其使用也得到了参照语料库 10 部英文小说的支持,笔者使用语料库统计软件对参照语料库进行了统计,结果显示,good-bye 作为名词的使用频次为 16 次,平均每部小说的使用频次为 1.6 次。邓译本、罗译本以及参照语料库 good-bye 的搭配如下:

bid/bade/bidding...good-bye:邓译本 0 次,罗译本 30 次,参照语料库 10 次。

say/said/saying good-bye:邓译本 2 次,罗译本 7 次,参照语料库 4 次。

表 92. 邓译本 good-bye 语境共现检索(共 2 次)

| So, Liu Bei said a hasty | good-bye | to his friend, called up |
| and when Liu Bei was saying | good-bye | , he whispered, "I will |

表 93. 罗译本 good-bye 语境共现检索(前 5 次,共 38 次)

Allow me to bid my mother	good-bye	," he said. Then
only for the chance to say	good-bye	to you. Our fortunate meeting
So, Lord Guan bid his host	good-bye	, saw the women into the
food and drink and bade them	good-bye	. He then issued an order
therefore, bade Yi Ji a grateful	good-bye	, summoned his followers, and

全译本母语译者的特色名词除与小说题材相关的政治军事词汇以及 good-bye 之外,一个值得关注的词是 complex。邓译本和罗译本 complex 的使用频次均为 5 次,其具体使用情况如表 94. 和表 95. 所示。其搭配如下:

palace complex:邓译本 4 次,罗译本 2 次。

从邓译本和罗译本 complex 的具体使用情况的统计中,我们可以发现,邓译本和罗译本的 complex 主要用来翻译建筑群,根据牛津新英汉词典,complex 是指 a group of buildings of a similar type together in one place(类型相似的)建筑群。邓译本和罗译本用 palace complex 来

· 179 ·

翻译皇宫、宫殿反映了其在母语思维模式和母语文化背景影响下的翻译风格和特征。

表94. 邓译本 complex 语境共现检索（共5次）

the building of a new palace	complex	to be called the Reflected Light
where he erected a large palace	complex	. The tale of these doings
name "Silver Pit". A palace	complex	had been built in the ravine
preparations to build himself a palace	complex	. At Luoyang he also built
Zhou erected a surpassingly beautiful palace	complex	and a Deer Terrace. But

表95. 罗译本 complex 语境共现检索（共5次）

, had remained in the imperial	complex	. Seeing the coup in progress
thousand men to the new palace	complex	at Mei and take custody of
The entire wealth of the new	complex	was confiscated: several hundred thousand
to Luoyang and built a palace	complex	there. Word soon reached Chengdu
Hao Zhao commands a well-fortified	complex	surrounded by an impenetrable network

《三国演义》四个英文节译本的母语译者（参照非母语译者）的独特名词包括：leaders（19,3-0,0）；sea（6,12-0,0）；mountains（11,5-0,0）；lines（7,6-0,0）；need（6,5-0,0）；everyone（4,6-0,0）；poet（2,8-0,0）；banquet（5,4-0,0）；miles（7,1-0,0）；occasion（3,5-0,0）；shout（3,5-0,0）；spans（5,3-0,0）；stations（2,6-0,0）；confidence（1,6-0,0）；defense（3,4-0,0）；favor（1,6-0,0）；patriarch（2,5-0,0）；patrol（1,6-0,0）；pity（5,2-0,0）；cliffs（2,4-0,0）；document（2,4-0,0）；Instructor（5,1-0,0）；navy（1,5-0,0）；oars（5,1-0,0）；rains（2,4-0,0）；response（1,5-0,0）；sailors（3,3-0,0）；salutations（3,3-0,0）；wealth（2,4-0,0）；weapon（1,5-0,0）；band（2,3-0,0）；bearer（3,2-0,0）；behalf（4,1-0,0）；Book（3,2-0,0）；brush（2,3-0,0）；concern（1,4-0,0）；crossbowmen（2,3-0,0）；discussions（1,4-0,0）；faction（3,2-0,0）；gale（3,2-0,0）；lips（2,3-0,0）；love（3,2-0,0）；mandate（1,4-0,0）；meeting（1,4-0,0）；pretense（3,2-0,0）；raven（2,

第四章　古典小说英译的母语译者和非母语译者的定量比较研究

3-0,0); roll (3,2-0,0); rumors (1,4-0,0); satisfaction (1,4-0,0); sorrow (4,1-0,0); spirits (1,4-0,0); towers (3,2-0,0); warrior (3, 2-0,0)共53个。

《三国演义》四个英文节译本的非母语译者(参照母语译者)的独特名词包括：lance (9,9-0,0); scouts (6,7-0,0); fire-ships (4,4-0,0); reinforcements (4,4-0,0); hostel (4,2-0,0); midnight (3,3-0,0); monastery(3,3-0,0); orators(3,3-0,0); ramparts(3,3-0,0); seas(3, 3-0,0); sweep (3,3-0,0); Dowager (2,3-0,0); servant-boy (3,2-0, 0)共13个。

从以上《三国演义》节译本的母语译者和非母语译者的独特名词的统计中，我们可以发现，节译本母语译者的独特名词数量都远大于非母语译者的独特名词数量。节译本母语译者的独特名词总数为53个单词，非母语译者的特色名词数为13个，两者相差40个，差异幅度比较显著。这说明在对于小说原作起重要作用的名词的种类方面，节译本母语译者在数量上要远大于非母语译者，其所使用的名词种类更为丰富。从名词使用种类数量的视角来看，母语译者在对于原作当中的名词及其相关信息的处理比非母语译者更为精确和细腻。全译本两位母语译者的特色名词数远大于非母语译者的特色名词数，节译本两位母语译者的特色名词数也远大于两位非母语译者的特色名词数，从这一意义上来说，节译本佐证了全译本相互佐证了母语译者在母语优势下的母语思维模式和母语文化背景影响的翻译风格和特征。

4.2.5.2　独特动词

《三国演义》三个英文全译本的母语译者(参照非母语译者)的独特动词包括：surprise(2,33-0); requite(2,21-0); coordinate(2,20-0); eyed (3,19-0); kneeled (1,17-0); pacifies (13,5-0); despaired (1, 15-0); memorialize (14,1-0); desist (2,12-0); retake (3,11-0); reversed (1,13-0); tender (2,12-0); conclude (7,6-0); suffice (1, 12-0); counseled (4,8-0); treasured (6,6-0); unsealed (1,11-0); waxed (11,1-0); betook (9,2-0); crave (6,5-0); refrained (2,9-0); communicated (1,9-0); Confound (2,8-0); empowered (1,9-0); howled (3,7-0); signify (1,9-0); detached (4,5-0); drop (4,5-0); figured(1,8-0); located(1,8-0); sustained(5,5-0); upholds(5,4-0);

designated（2,6-0）; establishes（3,5-0）; inspected（4,4-0）; loose（6,2-0）; penned（1,7-0）; performing（2,6-0）; providing（2,6-0）; unfold（6,2-0）; associated（1,6-0）; behooves（3,4-0）; bending（3,4-0）; destroys（4,3-0）; effect（4,3-0）; excuse（1,6-0）; interdict（1,6-0）; proffered（2,5-0）; quells（3,4-0）; steered（1,6-0）; swearing（1,6-0）; welcoming（2,5-0）; agreeing（1,5-0）; bethought（5,1-0）; communicate（2,4-0）; consummated（1,5-0）; counsel（3,3-0）; enjoined（2,4-0）; gotten（1,5-0）; initiated（2,4-0）; Liberate（1,5-0）; mistrusted（1,5-0）; patrolled（1,5-0）; pluck（2,4-0）; root（1,5-0）; screaming（2,4-0）; strung（2,4-0）; tossed（1,5-0）; unbound（1,5-0）; visiting（2,4-0）; vouchsafe（1,5-0）; wrested（3,3-0）; yearn（1,5-0）; anticipate（4,1-0）; augur（3,2-0）; caged（1,4-0）; clothed（4,1-0）; demoralized（1,4-0）; dismissing（2,3-0）; dove（4,1-0）; echoing（3,2-0）; Exhibits（2,3-0）; fashioned（1,4-0）; favoring（2,3-0）; gauge（2,3-0）; heeding（2,3-0）; immured（3,2-0）; imposed（2,3-0）; inaugurated（1,4-0）; inspire（3,2-0）; labored（4,1-0）; lash（3,2-0）; lays（3,2-0）; regaled（2,3-0）; relaxed（2,3-0）; replacing（1,4-0）; review（1,4-0）; rules（2,3-0）; sacrificing（1,4-0）; secures（1,4-0）; supposing（4,1-0）; adopting（1,3-0）; allayed（1,3-0）; Answers（1,3-0）; anticipates（2,2-0）; arrogated（2,2-0）; banquets（3,1-0）; chided（2,2-0）; complimented（3,1-0）; craved（2,2-0）; criticized（1,3-0）; daunt（1,3-0）; deign（2,2-0）; discerned（3,1-0）; discouraged（2,2-0）; disdain（2,2-0）; divest（1,3-0）; doubting（3,1-0）; drenching（3,1-0）; endangers（3,1-0）; excited（2,2-0）; fatigue（3,1-0）; feeds（1,3-0）; forbore（3,1-0）; frustrate（2,2-0）; leagued（2,2-0）; leveling（1,3-0）; massing（2,2-0）; master（1,3-0）; mistrust（2,2-0）; monopolized（2,2-0）; partake（1,3-0）; position（1,3-0）; praises（3,1-0）; purging（1,3-0）; reestablished（1,3-0）; repairing（2,2-0）; robed（3,1-0）; shouldered（2,2-0）; silvered（1,3-0）; smooth（2,2-0）; springing（2,2-0）; straining（1,3-0）; sue（1,3-0）; sued（1,3-0）; traversed（1,3-0）; vex（1,3-0）; wed（2,2-0）; whips（3,1-0）; yearns（1,3-0）共150个。

《三国演义》三个英文全译本的非母语译者（参照母语译者）的独特

第四章　古典小说英译的母语译者和非母语译者的定量比较研究

动词包括：mustn't（21-0,0）；attempts（6-0,0）；reunite（4-0,0）共3个。

我们首先从独特动词数量的角度来考察全译本母语译者和非母语译者各自的特征以及两者的差异。从以上《三国演义》全译本的母语译者和非母语译者的独特动词的统计中，我们可以发现，各自总计使用频次4次以上的独特动词中，母语译者的独特动词数量远大于非母语译者的独特动词数量。《三国演义》是一部以政治军事题材为主的历史小说，涉及诸多政治军事斗争场面的描写，动词在小说中占有重要地位，如何翻译小说原文中的动词以及相关的信息对于小说整体的翻译具有极为重要和关键的影响。全译本两位母语译者相较于非母语译者的独特动词数为150个单词，非母语译者相较于母语译者的独特动词数为3个单词，两者相差147个单词，差异幅度非常显著，这说明全译本母语译者使用的动词种类多于非母语译者使用的动词种类。从使用动词种类数量的角度来说，母语译者比非母语译者对于小说原作的动词以及相关信息的翻译更为精确和细腻。

除了独特动词数量的视角之外，我们再从独特动词的具体使用情况来进行分析。从母语译者和非母语译者的独特动词的对比中，我们可以发现，除了数量上的差异之外，两者之间最为显著的差异表现在非母语译者对于情态动词must的否定缩写形式的使用，其使用频次为21次。

表96. 虞译本mustn't语境共现检索（前5次，共21次）

course, he said. You	mustn't	act too rashly. Then the
scoundrel will suspect something. I	mustn't	stay too long, he said
you see Zhou Yu, you	mustn't	tell him that I have seen
assist me. No, you	mustn't	, replied Lu Su. We
point, he shouted. We	mustn't	abandon the ship.

《三国演义》四个英文节译本母语译者（参照非母语译者）的独特动词包括：placed（8,3-0,0）；retired（8,3-0,0）；watched（5,6-0,0）；share（2,8-0,0）；departed（1,7-0,0）；honored（3,5-0,0）；informed（1,7-0,0）；expressed（3,4-0,0）；hidden（5,2-0,0）；remove（4,3-0,0）；restored（5,2-0,0）；caught（2,4-0,0）；deny（1,5-0,0）；executed（1,5-0,0）；recognize（1,5-0,0）recognized（5,1-0,0）；render（4,2-0,0）；resolved（3,3-0,0）；rolled（4,2-0,0）；spared（2,4-0,0）；submitted（2,4-0,0）；approach（3,2-0,0）；begin（1,4-0,

0）; begins（2,3-0,0）; cause（3,2-0,0）; delay（2,3-0,0）; directed（1,4-0,0）; directing（3,2-0,0）; dismissed（1,4-0,0）; execute（2,3-0,0）; fitted（3,2-0,0）; formed（3,2-0,0）; leveled（2,3-0,0）; lowered（1,4-0,0）; play（4,1-0,0）; protect（4,1-0,0）; provided（2,3-0,0）; remembered（4,1-0,0）; rushed（1,4-0,0）; slain（3,2-0,0）; wept（2,3-0,0）; wonder（2,3-0,0）; wore（3,2-0,0）; awaited（2,2-0,0）; clad（3,1-0,0）; committed（1,3-0,0）; convey（1,3-0,0）; conveyed（1,3-0,0）; ensure（2,2-0,0）; feeling（3,1-0,0）; feign（2,2-0,0）; finish（1,3-0,0）; grieve（2,2-0,0）; guided（1,3-0,0）; happen（3,1-0,0）; lend（2,2-0,0）; penetrate（2,2-0,0）; place（1,3-0,0）; preceded（1,3-0,0）; recommend（3,1-0,0）; reentered（1,3-0,0）; regarded（3,1-0,0）; regret（2,2-0,0）; release（2,2-0,0）; remaining（2,2-0,0）; request（1,3-0,0）; stem（2,2-0,0）; threaten（3,1-0,0）共68个。

《三国演义》四个英文节译本非母语译者（参照母语译者）的独特动词包括：conquer（5,4-0,0）; leapt（5,4-0,0）; withdraw（4,5-0,0）; loosed（4,4-0,0）; withdrawn（5,3-0,0）; drag（3,3-0,0）; helping（3,3-0,0）; learned（2,4-0,0）; sighted（3,3-0,0）; offending（2,3-0,0）; swore（3,2-0,0）; banged（2,2-0,0）; bled（2,2-0,0）; chasing（2,2-0,0）; clasping（2,2-0,0）; convinced（2,2-0,0）; fasten（2,2-0,0）; injure（2,2-0,0）; inspect（2,2-0,0）; insult（2,2-0,0）; intercepted（2,2-0,0）; keeps（2,2-0,0）; mobilizing（2,2-0,0）; perish（2,2-0,0）; Proposes（2,2-0,0）; reconnoitre（2,2-0,0）; relieve（2,2-0,0）; retreat（2,2-0,0）; routed（3,1-0,0）; sacrificing（2,2-0,0）; shed（2,2-0,0）; shocked（2,2-0,0）; stomach（2,2-0,0）; troubling（2,2-0,0）共34个。

我们首先还是从独特动词数量的角度来考察节译本母语译者和非母语译者各自的特征以及两者的差异。从以上《三国演义》节译本的母语译者和非母语译者的独特动词的统计中，我们可以发现，各自总计使用频次4次以上的独特动词中，母语译者的独特动词数量远大于非母语译者的独特动词数量。节译本两位母语译者总计使用频次在4次以上的独特动词为68个单词，两位非母语译者的总计使用频次在4次以上的独特动词为34个，两者的差异幅度为34个单词，差异比较显著。节

第四章 古典小说英译的母语译者和非母语译者的定量比较研究

译本母语译者的独特动词的数量以较大幅度大于非母语译者,这与全译本是一致的。全译本和节译本共计两位母语译者和三位非母语译者,不论全译本还是节译本,母语译者的独特动词数都以较大幅度大于非母语译者,基于此,我们可以认为独特动词数较高是《三国演义》全译本和节译本母语译者相较于非母语译者的区别性特征。从独特动词的数量的角度来说,节译本母语译者对于小说原作的动词以及相关信息的翻译比非母语译者更为精确和细腻。

4.2.5.3 独特副词

《三国演义》三个英文全译本母语译者(参照非母语译者)的独特副词包括:thence(29,1-0);thereof(15,1-0);second(6,7-0);jointly(1,11-0);afire(1,9-0);precisely(1,9-0);harder(2,5-0);grimly(2,4-0);officially(1,5-0);wisely(3,3-0);wrong(3,3-0);disdainfully(2,3-0);due(1,4-0);eternally(1,4-0);prior(1,4-0);summarily(3,2-0);aye(3,1-0);doubtless(3,1-0);gaily(2,2-0);herein(2,2-0);naught(2,2-0);noisily(2,2-0);pretty(1,3-0);annually(1,2-0);brutally(1,2-0);currently(2,1-0);discreetly(2,1-0);exquisitely(1,2-0);feebly(1,2-0);forcibly(1,2-0);impudently(1,2-0);justly(2,1-0);plain(2,1-0);unbearably(1,2-0);uselessly(2,1-0);wantonly(1,2-0);aright(1,1-0);carelessly(1,1-0);ceremonially(1,1-0);devotedly(1,1-0);foully(1,1-0);fourth(1,1-0);gloriously(1,1-0);indifferently(1,1-0);insistently(1,1-0);kingly(1,1-0);marvelously(1,1-0);meticulously(1,1-0);pleasantly(1,1-0);resignedly(1,1-0);sidelong(1,1-0);singularly(1,1-0);willfully(1,1-0);worthily(1,1-0)共54个。

《三国演义》三个英文全译本非母语译者(参照母语译者)的独特副词包括:intentionally(7-0,0);exceptionally(6-0,0);ferociously(5-0,0);fourthly(4-0,0);inevitably(4-0,0);presumably(4-0,0);crosswise(3-0,0);definitely(3-0,0);provocatively(3-0,0);agreeably(2-0,0);incoherently(2-0,0);tragically(2-0,0);tremendously(2-0,0);wickedly(2-0,0);absentmindedly(1-0,0);alternatively(1-0,0);amazingly(1-0,0);appropriately(1-0,0);

aplenty（1-0,0）; comprehensively（1-0,0）; conveniently（1-0,0）; crossly（1-0,0）; disparagingly（1-0,0）; doubtlessly（1-0,0）; dubiously（1-0,0）; erroneously（1-0,0）; extensively（1-0,0）; externally（1-0,0）; exultantly（1-0,0）; geographically（1-0,0）; glibly（1-0,0）; grumpily（1-0,0）; heartbrokenly（1-0,0）; insultingly（1-0,0）; lamely（1-0,0）; monstrously（1-0,0）; onshore（1-0,0）; orderly（1-0,0）; persistently（1-0,0）; persuasively（1-0,0）; provokingly（1-0,0）; rapturously（1-0,0）共42个。

《三国演义》四个英文节译本母语译者（参照非母语译者）的独特副词包括：surely（9,3-0,0）; deeply（5,4-0,0）; perhaps（7,1-0,0）; kindly（5,2-0,0）; next（3,4-0,0）; perfectly（5,2-0,0）; personally（1,5-0,0）; thrice（4,2-0,0）; precisely（1,4-0,0）; privately（2,3-0,0）; respectfully（1,4-0,0）; silently（4,1-0,0）; afoot（3,1-0,0）; entirely（1,3-0,0）; expressly（3,1-0,0）; scarcely（3,1-0,0）; after（2,1-0,0）; anxiously（2,1-0,0）; early（2,1-0,0）; fairly（1,2-0,0）; handsomely（1,2-0,0）; harshly（2,1-0,0）; intently（1,2-0,0）; purposely（1,2-0,0）共24个。

《三国演义》四个英文节译本非母语译者（参照母语译者）的独特副词包括：promptly（4,4-0,0）; readily（4,4-0,0）; besides（2,2-0,0）; obviously（2,2-0,0）; closely（3,3-0,0）; abruptly（2,1-0,0）; hurriedly（1,2-0,0）共7个。

  从以上《三国演义》全译本和节译本母语译者和非母语译者的独特副词的统计中，我们可以发现不论是全译本还是节译本，母语译者的独特副词的数量都以较大幅度大于非母语译者独特副词数量。全译本两位母语译者的使用频次在6次以上的独特副词为10个单词，非母语译者使用频次在6次以上的独特副词为1个单词，两者相差9个单词，差异较为显著；节译本两位母语译者使用频次在3次以上的独特副词为24个单词，两位非母语译者使用频次在3次以上的独特副词为7个单词，两者相差17个单词，差异也比较显著。《三国演义》英译的母语译者独特副词数量大于非母语译者的独特副词数量，全译本和节译本可以相互对比佐证。同时，从独特副词数量的角度来说，不论是全译本还是节译本，母语译者对于原文副词或相关的信息的翻译更为精确和细腻。

  全译本母语译者的独特副词中，排首位的是thence。两位母语译者

第四章 古典小说英译的母语译者和非母语译者的定量比较研究

的使用频次总计为 30 次,其中邓译本 29 次,罗译本 1 次。其使用在某种程度上得到了参照语料库的支持,根据笔者对参照语料库 10 部英文小说的统计,其对 thence 的使用频次总计为 39 次,平均每部小说的使用频次为 3.9 次;根据笔者对《红楼梦》霍译和杨译的统计,thence 霍译的使用频次为 6 次,杨译的使用频次为 0 次。这说明不论是英文原创小说还是《红楼梦》的母语译者都对 thence 进行了一定程度的使用,而《三国演义》全译本、节译本以及《红楼梦》的非母语译者 thence 的使用频次均为 0 次。

表 97. 邓译本 thence 语境共现检索(前 5 次,共 29 次)

They then separated.	Thence	Dong Zhuo's power and influence increased
and near this he camped.	Thence	to Yejun was five miles.
a camp under their shelter.	Thence	he sent messengers to urge Ma
hordes from the Gobi Desert.	Thence	southward I would try for the
out to the hills near and	thence	had the drums beaten for a

表 98. 罗译本 thence 语境共现检索(共 1 次)

graced Three Gorges And two years	thence	was dead, in Yong'an Palace

表 99. 10 部英文小说 thence 语境共现检索(前 5 次,共 39 次)

傲慢偏见.	into the breakfast room; from	thence	to the library;—their
化身博士.	sure, destroyed my papers;	thence	I set out through the lamplit
化身博士.	quailing before his eye; and	thence	, when the night was fully
双城记.	sport of window-breaking, and	thence	to the plundering of public-
汤姆历险.	the roof of the woodshed and	thence	to the ground. Huckleberry

表 100.《红楼梦》霍译 thence 语境共现检索（共 6 次）

foot of the rear terrace and	thence	round the side of the house
and. orient pearl, and	thence	down to the very floor of
be performed, to convey them	thence	to the deceased's registered
' couple into the hall and	thence	to the bridal chamber. Here
Third Branch Yin comes Wood and	thence	Fire. The Signature " Offspring
menservants were waiting for him;	thence	he proceeded to the inner apartments

节译本母语译者的独特副词中，排首位的是 surely，邓译本的使用频次为 9 次，罗译本的使用频次为 3 次，两位母语译者的使用频次总计为 12 次。笔者对参照语料库 10 部英文小说 surely 的使用情况进行了统计，结果显示 10 部英文小说 surely 的使用频次总计为 92 次，平均每部小说的使用频次为 9.2 次。参照语料库 10 部英文小说对于 surely 的使用也在一定程度上支持了《三国演义》节译本对于 surely 的使用。

节译本非母语译者的独特副词中，值得关注的是 besides。besides 在全译本中，是非母语译者的特色副词，其对于 besides 的使用频次为 54 次，邓译本和罗译本对于 besides 的使用频次分别为 2 次和 5 次，全译本非母语译者对于 besides 的使用频次远高于两位母语译者，这在一定程度上支持了节译本中非母语译者对于 besides 的使用。

4.2.5.4 独特形容词

《三国演义》三个英文全译本母语译者（参照非母语译者）的独特形容词包括：forward（1,47-0）; liege（2,20-0）; especial（15,3-0）warlike（16,1-0）; boundless（1,15-0）; hardy（2,10-0）; concerted（3,8-0）; transverse（9,2-0）; tribal（2,9-0）; triple（6,4-0）; genuine（1,8-0）; lax（3,6-0）; lead（1,8-0）; ultimate（3,6-0）; central（3,5-0）; considerable（2,6-0）; alert（4,3-0）; auxiliary（1,6-0）; congratulatory（2,5-0）; regional（2,5-0）; stunning（1,6-0）; thankful（1,6-0）; thorny（6,1-0）; three-span（3,4-0）; coastal（3,3-0）; craven（2,4-0）; green-eyed（4,2-0）; harmless（3,3-0）; oncoming（1,5-0）; select（2,4-0）; solicitous（1,5-0）; speechless（2,4-0）; unclear（1,5-0）; bereft（1,4-0）; dearest（1,4-0）; established（1,4-0）; foster（1,4-0）; foster（1,4-0）; frantic（3,2-0）; gloomy

第四章 古典小说英译的母语译者和非母语译者的定量比较研究

(3,2-0); irregular (1,4-0); loath (2,3-0); reddish (1,4-0); scant (2,3-0); secondary (3,2-0); spare (3,2-0); storied (3,2-0); threatening (4,1-0); three-pronged (1,4-0); unchanged (1,4-0); unsteady (2,3-0)共51个。

《三国演义》三个英文全译本非母语译者(参照母语译者)的独特形容词包括:high-ranking(25-0,0); fastest(6-0,0); southeasterly(6-0,0); blue-eyed (5-0,0); well-versed (5-0,0)共5个。

《三国演义》四个英文节译本母语译者(参照非母语译者)的独特形容词包括:treacherous (6,3-0,0); various (7,2-0,0); greatest (4,4-0,0); capable (5,2-0,0); sacred (2,5-0,0); worthy (1,6-0,0); highest (3,3-0,0); huge (4,2-0,0); poor (3,3-0,0); profound (2,4-0,0); solid (4,2-0,0); critical (1,4-0,0); fierce (4,1-0,0); loud (4,1-0,0); marine (3,2-0,0); steady (2,3-0,0); superior (3,2-0,0); terrible (4,1-0,0); confident (2,2-0,0); deepest (2,2-0,0); familiar (1,3-0,0); fiery (2,2-0,0); generous (2,2-0,0); quick (2,2-0,0); secure (3,1-0,0); strange (2,2-0,0)共26个。

《三国演义》四个英文节译本非母语译者(参照母语译者)的独特形容词包括:lower (8,5-0,0); senior (3,3-0,0); ablaze (2,2-0,0); asleep (2,2-0,0); busy (2,2-0,0); middle (2,2-0,0); southeasterly (2,2-0,0); special (2,2-0,0)共8个。

从以上《三国演义》全译本和节译本母语译者和非母语译者的独特形容词的统计中,我们可以发现不论是全译本还是节译本,母语译者的独特形容词的数量都以较大幅度大于非母语译者所使用的独特形容词的数量。全译本两位母语译者的使用频次在5次以上的独特形容词为51个单词,非母语译者使用频次在5次以上的独特形容词为5个单词,两者相差46个单词,差异较为显著;节译本两位母语译者使用频次在4次以上的独特形容词为26个单词,两位非母语译者使用频次在4次以上的独特形容词为8个单词,两者相差18个单词,差异也比较显著。《三国演义》英译的母语译者独特形容词数量大于非母语译者的独特形容词数量,全译本和节译本可以相互对比佐证。同时,从独特形容词数量的角度来说,不论是全译本还是节译本,母语译者对于原文形容词或相关的信息的翻译更为精确和细腻。

全译本母语译者的独特形容词中,排首位的是forward。两位母语译者的使用频次总计为 48 次,其中邓译本 1 次,罗译本 47 次。Forward 在罗译本多用来翻译原文中"前军"等相关的军事用词,其搭配 forward army 为 19 次,forward unit 为 9 次,forward camp 为 4 次;邓译本的搭配也为相关的军事用词 forward movement,共 1 次。对全译本母语译者的独特形容词进行仔细考察之后,我们发现这些独特形容词有不少是与政治军事描写相关的词汇,这反映了两位母语译者在母语思维模式和母语文化背景下对于原文的政治军事词汇或与政治军事词汇相关信息的翻译更为精确和细腻。母语译者其他部分与政治军事相关的独特形容词的搭配情况和具体使用情况如下:

liege lord:邓译本 2 次,罗译本 3 次。
liege man/men:邓译本 0 次,罗译本 12 次。
warlike weapons:邓译本 3 次,罗译本 0 次。
warlike shouts:邓译本 0 次,罗译本 1 次。
warlike operations:邓译本 2 次,罗译本 0 次。
hardy men:邓译本 1 次,罗译本 0 次。
hardy warriors:邓译本 0 次,罗译本 5 次。

表 101. 邓译本 liege 语境共现检索(共 2 次)

| . So, Zhou Yu for his | liege | lord Got the victory. And |
| even his life to avenge his | liege | lord or his father? How |

表 102. 罗译本 liege 语境共现检索(前 5 次,共 20 次)

; Their plighted faith requites their	liege	lord's love. The sacred
than men to him were southern	liege	men; Alone, he faced
his genius sprang— Genius shared by	liege	men, brothers, sons!
" Withdraw for now; our	liege	lord needs rest. " The
Stern and grand, the royal	liege	man's likeness claims respect.

表 103. 邓译本 warlike 语境共现检索(前 5 次,共 16 次)

explaining, "By your virtue of	warlike	renown, I have recovered my
Guan Yu, both for his	warlike	abilities and his principles. I
sufferings of the people during the	warlike	operations. He sent up a
a son of Gongsun Du the	Warlike	, the General of Han.
be famous for literary grace and	warlike	exploits, secondly, handsome and

第四章　古典小说英译的母语译者和非母语译者的定量比较研究

表 104. 罗译本 warlike 语境共现检索（共 1 次）

| the second watch when they heard | warlike | shouts on all sides; Wang |

表 105. 邓译本 hardy 语境共现检索（共 2 次）

| which he manned with strong, | hardy | men armed with powerful bows and |
| in excellent state, the soldiers | hardy | , the horses strong. There |

表 106. 罗译本 hardy 语境共现检索（前 5 次，共 10 次）

:all of them brave and	hardy	warriors, veritable heroes. He
Sure, of catching the bold and	hardy	troops of Wu. Would Lu
response they sent several hundred thousand	hardy	warriors armed with shields and
troops are tough, our horses	hardy	;and our commanders—with the fierce
Han Xin's conquest of the	hardy	kingdom of Zhao. Therefore shall

除了以上与政治军事描写相关的词汇之外，全译本值得关注的特色形容词是 especial。especial 两位母语译者的使用频次总计为 18 次，其中邓译本为 15 次，罗译本为 3 次，除了与政治军事相关的描写词汇之外排第一位。其使用同样得到了参照语料库 10 部英文小说和《红楼梦》英译的支持，笔者使用语料库统计软件对参照语料库 10 部英文小说和《红楼梦》的霍译及杨译进行了统计，结果显示：参照语料库 10 部英文小说 especial 的使用频次总计为 12 次，平均每部小说的使用频次为 1.2 次；《红楼梦》霍译 especial 的使用频次为 2 次，杨译为 0 次。全译本母语译者对于作为独特形容词 especial 的使用与《红楼梦》母语译者霍译对于作为独特形容词 especial 的使用可以互为佐证，两者同时也得到了参照语料库 10 部英文小说作为原创小说的支持。邓译本、罗译本、《红楼梦》霍译以及部分参照语料库小说对于 especial 的具体使用情况如表 107. 至表 110. 所示。

表 107. 邓译本 especial 语境共现检索（前 5 次，共 15 次）

from the city, under his	especial	protection and saw that she did
. But Dian Wei, the	especial	guard of Cao Cao's tent,
himself into the arms of our	especial	enemy, Yuan Shu. These
the outer robe and held his	especial	weapon, while their escort followed
and he was confided to my	especial	care. Now this Guan Yu

表 108. 罗译本 especial 语境共现检索（共 3 次）

（Cao Pi）showed them	especial	kindness and generosity. Let us
he showed Ma Su's family	especial	concern and provided them with cash
main route and did not attach	especial	importance to the report, particularly

表 109.《红楼梦》霍译 especial 语境共现检索（共 2 次）

| as I said, of no | especial | value, they are-what shall I |
| Prince Heng's favourite with | especial | zeal was filled.' Neatly |

表 110. 10 部英文小说 especial 语境共现检索（共 12 次）

双城记.	, above all things to lay	especial	stress on the discharge of that
嘉莉妹妹.	, but there was no	especial	greeting. The newcomer nodded
嘉莉妹妹.	, but it was with no	especial	delight that Carrie remembered her
大卫科波.	these for my	especial	behoof, and as a piece
大卫科波.	, no longer moping in her	especial	corner, was busy preparing
简爱.	I, therefore, direct that	especial	care shall be bestowed on its
简爱.	Had he treated you as an	especial	favourite, you would have found
红字.	many other personages of	especial	sanctity, in all ages of
红字.	has become a fiend for his	especial	torment!" The unfortunate
红字.	of which Ann Turner, her	especial	friend, had taught her the
苔丝.	person who did not find her	especial	burden in material things.
苔丝.	that, reprobates being their	especial	care, the tenderness towards Tess

在节译本母语译者的独特形容词中，排首位的是 treacherous，两位母语译者的使用频次总计为 9 次，其中邓译本 6 次，罗译本 3 次。排第二位的是 various，两位母语译者的使用频次总计为 9 次，其中邓译本为 7 次，罗译本为 2 次。其具体使用情况如表 111. 至表 114. 所示，其部分搭配情况如下：

elder brother：邓译本 1 次，罗译本 4 次。

elder lords：邓译本 0 次，罗译本 2 次。

treacherous plot：邓译本 1 次，罗译本 0 次。

第四章　古典小说英译的母语译者和非母语译者的定量比较研究

treacherous slope：邓译本 0 次,罗译本 1 次。
treacherous letter：邓译本 2 次,罗译本 0 次。
various units：邓译本 1 次,罗译本 1 次。
various commanders：邓译本 1 次,罗译本 1 次。
various officers/gifts/noises/armies/flags：邓译本 5 次,罗译本 0 次。

对节译本这些独特形容词的搭配及其具体使用情况进行仔细考察之后我们可以发现,这些独特形容词大都修饰与政治军事相关信息的一些名词。母语译者使用这些非母语译者所没有使用的形容词来对这些小说原文中与政治军事相关的词汇或反映这些信息的词汇进行修饰,体现了其在母语思维模式和母语文化背景影响下的翻译风格和特征。

表 111. 邓译本(节译)treacherous 语境共现检索(共 6 次)

, "Zhou Yu is artful and	treacherous	, and there is no news
, But Zhou Yu was more	treacherous	, And caught him in a
beneath the sword. Zhou Yu's	treacherous	plot succeeded well; Dissension sown
Kan Ze Presents A	Treacherous	Letter; Pang Tong Suggests Chaining
of Kan Ze to present the	treacherous	letter to Cao Cao, as

表 112. 罗译本(节译)treacherous 语境共现检索(共 3 次)

, how could they negotiate the	treacherous	Great River? "Just then two
li shorter, but narrow and	treacherous	and hard-going." Cao Cao ordered some
Cao Cao. They passed a	treacherous	slope. The road began to

表 113. 邓译本(节译)various 语境共现检索(前 5 次,共 7 次)

and left the chamber. The	various	officers also went their several ways
place to place and keep the	various	units up to their work and
for Zhou Yu and offered the	various	gifts. The ceremony of reception
Gan lay and listened to the	various	camp noises without and his host's
squadron to receive orders. The	various	armies and squadrons were distinguished by

表 114. 罗译本（节译）various 语境共现检索（共 2 次）

| assignments had been made, the | various | commanders put their boats and armaments |
| and plied their swords. The | various | units maintained ranks under the discipline |

4.3 句子层面

句子是语篇的基本组成单位，是语言中表达一个完整语义的基本单位。如何对句子内部各部分进行组合是反映一个译者译文特征的重要指标。下面本研究将从句首词 and、标点符号以及非谓语动词 ing 形式的使用三个方面来对《三国演义》英译的母语译者和非母语译者在句子层面的特征进行考察。

4.3.1 句首词 and

对于句首词 and 的使用是英语相较于汉语的一个重要区别性特征。从语言学的视角来说，英语重形合，汉语重意合，英语多通过连词、代词等手段来达成句与句之间或句子内部的衔接关系。英语书面语尤其是文学文本中，句首词 and 具有一定的使用频率，其具体的使用情况对于句子内部的衔接，以及语篇的衔接具有重要作用和影响。根据句首词 and 在英语语言中对于语篇的衔接作用，译者对于其具体的使用特征应归于篇章层面进行研究，但鉴于句首词 and 归于句子当中的特征并且主要是依据句子来进行统计，本研究把其放在句子层面进行研究。下面本研究将从句首词 and 的使用的角度来对《三国演义》三个英文全译本和四个英文节译本的母语译者和非母语译者进行比较分析。

第四章 古典小说英译的母语译者和非母语译者的定量比较研究

表 115.《三国演义》三个英文全译本句首词 and 词频

	罗译本	虞译本	邓译本
Tokens	806	556	838
Types	8	7	7
. And	199	271	419
; and	189	73	223
"And	374	66	22
"And	0	126	161
? And	15	9	9
! And	14	11	4
' And	15	0	0

表 116.《三国演义》四个英文节译本句首词 and 词频

	张译本	杨译本	罗译本	邓译本
Tokens	18	17	67	46
Types	4	3	6	4
. And	15	15	23	26
"And	1	0	31	0
; and	2	2	7	19
? And	0	0	4	1
! And	0	0	2	0

从表 115. 和表 116. 的统计结果中我们可以发现,不论是《三国演义》全译本还是节译本,母语译者对于句首词 and 的使用频次远高于非母语译者。全译本对于句首词 and 的使用频次邓译为 838 次,罗译为 806 次,虞译为 556 次,两位母语译者的使用频次较为接近,非母语译者则以较大幅度低于两位母语译者。节译本两位母语译者对于句首词 and 的使用频次邓译为 46 次,罗译为 67 次;两位非母语译者对于句首词 and 的使用频次杨译为 17 次,张译为 18 次,两位母语译者的使用频次以较大幅度高于两位非母语译者。这表明两位母语译者在母语思维模式的影响下,在对于使用句首词 and 来对句子之间的关系进行衔接的频次较为接近,而另三位非母语译者则表现出明显的差异,使用频次远低于母语译者。

朱自清散文的葛译和其他三位译者在句首词 and 的使用方面也存在比较大的差异。这也为《三国演义》三个英文全译本和四个英文节译本母语译者对于句首词 and 使用频次较高的特征提供了有力支撑。由于统计方面的技术原因，本研究对于朱自清散文英译的句首词的统计包括了 and，而《三国演义》的英译则没有包括，但这并不影响本研究的结论。葛译的句式特征与其词汇特征密切相关，葛译对句首词 and 的使用频率比较高，这也是葛译句式区别于其他三位译者的一个重要特征。对于句首词 and 较低频率的使用是三位非母语译者相对于母语译者在句式上的共有特征。葛译和其他三位母语译者对于句首词 and 的使用情况如表 117. 所示，表 118. 至表 121. 是句首词 and 的具体使用情况。

表 117. 句首词 and 使用情况

	葛译	徐译	杨译	朱译
Tokens	21	13	18	8
Types	3	4	3	2
, and	18	8	13	6
. And	2	3	4	0
; and	0	1	0	2
? And	1	1	0	0
! And	0	0	1	0

表 118. 葛译句首词 and 语境共现检索（前 5 次，共 21 次）

was used to taking daily walks	, and	I imagined that it must look
the moon climbed in the sky	, and	beyond the wall the laughter of
the day few people use it	, and	at night it is even lonelier
me seemed to belong to me	, and	I could transcend my own existence
together, pushing back and forth	, and	they seemed to be a cresting

表 119. 杨译句首词 and 语境共现检索（前 5 次，共 18 次）

from the lane beyond our wall	, and	my wife was in the house
pleased or of nothing at all	, and	that gave me a sense of
must have been a delightful event	, and	it is a great pity we
the flared skirts of dancing girls	. And	starring these tiers of leaves were
hills—their general outline only	. And	between the trees appeared one or

第四章　古典小说英译的母语译者和非母语译者的定量比较研究

表 120. 徐译句首词 and 语境共现检索（前 5 次，共 13 次）

go myself, but he insisted	, and	therefore, I had to let
was young to seek a living	, and	he had always supported himself;
mist evaporate with the morning sun	. And	what mark have I left in the
— faintly recognizable at the most	. And	dripping through the sporadic gaps among
to catch cold during the trip	. And	he also told one of the

表 121. 朱译句首词 and 语境共现检索（前 5 次，共 8 次）

exquisite water is covered from view	, and	none can tell its colour;
oars are caught in dangling algae	, and	duckweed float apart the moment their
years since I last saw father	, and	what I can never forget is
universe seems in my possession now	; and	I myself seem to have been
treading on, lightly and furtively	; and	I am caught, blankly,

从 and 作为句首词的使用百分比来看，笔者使用 PowerConc 1.0 beta 25b 对 and 作为句首词进行统计，结果显示葛译 and 作为句首词的使用频率为 0.75%，徐译、杨译和朱译分别为 0.48%、0.74% 和 0.25%。把 and 作为句首词高频率的使用是葛译的一个重要特征，同时 and 作为一个具有较强句法功能的词，对于英语语篇的内在衔接和流畅性都具有重要作用。就葛译对于 and 作为句首词高频率使用的角度来看，其译文语篇的内在衔接和流畅性更为地道和出色。笔者使用 PowerConc 1.0 beta 25b 对《红楼梦》霍译和杨译的 and 作为句首词的使用情况分别进行统计发现：《红楼梦》霍译对 and 作为句首词的使用频率为 0.68%，《红楼梦》杨译对 and 作为句首词的使用频率为 0.50%，霍译明显高于杨译。使用 PowerConc 1.0 beta 25b 对 The Essays of Francis Bacon and 作为句首词进行统计发现其使用频率为 0.88%。以上结果显示《红楼梦》霍译和 The Essays of Francis Bacon 对 and 作为句首词的使用频率都比较高，有力支持了葛译和《三国演义》全译本和节译本母语译者 and 句首词使用频率较高的特征。

4.3.2 标点符号

英语中,逗号的使用是体现句子内部结构复杂度的一个重要指标。逗号在英语中主要用来连接句子中两个并列的词或短语,用来将主句和由分词短语、介词结构、独立主格结构等构成的状语隔开,或置于分句之前或并列连词之前用来将分句隔开。一般来说,英语中一个句子使用的逗号越多,其句子结构就越复杂,反之,则越简单。所以,译本句子逗号的使用次数可以在一定程度上反映句子结构的复杂程度。下面本研究将从句子内部逗号使用的角度来考察《三国演义》三个全译本和四个节译本母语译者相较于非母语译者的区别性特征。《三国演义》三个全译本和四个节译本的部分标点使用情况如表 122. 和表 123. 所示。

表 122.《三国演义》三个英文全译本部分标点符号使用情况

	邓译	罗译	虞译
,	75980	70282	61450
.	69444	68050	69324
?	5534	5874	5584
!	2598	3046	1766
;	2466	4724	1102

表 123.《三国演义》四个英文节译本部分标点符号使用情况

	邓译	罗译	杨译	张译
,	2399	2374	1805	1809
.	2127	2157	1856	1897
?	238	273	234	247
!	63	103	146	146
;	83	102	70	72

从上表中我们可以发现,不论是全译本还是节译本,母语译者的逗号使用频次都以较大幅度高于非母语译者。全译本邓译的逗号使用频次为 75980 次,罗译逗号的使用频次为 70282 次,虞译逗号的使用频次为 61450 次;节译本邓译逗号的使用频次为 2399 次,罗译逗号的使用频次为 2374 次,杨译逗号的使用频次为 1805 次,张译逗号的使用频次

第四章　古典小说英译的母语译者和非母语译者的定量比较研究

为1809次。通过统计句末标点符号,可以获得译文的句子总数,再用译文逗号的使用频次除以总句数,就可以获得译文句子的逗号平均使用频次。

从上表中我们可以发现,全译本邓译的句末标点符号总计为80042,用其逗号使用总频次75980与句末标点符号总数80042相比即可得出其译文句子的逗号平均使用频次为0.949次;使用同样的方法,我们可以发现罗译的句末标点符号总计为81694,句子的逗号平均使用频次为0.860次;虞译的句末标点符号总计为77776,句子的逗号平均使用频次为0.790次。节译本邓译(节译)的句末标点符号总计为2511,句子的逗号平均使用频次为0.955次;罗译(节译)的句末标点符号总计为2635,句子的逗号平均使用频次为0.901次;杨译(节译)的句末标点符号总计为2306,句子的逗号平均使用频次为0.783次;张译(节译)的句末标点符号总计为2362,句子的逗号平均使用频次为0.766次。

不论是全译本还是节译本母语译者句子的逗号平均使用频次明显高于非母语译者,这说明在一定程度上母语译者的句子结构比非母语译者更为复杂。

4.3.3 非谓语动词的 ing 形式

英语中动词的 ing 形式多用来作句子的伴随状语,表示谓语动词伴随的方式或目的等,是句子结构复杂程度的一个重要指标。下面本研究将通过对《三国演义》三个英文全译本和四个英文节译本的非谓语动词的 ing 形式的统计,从非谓语动词 ing 形式使用的角度对母语译者和非母语译者的句子结构进行比较分析。

表124.《三国演义》三个英文全译本非谓语动词 ing 形式使用情况

	邓译本	罗译本	虞译本
非谓语动词 ing 形式形符数	7034	7956	7336
总句数	80042	81694	77776
平均每句分词使用数	0.08787	0.09738	0.09432

表 125.《三国演义》四个英文节译本非谓语动词 ing 使用情况

	邓译本	罗译本	杨译本	张译本
非谓语动词 ing 形式形符数	442	542	404	406
总句数	2511	2635	2306	2362
平均每句分词使用数	0.1760	0.2056	0.1751	0.1718

从上表的统计结果中,我们可以发现《三国演义》英文全译本邓译的非谓语动词 ing 形式的使用次数为 7034 次,罗译为 7956 次,虞译为 7336 次,邓译的使用次数最高,邓译和虞译比较接近;邓译非谓语动词 ing 形式平均每句的使用次数为 0.08787 次,罗译为 0.09738 次,虞译为 0.09432 次。从整体上来看,罗译使用的非谓语动词的 ing 形式最多,平均每句的使用次数也最多,鉴于动词的 ing 形式用作状语的几率远大于作定语等其他成分的几率,这些统计结果表明罗译的句子相比较而言更多使用动词的 ing 形式作状语,而非通过并列谓语等其他方式,使其句子结构更为复杂;邓译本非谓语动词的 ing 形式最少,平均每句的使用次数也最少,说明邓译的句子多通过其他方式做伴随或目的状语;虞译的非谓语动词的 ing 形式和平均每句的使用次数都介于罗译和邓译之间。

《三国演义》英文节译本两位母语译者非谓语动词的 ing 形式的整体使用次数和平均每句的使用次数都以一定幅度多于两位非母语译者,表明两位母语译者的句子多使用动词的 ing 形式而非通过并列谓语等其他方式作状语,使其与两位非母语译者相比,句子结构更为复杂。

母语译者相较于非母语译者句式结构较为复杂的特征还可以从散文英译中得到佐证。笔者使用对参照语料库朱自清散文英译的母语译者和非母语译者的译文进行了统计分析,发现母语译者葛译的句式结构与其他三位非母语译者相比较为复杂。句式结构的复杂度除了取决于介词结构的使用之外,从属连词 that 的使用(包括其作为关系代词的使用)也是对句子结构进行构建的重要方法,对于其使用的多少也是影响文本句式结构的重要因素,同时也是衡量译文句式复杂程度的重要指标之一。笔者使用语料库统计软件 PowerConc 对葛译和杨译、朱译、徐译的从属连词 that 的使用情况进行了统计,结果显示:葛译对于从属连词 that 的使用频次为 19 次,杨译对于从属连词 that 的使用频次为 4 次,朱译对于从属连词 that 的使用频次为 9 次,徐译对于从属连词 that 的使

第四章 古典小说英译的母语译者和非母语译者的定量比较研究

用频次为 10 次。其具体的使用情况如表 126. 到表 129. 所示。

表 126. 葛译从属连词 that 的语境共现检索（前 5 次,共 19 次）

daily walks, and I imagined	that	it must look quite different under
yet I had the pleasant feeling	that	I had come to a fine
date from very early on but	that	flourished during the Six Dynasty period
love. It goes without saying	that	there were great numbers of lotus
events; it is a pity	that	we can no longer enjoy such

表 127. 杨译从属连词 that 的语境共现检索（共 4 次）

luggage. This was so bulky	that	we had to hire a porter
was such a bright young man	that	I thought some of his remarks
but I wiped them hastily so	that	neither he nor anyone else might
Counting up silently, I find	that	more than 8,000 days have already

表 128. 朱译从属连词 that 的语境共现检索（前 5 次,共 9 次）

cool, it occurred to me	that	the Lotus Pond, which I
their shirts tucked in for fear	that	the sampan might tilt. That
lotuses tonight, she could tell	that	the lilies here are high enough
cheeks. Father said, "Now	that	things've come to such a pass
but would ask a hotel waiter	that	he knew to accompany me there

表 129. 徐译从属连词 that 的语境共现检索（前 5 次,共 10 次）

was so preoccupied with this matter	that	he repeatedly spelled out the details
he was still worried, afraid	that	the attendant might make a mistake
myself — but I now recognize	that	I was too smug back then
move." I looked out and saw	that	beyond the guardrails of the platform
climbing down. This was not	that	difficult for him, but it

　　葛译对于从属连词 that 较高频率的使用得其与三位非母语译者相比句子结构更为复杂，同时句子所展现的层次感和节奏感更为明显。葛译的这些句式特征也是其再现原文的韵味和节奏的重要手段和方法。

4.4 篇章层面

it 在英语中有着重要的句法功能,对于句式的构造和语篇的衔接都具有重要作用。照应是"语篇中的指代成分与指称或所指对象之间的相互解释关系,是语篇实现其结构上的衔接和语义上的连贯的一种主要手段"。(董晓波,2013:55)从语篇衔接与连贯的角度来看,it 的照应功能决定了其在英语语篇衔接中的重要作用,从而在汉译英中对其使用频率的高低在某种程度上会影响语篇的衔接性。下面本研究将从 it 的使用角度对《三国演义》三个英文全译本和四个英文节译本的母语译者和非母语译者语篇衔接特征进行比较分析。

表 130.《三国演义》三个英文全译本代词 it 和 its 的使用情况

	邓译	罗译	虞译
it	2531	2235	2406
its	297	308	315
形符数	594696	549417	591730
it/its 占比	0.0047	0.0046	0.0045

表 131.《三国演义》四个英文节译本代词 it 和 its 的使用情况

	邓译	罗译	杨译	张译
it	184	148	131	138
its	17	26	7	8
形符数	36476	33202	30099	32474
it/its 占比	0.0055	0.0052	0.0045	0.0044

从以上两表的统计结果中我们可以发现,《三国演义》英文全译本以及节译本母语译者 it 和 its 的使用频次在译文中的占比都略大于非母语译者,这表明与非母语译者相比,母语译者相对更多使用 it 或 its 进行语篇的前后照应,在一定程度上增强了语篇的衔接性和连贯性。就

第四章 古典小说英译的母语译者和非母语译者的定量比较研究

it 和 its 的使用频次在译文中的占比来看,母语译者对于 it 和 its 较高频次的使用增强了其译文的衔接性和连贯性。

《三国演义》英文全译本以及节译本母语译者 it 和 its 的使用频次在译文中的占比都略大于非母语译者的特征也可以从朱自清散文英译中得到佐证。本研究使用 PowerConc 1.0 beta 25b 对朱自清散文英译进行统计发现,葛译 it 的使用频率为 1.05%,徐译、杨译和朱译分别为 0.65%、0.70% 和 0.68%。从葛译这些特色词比较高频率的使用来看,葛译的语言更为地道。本研究再以英语散文的经典培根散文集 The Essays of Francis Bacon 为参照进行比较分析。使用 PowerConc 1.0 beta 25b 对其 it 的使用进行统计发现:The Essays of Francis Bacon 对 it 的使用频率依次为 1.39%,显然葛译和 The Essays of Francis Bacon 两者的使用频率都比较高,而且 The Essays of Francis Bacon 还略大于葛译。以上的统计结果说明《三国演义》英文全译本以及节译本母语译者 it 和 its 的使用频次在译文中的占比都略大于非母语译者的特征以及葛译对 it 较高频率的使用并非偶然,而是其母语思维对译文影响的结果。

表 132. 葛译 it 的语境共现检索(共 35 次)

1.	I was used to taking daily walks, and I imagined that	it	must look quite different under the light of this full moon.
2.	me. Bordering the pond is a meandering little cinder path.	It	is a secluded path; during the day few people use it
3.	It is a secluded path; during the day few people use	it	, and at night it is even lonelier. There are great
4.	; during the day few people use it, and at night	it	is even lonelier. There are great numbers of trees growing on
5.	and forbidding, giving one an eerie feeling. But this evening	it	was quite nice, even though the rays of the moon were
6.	from their bath. A gentle breeze floated by, bringing with	it	waves of a crisp fragrance like strains of a vague melody sent
7.	was full, a light covering of clouds in the sky prevented	it	from shining brightly; yet I had the pleasant feeling that I
8.	. But the noise was theirs alone; I added nothing to	it	. All of a sudden I was reminded of lotus gathering.

续表

9.	who drifted in small boats and sang their songs of love.	It	goes without saying that there were great numbers of lotus gatherers as
10.	The Lotus Gatherers " by Emperor Yuan of the Liang dynasty tells	it	well: Princely lads and alluring maidens
11.	of those days. They must have been truly memorable events;	it	is a pity that we can no longer enjoy such pastimes.
12.	blossoms here too would " rise above their heads. " But	it	is not enough to have before me only these rippling shadows.
13.	steps had carried me to my own gate; I softly pushed	it	open and entered. I was greeted by complete silence; my
14.	The Silhouette of His Back	It	has been more than two years since the last time I saw
15.	stayed with me the longest is the silhouette of his back.	It	was during the winter of that year; Grandmother had just died
16.	had journeyed to and from Beijing two or three times, so	it	wasn't such a major affair. He vacillated for a while
17.	the luggage, of which there was so much that he found	it	necessary to offer a tip to a porter before we could pass
18.	and, feeling that his speech wasn't all that elegant,	it	was necessary for me to interject some words of my own.
19.	them for favors is absolutely useless! What's more, was	it	possible that a fellow as old and mature as I was would
20.	take care of himself? Ai! As I think back on	it	now, I was really too smart for my own good then
21.	first I wanted to go myself, but he wouldn't allow	it	, so all I could do was let him go.
22.	platform, that was no easy matter. He grabbed hold of	it	with two hands, then hoisted up both of his legs,
23.	to the left and showing the great strain he was exerting.	It	was then that I noticed the silhouette of his back, and
24.	picked up the oranges and started out again. When he made	it	over to this side, 1quickly went over and gave him a
25.	, but I am bothered by a rather painful shoulder that makes	it	difficult to raise my chopsticks or lift a pen; probably the

第四章 古典小说英译的母语译者和非母语译者的定量比较研究

续表

26.	are wiser than I, tell me, then: why is	it	that the days, once gone, never again return? Are
27.	what is gone to what is yet to come, why must	it	pass so quickly? In the morning when I get up,
28.	of sunlight slanting into my small room. The sun, does	it	have feet? Stealthily it moves along, as I too,
29.	small room. The sun, does it have feet? Stealthily	it	moves along, as I too, unknowingly, follow its progress
30.	eyes carefully follow its progress past me. I can sense that	it	is hurrying alone, and when I stretch out my hands to
31.	, and when I stretch out my hands to cover and hold	it	, it soon emerges from under my hands and moves along.
32.	when I stretch out my hands to cover and hold it,	it	soon emerges from under my hands and moves along. At night
33.	. At night, as I lie on my bed, agilely	it	strides across my body and flies past my feet. And when
34.	this world, and in a twinkling still naked I will leave	it	. But what I cannot accept this: why should I make
35.	? You who are wiser than I, please tell me why	it	is that once gone, our days never return.

表133. 徐译从属连词that的语境共现检索（共20次）

1.	while I sit in our yard and enjoy the cool air,	it	strikes me that the lotus pool that I pass by every day
2.	very few pedestrians, even during the daytime, and therefore,	it	is quieter at night. Encircling the pool are dense clusters of
3.	across from ours to reach them. Father was stout, so	it	would be quite something for him to get there. I told
4.	he insisted, and therefore, I had to let him do	it	. So I watched him, in his small black cloth hat
5.	climbing down. This was not that difficult for him, but	it	was quite something for him to climb onto the other platform after
6.	his later life would be so dispiriting. Seeing his situation,	it	was natural for him to be sad and unable to control his

· 205 ·

续表

7.	unable to control his emotions; when one was unhappy inside,	it	was natural that the feeling would find a way out. So
8.	my health, except for the sharp pain in my arm, which makes	it	hard for me to handle chopsticks or pens. Maybe I am
9.	light streaming into my room. The sun also has feet;	it	moves away on tiptoe and I follow it aimlessly. When I
10.	also has feet; it moves away on tiptoe and I follow	it	aimlessly. When I wash my hands, my days wash off
11.	to hold them back before they are beyond my grasp. When	it	is dark, I lie upon my bed and watch days cleverly
12.	naked, soon I'll leave here naked too. But,	it	's unfair to me... why did I come
13.	On a moonless night, this path appears eerily somber, but	it	is fine tonight, although the moonlight is pale. I am
14.	slight shiver from among the leaves and flowers. Like lightning,	it	flashes to the other side of the pool in the blink of
15.	dream. Although a full-orbed moon sails in the sky tonight,	it	cannot shine brightly, because of the clouds, flimsy though they
16.	its own appeal. As the moon shines through the trees,	it	casts across the pool irregular and mottled shadows from the bosky shrubs
17.	only a lot of lotus gatherers, but also many spectators.	It	must have been a joyful and romantic event. In his verse
18.	This verse clearly reveals the merry spectacle of such an event.	It	must have been an interesting event, but we now do not
19.	event, but we now do not have the fortune to enjoy	it	. This reminds me of a few lines from The Song of
20.	again, and tears kept rolling down my cheeks. Father said. "	It	's no use crying over what's already happened, but

表 134. 杨译 it 的语境共现检索(共 19 次)

| 1. | evening as I sat in the yard to enjoy the cool, | it | struck me how different the lotus pool I pass every day must |
| 2. | cinder—path winds along by the side of the pool. | It | is off the beaten track and few pass this way even by |

· 206 ·

第四章 古典小说英译的母语译者和非母语译者的定量比较研究

续表

3.	and few pass this way even by day, so at night	it	is still more quiet. Trees grow thick and bosky all around
4.	is no moon the track is almost terrifyingly dark, but tonight	it	was quite clear, though the moonlight was pale. Strolling alone
5.	but this animation was theirs alone, I had no part in	it	. Then lotus-gathering flashed into my mind. This was an old
6.	festival and a romantic one. We have a good account of	it	in a poem by Emperor Yuan of the Liang dynasty called Lotus
7.	merry excursions. This must have been a delightful event, and	it	is a great pity we cannot enjoy it today. I also
8.	delightful event, and it is a great pity we cannot enjoy	it	today. I also remember some lines from the poem West Islet
9.	looked up to discover I had reached my own door. Pushing	it	softly open and tiptoeing in, I found all quiet inside,
10.	My Father's Back Though	it	is over two years since I saw my father, I can
11.	What's past is gone," said my father. "	It	's no use grieving. Heaven always leaves us some way out
12.	But when I volunteered to go instead he would not hear of	it	. So I watched him in his black cloth cap and jacket
13.	is all right, only my arm aches so badly I find	it	hard to hold the pen. Probably the end is not far
14.	? Perhaps they have been stolen by someone. But who could	it	be and where could he hide them? Perhaps they have just
15.	too, edging away softly and stealthily. And, without knowing	it	, I am already caught in its revolution. Thus the day
16.	reverie. Aware of its fleeting presence, I reach out for	it	only to find it brushing past my outstretched hands. In the
17.	its fleeting presence, I reach out for it only to find	it	brushing past my outstretched hands. In the evening, when I
18.	. In the evening, when I lie on my bed,	it	nimbly strides over my body and flits past my feet. By
19.	back as stark naked as ever. However, I am taking	it	very much to heart: why should I be made to pass

· 207 ·

表 135. 朱译 it 的语境共现检索（共 21 次）

1.	, when I was sitting in the yard enjoying the cool,	it	occurred to me that the Lotus Pond, which I pass by
2.	me. Alongside the Lotus Pond runs a small cinder footpath.	It	is peaceful and secluded here, a place not frequented by pedestrians
3.	frequented by pedestrians even in the daytime; now at night,	it	looks more solitary, in a lush, shady ambience of trees
4.	like being in solitude, as much as in company. As	it	is tonight, basking in a misty moonshine all by myself,
5.	, or like a dream wrapped in a gauzy hood. Although	it	is a full moon, shining through a film of clouds,
6.	film of clouds, the light is not at its brightest;	it	is, however, just right for me—a profound sleep
7.	have nothing. Suddenly, something like lotus-gathering crosses my mind.	It	used to be celebrated as a folk festival in the South,
8.	can pick up some outlines of this activity in the poetry.	It	was young girls who went gathering lotuses, in sampans and singing
9.	them doing the gathering, apart from those who were watching.	It	was a lively season, brimming with vitality, and romance.
10.	might tilt. That is a glimpse of those merrymaking scenes.	It	must have been fascinating; but unfortunately we have long been denied
11.	The Sight of Father's Back	It	is more than two years since I last saw father, and
12.	, "Now that things 've come to such a pass,	it	's no use crying. Fortunately, Heaven always leaves one a
13.	to the station. I repeatedly tried to talk him out of	it	, but he only said, "Never mind! It won
14.	of it, but he only said, "Never mind!	It	won't do to trust guys like those hotel boys!"
15.	me. I sniggered at father for being so impractical, for	it	was utterly useless to entrust me to those attendants, who cared
16.	those attendants, who cared for nothing but money. Besides,	it	was certainly no problem for a person of my age to look

· 208 ·

第四章 古典小说英译的母语译者和非母语译者的定量比较研究

续表

17.	look after himself. Oh, when I come to think of	it	, I can see how smarty I was in those days!
18.	. He had little trouble climbing down the railway track, but	it	was a lot more difficult for him to climb up that platform
19.	. I even have trouble using chopsticks or writing brushes. Perhaps	it	won't be long now before I depart this life."
20.	?——If they had been stolen by someone, who could	it	be? Where could he hide them? If they had made
21.	back, in a blink, in the same stark nakedness?	It	is not fair though: why should I have made such a

《三国演义》英文全译本以及节译本母语译者 it 和 its 的使用频次在译文中的占比都略大于非母语译者的特征也可以从《红楼梦》霍译和杨译中得到佐证。

本研究使用 PowerConc 对《红楼梦》霍译和杨译的 it 分别进行统计发现:《红楼梦》霍译对 it 的使用频率分别为 1.06%;《红楼梦》杨译对 it 的使用频率分别为 0.84%。从统计结果来看,母语译者霍克斯与葛浩文对 it 的使用频率接近,均大于非母语译者。我们再看参照语料库中,it 的使用频率如何。10 部英文经典小说中 it 的使用频率与霍译的大致相当,都集中在 0.97% 到 1.46% 之间,具体结果依次为《大卫·科波菲尔》1.12%,《傲慢与偏见》1.05%,《简·爱》1.05%,《化身博士》1.18%,《嘉莉妹妹》1.09%,《汤姆·索亚历险记》1.46%,《德伯家的苔丝》0.97%,《红字》1.12%,《鲁宾逊漂流记》1.28%,《双城记》1.22%,平均使用频率为 1.13%。这 10 部小说都是英文经典原著,在某种程度上可以说是英文小说语言的代表,其对于语言的运用可以认为是代表了英文小说语言的使用风格。从对于 it 的使用频率来看,霍译作为母语译者和英语原著语言的使用风格相一致。我们再结合具体的例句进行分析。

例 20:

原文:次后忽然宝玉去了,他二人又是那般景况,他母子二人心下更明白了,越发石头落了地,而且是意外之想,彼此放心,再无赎念了。

霍 译: Later, when Baoyu unexpectedly arrived on the scene and they saw how it was between him and Aroma, the reason for her reluctance to leave service at once became apparent.

· 209 ·

It was a factor they had not foreseen; but now they recognized it, it is a great weight off their minds, and it was not without feelings of relief that they abandoned all further thought of attempting to purchase her freedom.

杨译：Baoyu's unexpected visit and the apparent intimacy between maid and master opened their eyes to the true situation, leaving them much reassured. In fact, this was something they had not even hoped for. So they abandoned all thought of buying her freedom.

例21：

原文：雪雁道："这会子就去的,只怕此时已去了。"紫鹃点点头。雪雁道："姑娘还没醒呢,是谁给了宝玉气受,坐在那里哭呢。"紫鹃听了,忙问在那里。雪雁道："在沁芳亭后头桃花底下呢。"

霍译：'Now,' said Snowgoose. 'She's probably already left.'
Nightingale nodded.
'It looks as if Miss Lin's still asleep,' said Snowgoose.
'If it wasn't her, I wonder who it was that made Baoyu so upset. He was sitting Out there in the Garden crying.
'Oh?' said Nightingale sharply. 'Where?'
'Under that peach-tree behind Drenched Blossoms Pavilion.'

杨译：'She was just setting off. I expect she's gone by now.'
Zijuan nodded in silence.
'If our young lady's still asleep, who's been upsetting Baoyu?' continued Xueyan. 'He's sitting out there crying.'
'Out where?'
'Under the peach-blossom behind Seeping Fragrance Pavilion.'

《双城记》：It was n't ending it, I suppose?

I say, when you began it, it was hard enough; not that I have any fault to find with Doctor Manette, except that he is not worthy of such a daughter, which is no imputation on him, for it was not to be expected that anybody should be, under any circumstances.

But it really is doubly and trebly hard to have crowds and multitudes of people turning up after him (I could have forgiven him), to take Ladybird's affections away from me.

第四章　古典小说英译的母语译者和非母语译者的定量比较研究

从以上两例我们可以发现,霍译和杨译对于同样的原文进行了完全不同的处理,显示了两位译者的不同风格。除了霍译的字数多于杨译之外,一个明显的差异就是,霍译对于 it 的使用明显多于杨译。在例 20 中,霍译使用 it 为 5 次,杨译为 0 次,在例 21 中,霍译使用 it 为 5 次,杨译为 2 次。我们再看参照语料库的例句,参照语料选取的是《双城记》中的一段话,it 共计使用 6 次。我们可以发现,霍译明显多于杨译,霍译在母语思维模式下对 it 的使用不同于非母语译者杨译,其对 it 的使用次数明显与《双城记》相接近。

下面再看几例。

例 22:

原文:次后忽然宝玉去了,他两个又是那个光景儿,母子二人心中更明白了,越发一块石头落了地,而且是意外之想,彼此放心,再无别意了。(霍译参考蓝本)

原文:次后忽然宝玉去了,他二人又是那般景况,他母子二人心下更明白了,越发石头落了地,而且是意外之想,彼此放心,再无赎念了。(杨译参考蓝本)

霍译: Later, when Baoyu unexpectedly arrived on the scene and they saw how it was between him and Aroma, the reason for her reluctance to leave service at once became apparent. (Paragraph 6653)

It was a factor they had not foreseen; but now they recognized it, it is a great weight off their minds, and it was not without feelings of relief that they abandoned all further thought of attempting to purchase her freedom.

杨译: Baoyu's unexpected visit and the apparent intimacy between maid and master opened their eyes to the true situation, leaving them much reassured. In fact, this was something they had not even hoped for. So they abandoned all thought of buying her freedom.

例 23:

原文:"我想,如今长安节度云老爷,和府上相好,怎么求太太和老爷说说,写一封书子,求云老爷和那守备说一声,不怕他不依。要是肯行,张家那怕倾家孝顺,也是情愿的。"(霍译参考蓝本)

原文:"我想如今长安节度云老爷与府上最契,可以求太太与老爷说声,打发一封书去,求云老爷和那守备说一声,不怕那守备不依。若是

· 211 ·

肯行,张家连倾家孝顺也都情愿。"(杨译参考蓝本)

霍译:"Well, it occurred to me that the Area Commander for Chang-an, General Yun, is on very good terms with your husband's family, and I thought I might try to find some way of persuading Her Ladyship to talk to Sir Zheng about this and get him to write a letter to General Yun and ask him to have a word with this captain.

It is hardly likely that he would refuse to obey his commanding officer.

The Zhangs would gladly pay anything—even if it meant bankrupting themselves -in return for this kindness."

杨译:"Well, I understand that General Yun the Military Governor of Changan is on friendly terms with your family. If Lady Wang would get His Lordship to write to General Yun, asking him to have a word with the inspector, I'm sure he'd drop the suit. And the Zhangs would gladly give anything—even their whole fortune—in return for this favour."

例24:

原文:贾母因舍不得湘云,便留下他了,接到家中。原要命凤姐儿另设一处与他住,史湘云执意不肯,只要和宝钗一处住,因此也就罢了。

此时大观园中、比先又热闹了多少,(霍译参考蓝本)

原文:贾母因舍不得湘云,便留下他了,接到家中,原要命凤姐儿另设一处与他住。史湘云执意不肯,只要与宝钗一处住,因此就罢了。

此时大观园中比先更热闹了多少。(杨译参考蓝本)

霍译:Grandmother Jia could not bear the idea of a permanent separation from her great-niece, and so it was agreed that Xiang-yun, too, should move into residence with the Jias.

It was Grandmother Jia's original intention that Xi-feng should set up a separate establishment for her in the Garden; but as Xiang-yun herself rigorously opposed this idea and insisted on living with her beloved Bao-chai, she was allowed to have her way.

The Garden's society was now larger and livelier than it bad ever been before.

杨译: Not wanting to part with Xiangyun, the Lady Dowager kept her and had her fetched to their house, directing Xifeng go to give her

第四章 古典小说英译的母语译者和非母语译者的定量比较研究

a separate establishment. This Xiangyun resolutely declined, however, and at her insistence they let her move in with Baochai instead. Things were livelier in Grand View Garden now that thirteen people, counting in Xifeng, lived there.

例 25：

原文：雪雁道："这会子就走，只怕此时已去了。"紫鹃点头。雪雁道："只怕姑娘还没醒呢。是谁给了宝玉气受？坐在那里哭呢！"紫鹃听了，忙问："在那里？"雪雁道："在沁芳亭后头桃花底下呢。"（霍译参考蓝本）

原文：雪雁道"这会子就去的，只怕此时已去了。"紫鹃点点头。雪雁道："姑娘还没醒呢，是谁给了宝玉气受，坐在那里哭呢。"紫鹃听了，忙问在那里。雪雁道："在沁芳亭后头桃花底下呢。"（杨译参考蓝本）

霍译：Now, said Snowgoose. "She's probably already left." Nightingale nodded.
"It looks as if Miss Lin's still asleep", said Snowgoose.
"If it wasn't her, I wonder who it was that made Baoyu so upset. He was sitting Out there in the Garden crying."

杨译：'She was just setting off. I expect she's gone by now.'
Zijuan nodded in silence.
'If our young lady's still asleep, who's been upsetting Baoyu?' continued Xueyan. 'He's sitting out there crying.'

例 26：

原文：二人计议已定，那天气已是掌灯时分，出来又看他们玩了一回牌。算账时，却又是秦氏、尤氏二人输了戏酒的东道，言定后日吃这东道，一面又吃了晚饭。（霍译参考蓝本）

原文：那天气已是掌灯时候，出来又看他们玩了一回牌。算账时，却又是秦氏尤氏二人输了戏酒的东道，言定后日吃这东道。一面就叫送饭。（杨译参考蓝本）

霍译：They had concluded their discussion in gathering dusk, and now moved back into the lamplit outer room and watched the ladies at their cards for a while. When the latter had finished and had added up their scores, it appeared that Qin-shi and You-shi had lost to Xi-feng and owed her a dramatic entertainment at which the players and the drinks were to be provided at their expense.

In the course of dinner, which was now served and at which they were joined by the two boys, it was decided that this should take place in two day's time.

杨译：By the time this was settled, lamps were being lit and they went out to watch the game. When the score was reckoned, Keqing and Madam You had lost again and it was agreed that they should stand treat to a meal and an opera show in two days' time.

例 27：

原文：若采置别的地方去，那更费事，且不成体统。你回去说，这样很好，若老爷们再要改时，全仗大爷深阻，万不可另寻地方。（霍译参考蓝本）

原文：若采置别处地方去，那更费事，且倒不成体统。你回去说这样很好，若老爷们再要改时，全仗大爷谏阻，万不可另寻地方。（杨译参考蓝本）

霍译：It would mean very much more trouble if we were to build on land outside, yet at the same time we should lose the convenience this present scheme gives us of a single layout.

Tell him when you get back that I think it is an excellent proposal, and that I leave it to him to protest in any way he thinks fit if the others show signs of going back on it.

杨译：Any other site would entail more work without such good results. Tell him when you get back that I thoroughly approve, and if the old gentlemen have second thoughts I hope he will dissuade them from looking for another site.

例 28：

原文：我也解不过来，也从未见过这样的孩子。别的淘气都是应该的，只他这种和丫头们好却是难懂。我为此也耽心，每每冷眼查看他。只和丫头们闹，必是人大心大，知道男女的事了，所以爱亲近他们。既细细查试，究竟不是为此。岂不奇怪。想必原是个丫头错投了胎不成。

霍译：His other kinds of naughtiness I can understand; it's this passion for spending all his time with maids that I find so hard to make out.

It used at one time to worry me: I thought it must be because he had reached puberty and was having experiences with them; but after watching him very carefully, I came to the conclusion that it wasn't that at all.

It's very, very strange. Perhaps he was a maid himself in some past life. Perhaps he ought to have been a girl.

杨译：I can't understand him either. I've never known another child like him. One expects a boy to be mischievous, but this extraordinary liking he has for maids has been preying on my mind. I'm for ever finding him fooling about with them. At first I thought this intimacy was because he'd grown big enough to know about sex; but watching him more closely I realized that wasn't the reason, which makes it even odder. Could it be that he was really meant to be born a girl...

4.5 本章小结

本章研究是本研究的重要环节和组成部分，所占篇幅也最大，是整个研究的基础和关键环节。为进一步发现并厘清母语译者相较于非母语译者的区别性特征，验证"母语优势"，认知母语优势的具体特征等研究目标，本章研究详细制订了研究方法，确定了研究范式，建立了研究所用的语料库，拟定了研究步骤，进一步提高了对母语译者和非母语译者定量研究的科学性，确保定量统计所获得数据的准确性和客观性。

语料库方法相较于以往的翻译研究方法，增强了结论的科学性和客观性，有效避免了传统翻译研究的感悟式、印象式的主观性和个案描写、主观哲学思辨的片面性。研究所用的语料库包括：《三国演义》的三个英文全译本邓罗译本、罗慕士译本、虞苏美译本和四个英文节译本邓罗节译本、罗慕士节译本、杨宪益节译本、张亦文节译本，参照语料库10部英文小说原著，《红楼梦》霍克斯译本和杨宪益译本，朱自清散文的葛译、杨译、徐译和朱译。研究步骤包括：定向观察、定量分析和统计、定性阐释。

本章研究通过使用语料库统计分析软件对《三国演义》三个英文全

译本和四个英文节译本的定量统计分析发现母语译者和非母语译者在词汇、句子、篇章层面存在较大差异。在词汇层面,母语译者相较于非母语译者的区别性特征主要包括:《三国演义》母语译者的形符数和类符数都以一定幅度大于非母语译者的形符数和类符数。《三国演义》的三个英文全译本和四个英文节译本母语译者的类符数都以较大幅度大于非母语译者类符数;形符数方面,除了虞译的形符数以一定幅度高于罗译外,其余不论全译本还是节译本所有母语译者的形符数都以较大幅度大于非母语译者。虞译本的形符数大于罗译本并不影响母语译者译文的形符数较多的倾向性。母语译者的类符数较多是母语译者相较于非母语译者在词汇层面最为显著的特征之一,全译本中的邓译本和罗译本的类符数都以较大幅度多于虞译本,邓译本和罗译本的第 43-50 回内容的类符数也以较大幅度多于杨译本和张译本。母语译者类符数较高的特征除了表现为类符数的总量较多之外,还表现为其动词、名词、形容词、副词、介词和连词的类符数也多于非母语译者。这说明母语译者所使用的词类更为丰富,从词汇丰富的角度来说,对于原文的再现更为细腻。

在词汇层面,母语译者相较于非母语译者的区别性特征主要包括:母语译者对于句首词 and、逗号、非谓语动词 ing 形式的使用频次较高,增强了其译文句子结构的复杂度和语篇的衔接性和流畅性。

在篇章层面:母语译者相较于非母语译者的区别性特征主要包括:母语译者 it 和 its 的使用频次在译文中的占比都略大于非母语译者,这表明与非母语译者相比,母语译者相对更多使用 it 或 its 进行语篇的前后照应,在一定程度上增强了语篇的衔接性和连贯性。

第五章 古典小说英译的母语译者和非母语译者的定性比较研究

5.1 方法与路径

定量研究和定性研究是对文本进行分析研究的两种方法,这两种方法相辅相成,互为印证。本研究的第四章对《三国演义》的三个全译本和四个节译本的母语译者和非母语译者的译文特征进行了词汇、句式、篇章层面的定量分析,发现了母语译者相较于非母语译者的区别性特征。本章将对其从战斗场面描写、否定词、自然环境描写 4 个有代表性的视角进行定性分析,从定性描写研究的视角,来探讨母语译者相较于非母语译者的区别性特征,并用第四章定量分析的数据作支撑,从而使母语译者和非母语译者的比较研究更为全面和系统。

5.1.1 研究目标与范围

定量研究使用语料库统计分析软件对特定文本进行统计和定量分析,获得文本的词汇、句式、篇章等层面的相关数据特征,定量分析由于借助计算机技术,以及特定语料的数据支撑,其所得出的结论更为科学和客观;定性分析则对文本进行定性的质性分析,具有主观性和哲学思辨的性质。这两种方法相辅相成,互为印证,没有定性分析,定量分析就缺乏质性的判断和界定,其数据也失去意义,定性分析如果没有定量分析作支撑,就会滑向主观片面性。

　　本章节的研究目标旨在使用定性研究的主观分析判断、哲学思辨以及个案描写研究的质性分析来对《三国演义》的三个英文全译本和四个英文节译本的母语译者和非母语译者进行比较研究,从定性分析的视角来考察母语译者相较于非母语译者的区别性特征,从而对第四章的定量比较研究的数据做出定性的质性阐释和判断,同时赋予定量研究所得出的数据结论以质性意义。《三国演义》是一部以政治和军事斗争为主轴的历史小说,小说多以政治和军事斗争场面的描写为主,所以关于政治和战争场面、人物心理活动以及动作描写在整个小说的描写中便占有很大比重。此外,小说原作中对于自然环境的描写虽然比重较小,但对于小说具有烘托人物心理和形象,渲染政治军事等场面的斗争氛围的重要作用;同时本研究在第四章对于《三国演义》英译本母语译者和非母语译者的定量比较研究中发现,非母语译者相较于母语译者的独特动词中,助动词、情态动词和系动词的否定缩写形式排位比较靠前,基于此,本研究针对《三国演义》小说原作的题材和描写内容的特征,拟从战斗场面描写、动词以及否定词和自然环境描写共四个有代表性的角度进行定性分析研究,并以第四章定量分析的数据为支撑,使用其客观和科学的文本数据支持定性研究的质性分析,使定性分析具有坚实的客观、科学的数据基础,避免其感悟式、印象式的主观性和个案描写、主观哲学思辨的片面性。

　　通过对《三国演义》的三个英文全译本和四个英文节译本的母语译者和非母语译者进行上述四个视角的定性考察,并结合第四章的定量研究所得出的结论,本研究将实现对母语译者和非母语译者全面、系统的描写性比较研究,发现母语译者相较于非母语译者的区别性特征,为后续章节的母语优势下的汉籍英译翻译策略研究提供全面坚实的基础。

5.1.2 语料筛选

　　定性研究主要是抽取有代表性的个案对文本进行定性分析研究,就母语译者相较于非母语译者的比较研究而言,应该选取能够代表小说原作主要描写内容和在小说原作中具有关键作用的描写视角的语料个案,从而考察在小说的整体翻译中母语译者相较于非母语译者的区别性特征。

《三国演义》是一部以政治和军事斗争为主轴的历史小说,政治和军事斗争贯穿了小说的始终,政治和军事斗争场面的描写在小说中占有很大比例,即使是政治人物的对话所涉及的也多为政治军事内容。所以,关于政治和战争场面、人物心理活动以及动作的描写在整个小说的描写中便占有很大比重。此外,小说原作尤其是军事战争场面的描写中,不可避免地会涉及对于自然环境的描写,虽然比重较小,但对于小说具有烘托人物心理和形象,渲染政治军事等场面斗争氛围的重要作用。基于此,本研究从译文中涉及以上几个方面的描写中选取个案研究的语料,具体包括战斗场面描写、动词、自然环境描写以及否定词共4个有代表性的描写语料。

　　定性研究的主要目的是对《三国演义》英文译本的母语译者和非母语译者进行定性的比较研究,同时对第四章的定量研究进行质性的阐释和佐证。所以,本章的定性研究的语料选取除了考虑其能够代表小说原作主要描写内容和在小说原作中具有关键作用的描写视角以外,还要考虑语料的选取具有随机性和经济性,所选取的语料能够代表母语译者或非母语译者在以上5个方面整体的翻译风格和特征。

5.1.3 研究方法与步骤

　　定性研究主要通过具有代表性的个案研究,总结归纳出文本的特征和风格,采取的是自下而上的归纳法。就《三国演义》三个英文全译本和四个英文节译本来说,本研究将通过对所选取的母语译者和非母语译者的针对原作主要描写内容的有代表性的语料进行定性的个案分析,并对母语译者和非母语译者的翻译风格和特征进行比较分析,以期在质性分析方面,发现母语译者相较于非母语译者的区别性特征。

　　就《三国演义》三个英文全译本和四个英文节译本的母语译者和非母语译者定性比较研究来说,本研究拟采取以下步骤:第一,确定研究目标和范围,针对母语译者和非母语译者比较研究的需要,确定定性研究的目标,基于《三国演义》原作的题材和主要描写内容,选取足够数量的有代表性的个案研究例证;第二,通过语料库检索出例证对应的母语译者和非母语译者的英语译文;第三,对例证对应的母语译者和非母语译者的英文译文进行定性的比较分析,以期发现母语译者相较于非母语译者的质性方面的区别性特征;第四,结合第四章定量研究的结果,对例证对应的母语译者和非母语译者的英语译文进行全面系统的比较研究,以期全面系统地发现母语译者相较于非母语译者的区别性特征。

5.2 战争场面描写英译比较

《三国演义》是一部以政治军事斗争为主轴的历史小说,描写了从东汉末年到西晋初年近100年的历史风云,其结构宏伟,内容丰富庞杂,其中战斗场面的描写所占比例较大,在整个小说的描写中占有重要地位。政治军事斗争是《三国演义》原作的主轴,也是小说描写的主要内容,政治斗争反映了从东汉末年到西晋初年的政治风云变幻,军事斗争是政治斗争的延伸和反映,政治斗争最终表现为军事斗争,并通过军事斗争来实现其目标,所以小说中充满了各种大小不一的战争或战斗场面的描写。战争或战斗场面的描写涉及各种人物以及人物的各种战斗行为的描写,对战争或战斗场面描写的翻译对《三国演义》小说整体的翻译具有重要意义。下面我们就通过对小说原作当中具有代表性的战争或战斗场面描写的母语译者和非母语译者的译文的定性比较研究,来考察母语译者相较于非母语译者的区别性特征。

例29是选取自《三国演义》原作中最为重要和精彩的战争场面之一赤壁之战中的一个战争场面的描写原文以及两个母语译者的译文和三个非母语译者的译文。

例29:

原文:却说焦触、张南凭一勇之气,飞棹小船而来。韩当独披掩心,手执长枪,立于船头。焦触船先到,便命军士乱箭往韩当船上射来;当用牌遮隔。焦触捻长枪与韩当交锋,当手起一枪,刺死焦触。张南随后大叫赶来;隔斜里周泰船出。张南挺枪立于船头,两边弓矢乱射。周泰一臂挽牌,一手提刀,两船相离七八尺,泰即飞身一跃,直跃过张南船上,手起刀落,砍张南于水中,乱杀驾舟军士。众船飞棹急回,韩当、周泰催船追赶,到半江中,恰与文聘船相迎,两边便摆定船厮杀。(第四十八回)

第五章　古典小说英译的母语译者和非母语译者的定性比较研究

邓译: The two braggarts from the north, Jiao Chu and Zhang Neng, really only trusted to their boldness and luck. Their ships came down under the powerful strokes of the oars.

　　As they neared, the two leaders put on their heart-protectors, gripped their spears, and each took his station in the prow of the leading ship of his division. Jiao Chu's ship led and as soon as he came near enough, his troops began to shoot at Han Dang, who fended off the arrows with his buckler. Jiao Chu twirled his long spear as he engaged his opponent. But, at the first thrust, he was killed. His comrade Zhang Neng with the other ships was coming up with great shouts, when Zhou Tai sailed up at an angle, and these two squadrons began shooting arrows at each other in clouds. Zhou Tai fended off the arrows with his shield and stood gripping his sword firmly till his ships came within a few spans of the enemy's ships, when he leaped across and cut down Zhang Neng. Zhang Neng's dead body fell into the water. Then the battle became confused, and the attacking ships rowed hard to get away. The southerners pursued but soon came in sight of Wen Ping's supporting fleet. Once more the ships engaged and the forces fought with each other.

罗译: Now Cao's volunteers, Jiao Chu and Zhang Nan, were relying on little more than raw nerve.

　　As their swift-oared boats approached the southern craft, Han Dang, wearing a breastplate, stood on the prow of his boat, a long spear in hand. Jiao Chu arrived first and ordered his archers to shoot, but Han Dang defended himself with his shield. Next, Jiao Chu crossed spears with Han Dang, but Dang slew him with a single thrust. Then Zhang Nan came forth, shouting, and Zhou Tai darted out from the side. Zhang Nan stood at the prow, his spear leveled. Arrows flew in volleys and counter-volleys. Plying his shield with one arm, his sword with the other hand, Zhou Tai leaped onto Zhang Nan's approaching boat and handily cut him down. Zhang Nan's body sank in the river, as Zhou Tai slashed wildly at his crew. The other attackers rowed swiftly back to the north shore. Han Dang and Zhou Tai gave chase but were checked in the middle of the river by Wen Ping. The boats of both sides took battle formation and set about the slaughter.

杨译: Meanwhile the small craft of bold Jiao Chu and Zhang Nan were bearing down on them swiftly.

Wearing armour, his lance in his hand, Han Dang stood in the prow of his boat. Jiao Chu, who was ahead of Zhang Nan, ordered his men to shoot once they came within range, but Han Dang warded off the arrows with his shield. And when Jiao Chu attacked with his lance, with one thrust Han Dang killed him. Zhang Nan was coming up with great shouts when Zhou Tai intercepted him. The northern officer was standing in the prow with his lance, while his men were shooting wildly. When the two boats were still some seven or eight feet apart, Zhou Tai, his shield in one hand, a sword in the other, leapt on to the enemy's boat. One sweep of his sword and Zhang Nan toppled into the river. Then Zhou set about killing the rest of the crew. The other boats turned and rowed hard for the north bank. Han Dang and Zhou Tai pursued them as fast as they could. In midstream, Wen Pin's squadron came up, and the battle was on again.

张译: Meanwhile the small craft of bold Jiao chu and Zhang Nan were bearing down on them swiftly.

Wearing armour, his lance in his hand, Han Dang stood in the prow of his boat. Jiao Chu, who ahead of Zhang Nan ordered his men to shoot once they came within range, but Han Dang warded off the arrows with his shield. And when Jiao Chu attacked with his lance, with one thrust Han Dang killed him. Zhang Nan was coming up with great shouts when Zhou Tai intercepted him. The northern officer was standing in the prow with his lance, while his men were shooting wildly. When the two boats were still some seven or eight feet apart, Zhou Tai, his shield in one hand, a sword in the other, leapt on to the enemy's boat. One sweep of his sword and. Zhang Nan toppled into the river. Then Zhou set about killing the rest of the crew. The other boats turned and rowed hard for the north bank. Han Dang and Zhou Tai pursued them as fast as they could. In midstream, Wen Pins squadron

第五章　古典小说英译的母语译者和非母语译者的定性比较研究

came up, and the battle was on again.

虞译：Meanwhile, the two braggarts from the north, driven by a desire to seem brave, came down swiftly under the powerful strokes of the oars.

As they neared, Han Dang, wearing armor to protect his heart, stood in the prow of his boat, gripping a spear. Jiao Chu, who was ahead of his friend, ordered his men to shoot at Han Dang, who fended off the arrows with his shield. Jiao Chu twirled his long spear as he engaged his opponent. But, at the first thrust, he was killed. His friend Zhang Nan was coming up with great shouts when Zhou Tai arrived from the side and intercepted him and these two squadrons began shooting arrows at each other in clouds. When his boat was still some seven or eight feet away from his opponent's, Zhou Tai, with his shield in one hand and his sword in the other, leaped across and cut down Zhang Nan, who fell into the water. Then he started killing the soldiers on the boat. All the other northern boats rowed hard to get away. The southerners pursued but soon came in sight of Wen Ping's supporting squadron. Once more fighting broke out between the opposing forces.

原文的这段战斗场面的描写是小说原作战斗场面的典型代表，其描写的是赤壁之战时在周瑜火烧连营之前曹军和吴军的一次水上战斗，最后以吴军的获胜告终。这段战斗场面的描写充满了双方战斗人员的各种战斗行为和动作的描写，译文对这些描写如何处理体现了译者的翻译风格和策略，对于母语译者和非母语译者来说，译文反映了影响其翻译过程的母语思维模式。

原文是战斗场面的描写，充满了各种战斗行为和动作的描写，动词占有了很大比重，包括披、执、立、到、命、射、遮隔、捻、交锋、刺、叫、赶来、出、挺、挽、提、跃等。这些动词，前后相接，构成人物战斗中的一连串的动作行为，将人物的战斗行为描写得生动形象。同时，原文的这些动词用词精确，对于人物战斗行为的描写准确到位，十分形象。我们首先比较 5 个译文对于动词的使用情况。5 个译文中的动词和动词短语（包括动词的分词形式和不定式，但不包括 be 动词），笔者都用黑体标示出来，从中我们可以发现，邓译共使用了 25 种 34 个动词；罗译共使用

· 223 ·

了24种27个动词;杨译共使用了15种20个动词;张译共使用了15种20个动词;虞译共使用了21种24个动词。从动词使用的种类来看,邓译和罗译最多,分别为25种和24种,杨译和张译最少,为15种,虞译居中,为21种;从动词使用的数量来看,也是邓译和罗译最多,分别为34个和27个,杨译和张译最少,为20个,虞译居中为24个;动词的种类和数量越多,说明译文对于原文动作描写的再现越细腻、精确。

  下面我们再从非谓语动词、独立主格结构、介词短语的使用情况,来考察比较母语译者和非母语译者的风格特征。在英语语言中,表示人物行为动作的谓语动词的方式、状态、目的、时间、地点、结果等多用非谓语动词、独立主格结构、介词短语和副词等来描述,在涉及充满了一连串人物战斗行为和动作的战斗场面描写的原文的译文当中,非谓语动词、独立主格结构和介词短语使用的数量和方式,对于原文的人物战斗行为和动作描写场面再现的精确性和细腻性具有重要的影响。5个译文中的非谓语动词、独立主格结构、介词短语笔者都用斜体加下划线的方式标示出来,从中我们可以发现邓译和罗译的最多,邓译为16个,罗译为21个;杨译为17个,张译为17个;虞译为17个;如果就每位译者来说,罗译最多,邓译、杨译、张译、虞译数量上大体相当,差异不大,就母语译者和非母语译者来说,母语译者平均为18.5个,非母语译者平均为17个,母语译者略多于非母语译者。

  在战争场面的描写当中,除了动词和非谓语动词、独立主格结构、介词短语之外,连词的使用对于人物一连串战斗行为和动作的描写也起着重要作用。连词对于句子之间以及句子内部之间的衔接起重要作用,根据句子之间或句子内部不同的连接需要,使用的连词也不同。一般来说,连词可以表示顺接、转折、时间、原因等连接关系。5个译文中的连词,笔者也使用黄颜色标示出来,从中我们可以发现邓译使用的连词共8种16个,罗译使用的连词共5种11个,杨译使用的连词共6种11个,张译使用的连词共6种11个,虞译使用的连词共5种9个。从数量上来看,邓译所使用连词的数量和种类都最多,罗译、杨译、张译、虞译连词的种类大体相当,连词的数量虞译最少,罗译、杨译、张译相同。总体来看,母语译者连词的平均使用种类为6.5种,平均使用数量为13.5个,非母语译者连词的平均使用种类为5.7种,平均使用数量为10个,母语译者略多于非母语译者。

  就连词的使用方式来看,母语译者和非母语译者最显著的差异是母

第五章　古典小说英译的母语译者和非母语译者的定性比较研究

语译者对于 and 和 but 的使用次数比较多，when 的使用次数相对较少，非母语译者对 and 和 but 的使用次数相对较少，对 when 的使用次数相对较多。邓译使用 and 共计 7 次，but 共计 2 次，when 共计 2 次；罗译使用 and 共计 4 次，but 共计 3 次，when 共计 0 次；杨译使用 and 共计 4 次，but 共计 1 次，when 共计 3 次；张译使用 and 共计 4 次，but 共计 1 次，when 共计 3 次；虞译使用 and 共计 2 次，but 共计 2 次，when 共计 2 次。此外，母语译者对于 and 的使用分布比较均匀，非母语译者对于 when 的使用分布则比较集中。母语译者在使用 and 和 but 时多用于句子之间或句子中连接两个先后发生的或具有转折关系的行为或动作，使译文对于人物行为和动作的描述更为连贯、流畅和生动；母语译者 when 使用的次数相对较少，而且与 as，as soon as，till，then 等词交错使用，分布较为均匀，使译文对于行为或动作之间的时间关系的连接更为多样、细腻和精确。非母语译者 when 的使用次数相对较多，而且与 as，while 意义相近的词使用分布相对比较集中，影响语篇整体的生动性和流畅性。

5.3　否定词的英译比较

否定词不论在汉语中还是英语中，都占有重要地位。对于文学作品尤其是篇幅较大的小说来说，更离不开否定词的使用。根据本研究在第四章的定量研究结果，非母语译者对于部分情态动词否定缩写形式 mustn't 的使用远多于母语译者。译文对于原文否定意义的词如何处理，在一定程度上体现了译者的翻译风格，就母语译者和非母语译者而言，对于否定意义词处理的差异，在一定程度上也反映了两者思维模式的差异。下面本研究将以具体例子对母语译者和非母语译者在否定词的使用方面进行定性的比较分析，从定性分析的角度来探究母语译者相较于非母语译者的区别性特征，并对第四章定量研究的结果进行验证，具体情况如下。

例 30：

原文：周瑜曰："子敬休忧，瑜自有主张。今可速请孔明来相见。"鲁肃上马去了。（第四十四回）

邓译："Have no anxiety," said Zhou Yu. "I shall be able to decide this. But go quickly and beg Zhuge Liang to come to see me." So Lu Su went to seek out Zhuge Liang.

罗译："No need to worry," Zhou Yu reassured Lu Su, "I think I know what we have to do. But you must get Kongming here for a meeting right away." Lu Su rode off to find him.

杨译："Don't worry," said Zhou Yu. "I know what to do. Just go at once and ask Zhuge Liang to come here." So Lu Su mounted his horse and rode off.

张译："Don't be worried," said Zhou Yu, "I shall be able to make a decision. Now go quickly and ask Zhuge Liang to come to see me." So Lu Su mounted his horse and rode off.

原文中的"子敬休忧"是周瑜对鲁肃所说，其背景是当时曹操取得荆州之后，准备攻打东吴，吴国所有的文官都主张降曹，主降派势力较大，而孙权正因不能决断而苦恼，准备邀请周瑜从鄱阳赶回商议，鲁肃因与周瑜相厚，最先迎接，同时对于主降派及当时的形势表示了担忧。周瑜对于对抗曹操暗中决心已定，成竹在胸，因而对鲁肃说"子敬休忧"，其语气是较为肯定和强烈的，表现了周瑜抗曹的决心和气魄以及对于战胜文官主降派的信心和决心。所以，在译文中如何处理其否定意义，对于再现原文中周瑜的信心、决心和气魄至关重要。对于例文中的"子敬休忧"，母语译者和非母语译者的处理存在较大差异，对于原文中的否定词，两位母语译者在译文中都使用 no 来进行再现，两位非母语译者都使用 don't 来进行再现。相较于 don't，母语译者所使用的 no 所表现的说话人的语气更为坚决和强烈，更为有效地再现了原文中周瑜的抗曹决心和气魄以及战胜文官主降派的信心和决心，在表现人物的语气和口吻方面与原文更为接近。

例 31：

原文：张飞大叫曰："偏子龙干得功，偏我是无用之人？只拨三千军与我，去取武陵郡，活捉太守金旋来献。"孔明大喜曰："翼德要去不妨，但要依一件事。"（第五十二回）

第五章　古典小说英译的母语译者和非母语译者的定性比较研究

邓译：But Zhang Fei was angry and disappointed. "So Zhao Zilong gets all the praise, and I am worth nothing," cried he. "Just give me three thousand soldiers, and I will take Wuling and bring you the Governor." This pleased Zhuge Liang, who said, "There is no reason why you should not go, but I will only require one condition of you."

罗译：Now Zhang Fei thundered in dismay："Let Zilong have all the credit! And let me remain a useless man! Oh, give me but three thousand to take Wuling, and I'll bring that governor Jin Xuan back alive!" Kongming was delighted with Zhang Fei's zeal. "There is no reason you should not go, Yide," he said.

虞译：But Zhang Fei was angry and disappointed. "So Zi-long gets all the credit and I'm worth nothing," he cried. "Just give me 3,000 men and I will take Wuling and bring you its prefect." This pleased Zhuge Liang, who said, "There is no reason why you shouldn't go, but you must fulfill one requirement."

对于例文中的"翼德要去不妨"，三位译者都以 There is no reason why... 的结构进行处理，但在否定词的使用方面，母语译者和非母语译者存在差异。两位母语译者使用 should not 的否定形式，非母语译者使用的是其否定式的缩写形式 shouldn't。三位译者使用 you should not/shouldn't go，实际上是将原文中否定对象进行了转换，原文中否定的是"妨"，译文中否定的是 go（去）。原文中，张飞强烈要求被派去攻取武陵郡，诸葛亮使用激将法起先故意没有给其分派攻取武陵郡的任务，张飞因而恼怒并质问为何没有被分派任务，其语气强烈，因而母语译者的译文所使用的 should not 与非母语译者所使用的 shouldn't 相比，其语气更为强烈，更为恰当地再现了原文中张飞愤怒的语气。

例32：

原文：回来正遇吕布之使，呈上书札，玄德大喜。关、张曰："吕布乃无义之人，不可信也。"玄德曰："彼既以好情待我，奈何疑之？"（第十五回）

邓译：When the messenger from Lu Bu came, Liu Bei read the letter. He was quite content with the offer, but his brothers were not inclined to trust Lu Bu. "Such a dishonorable man must have a motive," said Guan Yu and Zhang Fei. "Since he treats me kindly, I cannot but trust him," replied Liu Bei.

罗译：so Lü Bu's offer of Xiaopei was most welcome to Xuande, but not to his brothers. "A man so dishonorable cannot be trusted," they protested. Xuande replied, "He makes us a fair offer in good will. Why question his motives?"

虞译：On his way back he met the messenger sent by Lu Bu, who presented the letter. Liu Bei was quite content with the offer but his brothers were not inclined to trust Lu Bu. "Since he treats me kindly, I shouldn't suspect him," said Liu Bei. So he went back to Xuzhou.

原文是选自刘备刚刚被袁术劫寨，折兵大半之时，遇到吕布派人送来结好的书信。当时正值群雄逐鹿之时，袁术、吕布和刘备三方势力相互拉拢，攻伐，吕布准备攻打袁术之际，陈宫建议其结好刘备，使其为先锋，共同对付袁术，吕布便派人送书信给刘备。因为吕布在政治斗争中多次背叛，关羽和张飞对其不信任，建议拒绝吕布的邀请，而刘备则持相反的意见，所以原文中的"吕布乃无义之人，不可信也"突出体现了关羽和张飞的不信任，其强烈反对的语气和口吻跃然纸上，其中的否定意义词，"无"和"不"语气强烈，在译文中如何处理对于译文能否再现原文人物的语气和口吻具有重要影响，对于人物形象的塑造也起重要作用。"无义"一词是关羽和张飞不信任吕布的原因，两位母语译者都使用 dishonorable 一词来处理，前面加上修饰语 such 或 so 以突出强调的语气，这种处理方式有效再现了原文人物的语气和口吻；非母语译者则没有相对应的译文，这种略去不译的处理方式导致了原文重要信息在译文中的缺失，不利于译文再现原文人物强烈的语气和口吻以及人物形象的塑造。

原文"不可信也"体现了关羽和张飞强烈反对的语气和口吻，母语译者邓译使用 must have a motive 来处理，这种处理方式以 must 一词十分强烈地突出了说话人对于吕布的不信任以及对于其背后动机的怀疑；罗译使用 cannot be trusted 来处理，cannot 一词也较为有效地再现了说话人强烈的语气和口吻。两位母语译者的处理较为有效地再现原文中说话人强烈的不信任的语气和口吻。非母语译者虞译使用 his brothers were not inclined to trust Lu Bu 进行处理，主要侧重于对说话人的态度进行陈述，与两位母语译者直接用强烈的否定词翻译原文人物的话语相比，在再现说话人不信任的语气和口吻方面，没有那么强烈的

· 228 ·

第五章　古典小说英译的母语译者和非母语译者的定性比较研究

效果；从整体效果上来看，母语译者的处理方式使其译文与非母语译者的相比更为生动，也更有利于人物形象的塑造。

《三国演义》原作中，人物的对话占有很大比例，小说许多情节的推动，人物的之间的关系，人物之间的交锋，相关重要背景信息的介绍都是通过人物的对话来实现的；同时，原文中人物的对话是展现人物性格、格局、视野的重要手段，对于人物形象的塑造具有重要作用。《三国演义》原作中的人物对话往往语言精练，言简意赅，用较少的语言表现了人物强烈的态度和情感，译文如何处理对于再现原文人物对话的以上特征具有重要影响。原文"奈何疑之？"是刘备针对关羽和张飞对吕布的强烈的不信任，在给出自己的理由之后，所说的话。刘备的回答给出了他对吕布邀请的态度，使用的是反问句，语气比较强烈，极大地强化了刘备愿意接受邀请的态度，及其对自己所持理由的认可。对于原文"奈何疑之？"，邓译的处理为 I cannot but trust him，罗译的处理为 Why question his motives? 虞译的处理为 I shouldn't suspect him。邓译使用 cannot but trust 表示别无选择，只能如此，从反面承托必须如此的强烈语气，与原文有异曲同工之妙；罗译使用与原文相同的反问句来处理，再现了说话人只能如此的强烈态度和口吻；虞译使用 should 的否定缩写形式，与两位母语译者相比，对于原文说话人强烈的语气和口吻以及坚决态度的再现则略显不足。

例33：

原文："若聚五家僮仆，可得千馀人，乘今夜府中大宴，庆赏元宵，将府围住，突入杀之。不可失此机会。"承大喜，（第二十三回）

邓译："There is a great banquet in his palace tonight. If we get together our young men and servants, we can muster more than a thousand, and we can surround the palace, while Cao Cao is at the banquet, and finish him off. We must not miss this." Dong Cheng was more than delighted.

罗译："If we marshal a thousand servants and young attendants from our five households, we can surround the prime minister's residence this evening while the full moon festival is being held, and charge in and kill him. We have a unique opportunity." Enthusiastically Dong Cheng gathered the men of the household. Arms were collected. Dong Cheng was mounted and dressed for battle, spear couched for action.

虞译:"If we gather the servants of our five families, we can muster more than a thousand men, and while he's at the banquet we can surround his place and finish him off. We mustn't miss this chance!" Dong Cheng was more than delighted.

例文中的"不可失此机会"是国舅董承在梦中,与王子服等几人商议趁京城空虚之际,如何集结家仆等人,围攻曹操时,对其他几人所说的话。董承作为国舅,对汉室衰微,曹操专权感愤成疾,十分痛心,所以在梦中与王子服等人商议围攻曹操时,情词恳切,语气强烈。两位母语译者所使用的处理方式,其语气相较于非母语译者的处理方式,在效果上更能体现出说话人的急切、焦灼的心情和口吻,与原文用词和描写方式的效果更为接近。

5.4 动词的英译比较

《三国演义》是一部以政治和军事斗争为主轴的历史小说,政治和军事斗争贯穿了小说的始终,小说中的许多内容都是围绕政治军事斗争展开的,政治和军事斗争场面的描写在小说中占有很大比例。所以,关于政治和战争场面、人物行为和动作的描写在整个小说的描写中占有很大比重。笔者通过仔细比较母语译者和非母语译者的译文,发现两者对于动词的处理存在较大差异,下面是一些典型例子的具体情况。

例 34:

原文:待至日高雾散,孔明令收船急回。二十只船两边束草上排满箭枝。孔明令各船上军士齐声叫曰:"谢丞相箭。"比及曹军寨内报知曹操时,这里船轻水急,已放回二十馀里,追之不及。(第四十六回)

邓译:Zhuge Liang ordered the drums to be kept beating till the sun was high and the fog began to disperse, when the boats got under way and sailed down stream. The whole twenty boats were bristling with arrows on both sides. As they left, Zhuge Liang asked all the crews to shout derisively, "We thank you, Sir Prime Minister, for the arrows!" They told Cao Cao, but by the time he came, the light boats helped by

第五章　古典小说英译的母语译者和非母语译者的定性比较研究

the swift current were seven miles long down the river and pursuit was impossible.

罗译：When the sun climbed, dispersing the fog, Kongming ordered the boats to hurry homeward. The straw bundles bristled with arrow shafts, for which Kongming had each crew shout in unison: "Thanks to the prime minister for the arrows!" By the time this was reported to Cao Cao, the light craft, borne on swift currents, were twenty li downriver, beyond overtaking.

杨译：When the sun rose and the mist began to scatter, he gave orders for a speedy return. By then the straw on all the boats was bristling with arrows, and Zhuge Liang ordered the crews to shout, "Thank you, Cao Cao, for your arrows!" By the time this was reported to Cao Cao, the swift light boats were more than twenty li downstream, and it was impossible to overtake them. Cao Cao was sorry, but there was no help for it.

张译：When the sun rose and the mist began to scatter, he gave orders for a speedy return. By then the straw on all the boats was bristling with arrows, and Zhuge Liang ordered the crews to shout, "Thank you, Cao Cao, for your arrows!" By the time this was reported to Cao Cao, the swift light boats were more than twenty "li" downstream, and it was impossible to overtake them. Cao Cao was sorry, but there was no help for it.

原文是小说原作当中草船借箭的一段描写。草船借箭是小说原作最为精彩的战争故事之一，例文所选取的是故事接近尾声的一段描写，日高雾散、收船急回、船轻水急是其中比较重要的包含动词的描写。对于这3个4字格描写的处理，母语译者和非母语译者存在较大差异。日高雾散，邓译和罗译的处理分别为 the sun was high and the fog began to disperse 和 the sun climbed, dispersing the fog，杨译和张译都将其处理为 the sun rose and the mist began to scatter，邓译和罗译处理"雾散"都使用 disperse，杨译和张译都使用 scatter，《牛津高阶英语词典》对 disperse 和 scatter 的释义如下：

· 231 ·

1. disperse: verb

to move apart and go away in different directions; to make sb/sth do this: [V] The fog began to disperse. The crowd dispersed quickly. [VN] Police dispersed the protesters with tear gas.

to spread or to make sth spread over a wide area: [VN] The seeds are dispersed by the wind. [also V]

2. scatter: verb

[VN] ~ sth. (on/over/around sth)

~ sth. (with sth) to throw or drop things in different directions so that they cover an area of ground: Scatter the grass seed over the lawn. Scatter the lawn with grass seed. They scattered his ashes at sea.

to move or to make people or animals move very quickly in different directions: [V] At the first gunshot, the crowd scattered. [VN] The explosion scattered a flock of birds roosting in the trees.

从以上释义所给的例句中我们可以发现，牛津高阶英语词典在表述"雾散"时使用的是 disperse 一词，例文中母语译者的用词与其是一致的。

对于"日高"，邓译处理为 the sun was high，其静态的表述与原文更为接近，罗译处理为 the sun climbed，与杨译和张译的 the sun rose 相比，较为生动、形象，更具动态感。

"收船急回"邓译处理为 the boats got under way and sailed down stream，罗译处理为 to hurry homeward，杨译和张译都处理为 for a speedy return。邓译和罗译都以动词来再现原文中"收船急回"的行为，杨译和张译使用介词短语来再现这一行为，在表现战争场面的紧急状态和动态感以及对读者的冲击力的效果方面，笔者认为使用动词再现的效果相对更为明显。

"船轻水急"邓译处理为 the light boats helped by the swift current，罗译处理为 the light craft, borne on swift currents，杨译和张译都将其处理为 the swift light boats。两位母语译者具有共同之处，其 light craft 和 swift current/currents，将船轻和水急的意义都较为完整地再现出来，与两位非母语译者相比，对于原文信息的再现更为完整、精确和细腻。

从以上母语译者和非母语译者对于例文中包含动词的重要描述的

第五章　古典小说英译的母语译者和非母语译者的定性比较研究

译文比较分析中,我们可以发现母语译者在母语思维和母语文化背景的影响下,其对于原文中的动词如何在译文中进行再现把握得更为全面、精确和细腻。译者不仅作为译文的创作者,同时也作为译文的读者,以母语读者的思维模式和文化视角去审视译文的效果和艺术特色。邓译和罗译作为母语译者能够以母语思维站在母语读者的立场去审视其译文,在再现原文意义的同时,基于思维模式的影响,与非母语译者相比,能够把意义之外的艺术效果和感染力也予以相对完整和精确地再现出来。所以,从译文对于动词处理的效果来看,母语译者在这方面与非母语译者相比具有其自身的优势。

例 35:

原文:瑜受讫,设宴款待糜竺。竺曰:"孔明在此已久,今愿与同回。"瑜曰:"孔明方与我同谋破曹,岂可便去?"(第四十五回)

邓译: The ceremony of reception was followed by a banquet in honor of the guest. Mi Zhu said, "Zhuge Liang has been here a long time, and I desire that he may return with me." "Zhuge Liang is making plans with me, and I could not let him return," said Zhou Yu.

罗译: Zhou Yu accepted the gifts and called a banquet to welcome Mi Zhu. "Kongming has been here too long," Mi Zhu declared. "I would like to bring him back with me." "But he is consulting with us on the campaign against Cao Cao," said Zhou Yu,

杨译: Zhou Yu, having accepted these, gave a feast to entertain him. "Zhuge Liang has been here a long time," said Mi Zhu. "I should like to take him back with me." Zhou Yu said, "He is advising me on the best way to defeat Cao Cao."

张译: Zhou Yu, having accepted these, gave a feast to entertain him. "Zhuge Liang has been here a long time," said Mi Zhu. " I should like to take him back with me." Zhou Yu said, "He is advising me on the best way to defeat Cao Cao."

原文选取的是曹操占领荆州之后,刘备与孙权准备共同抵抗曹操时的一段描写。当时曹操已经占领荆州,刘备令刘琦守江夏,自己与众将领带兵前往夏口,而被其派往东吴游说孙权抗曹的诸葛亮一直没有消息,刘备便决定派糜竺带上羊酒礼物去东吴,以犒军为名打探虚实。糜竺的身份实际上是刘备一方的特使,其去东吴是具有政治性质的外交活动,所以周瑜设宴款待也是縻竺外交活动的一部分,同时也是其中一个重要环节,参加宴会的应该双方所有的重要官员和将领。基于此,原文中所说的宴会应该具有规模较大、人数较多、比较正式和官方性质等特征。原文的"设宴款待縻竺",邓译处理为 was followed by a banquet in honor of the guest,罗译处理为 called a banquet to welcome Mi Zhu,杨译和张译都处理为 gave a feast to entertain him。两位母语译者将原文的核心词"宴"用 banquet 来处理,两位非母语译者则都用 feast 来处理。牛津高阶英语词典对 banquet 和 feast 作为名词的释义如下:

Banquet: noun, a formal meal for a large number of people, usually for a special occasion, at which speeches are often made: a state banquet in honour of the visiting President, a large impressive meal.

feast: noun (formal), a large or special meal, especially for a lot of people and to celebrate sth: a wedding feast; a day or period of time when there is a religious festival: the feast of Christmas, a feast day; [usually sing.] a thing or an event that brings great pleasure: a feast of colours, The evening was a real feast for music lovers.

根据以上牛津高阶英语词典的释义,我们可以发现与非母语译者的处理相比,母语译者的处理与原文设宴的规模较大、人数较多、比较正式和官方性质等特征更为接近。

例 36:

原文:操大惊,急聚众谋士商议曰:"吾引兵南征,心中所忧者,韩遂、马腾耳。军中谣言虽未辨虚实,然不可不防。"(第四十八回)

邓译:This troubled Cao Cao, who called together his advisers to council. Said he, "The only anxiety I have felt in this expedition was about the possible doings of Han Sui and Ma Teng. Now there is a rumor running among the soldiers, and though I know not whether it be true or false, it is necessary to be on one's guard."

罗译:Alarmed, Cao Cao summoned his advisers. "My greatest concern when I undertook this expedition," he said, "was the danger from the west, Han Sui and Ma Teng. Whether the current rumors are true or not, we must take measures."

杨译:Startled by this news, Cao Cao promptly summoned his advisers and said, "My one anxiety on this expedition has been Han Sui

第五章 古典小说英译的母语译者和非母语译者的定性比较研究

and Ma Teng in the rear. Now this rumour has spread through the army. Though there may be no truth in it, we must be on our guard."

张译：Startled by this news, Cao Cao promptly summoned his advisers and said, "My one anxiety on this expedition has been Han Sui and Ma Teng in the rear. Now this rumour has spread through the army. Though there may be no truth in it we must be on our guard."

原文选自赤壁之战中庞统向曹操献上连环计之后，徐庶向其请教脱身之策，庞统教其在军中散布韩遂、马腾谋反的流言，在曹操担忧并抽调人马设防之时，趁机自荐去散关把守隘口，从而得以免受火烧连营的牵连。当时曹操攻打东吴，大后方的稳定对其前方战事的顺利推进最为重要，而西北的韩遂、马腾是其在后方最为担心和忌惮的力量，一旦有这两人谋反的谣言出现，其便不得不防。原文"吾引兵南征，心中所忧者，韩遂、马腾耳。军中谣言虽未辨虚实，然不可不防"正反映了当时曹操担忧的心态，其中"心中所忧者"恰如其分地表现了韩遂、马腾是其南征最为担忧和忌惮的力量的事实。原文的"心中所忧者"隐含了说话人曹操担忧的两个方面：一是其南征最担心的是韩遂、马腾，体现了对于韩遂、马腾担忧的程度，因为其在实力上和军队数量上远胜东吴，所以对于战胜东吴并不是很担心；二是突出了说话人曹操对于韩遂、马腾担忧的唯一性，这并不是说曹操没有其他的担忧，而是说其真正担忧的是韩遂、马腾。《三国演义》原文语言精练，往往字数不多，但其含义深刻、凝练，所以译者在翻译时，需要精确再现原文的意义和遣词造句的风格。

对于"心中所忧者"，母语译者邓译处理为 The only anxiety，较为有效地再现了原文说话人曹操对韩遂、马腾担忧的程度和唯一性特征，很好地诠释了当时曹操南征时必胜的信心和对于韩遂、马腾担忧的心态；罗译处理为 My greatest concern，突出再现了原文说话人曹操担忧的程度，同时隐含了其真正担忧的唯一性，较为有效地再现了原文的意义和风格。非母语译者杨译和张译的处理方式一致，都将其处理为 My one anxiety，较为有效地再现了原文的意义和说话人曹操担忧的程度。与非母语译者的处理相比，两位母语译者的处理在再现原文意义的精确性和曹操担忧的程度及唯一性的特征方面更为有效，对于人物当时的心态和战争局势的衬托以及人物形象的塑造更为出色。

5.5 自然环境描写的英译比较

  自然环境的描写在小说中一般都占有重要的地位。自然环境描写是反映作品所处的时代背景以及故事场景所在的自然风貌的最基本的手段和方法，此外，自然环境的描写对故事情节的推动以及烘托氛围和人物的形象等都具有不可替代的重要作用，同时，自然环境的描写还可以反映作者独特的观察事物的方法和视角及其描写手法，是小说中重要的描写内容。就《三国演义》来说，人物对话和政治军事斗争场面的描写占有很大比例，自然环境的描写所占比例较小，但其对小说人物形象的塑造和烘托，对各种政治军事战斗场面的烘托等都具有重要作用。此外，《三国演义》的自然环境描写，在小说中所占比例较小，但其语言精练，言简意赅，用较少的文字浓缩了所描写对象的整体风貌和特征。笔者通过仔细比较《三国演义》的三个全译本和四个节译本，发现母语译者和非母语译者对于自然环境描写的处理也存在较大差异，例37是比较有代表性的例子，其具体情况如下。

  例37：
  原文：是时东风大作，波浪汹涌。操在中军遥望隔江，看看月上，照耀江水，如万道金蛇翻波戏浪。操迎风大笑，自以为得志。（第四十九回）
  邓译：The wind was strong and the waves ran high. Cao Cao in the midst of the central squadron eagerly scanned the river which rolled down under the bright moon like a silver serpent writhing in innumerable folds. Letting the wind blow full in his face, Cao Cao laughed aloud for he was now to obtain his desire.
  罗译：By now the gale was in full motion. Waves and whitecaps surged tumultuously. Cao Cao scanned the river and watched the rising moon. Its reflections flickered over the waters, turning the river into myriad golden serpents rolling and sporting in the waves. Cao faced the wind and smiled, thinking he would achieve his ambition.

第五章 古典小说英译的母语译者和非母语译者的定性比较研究

杨译：The strong easterly wind was making the waves pitch and toss. Cao Cao from his camp was watching the opposite shore. When the moon rose over the river, countless golden serpents seemed to be rolling in the waves. With the wind in his face, Cao Cao laughed aloud, sure of success.

张译：The strong easterly wind was making the waves pitch and toss. Cao Cao from his camp was watching the opposite shore. When the moon rose over the river, countless golden serpents seemed to be rolling in the waves. With the wind in his face. Cao Cao laughed aloud, sure of success.

原文描写的是周瑜火烧赤壁的当夜，曹操得到黄盖的书信，约定当夜二更前来投降，曹操大喜过望，在军中遥望对岸，等待黄盖船只时的情景。其中自然环境的描写对当时战前自然条件的说明，对战争主角之一曹操当时心情和心态的烘托，对战前和战后场景的对比都具有重要作用。当时周瑜准备火烧曹操连营的一切准备都已就绪，但当时正值隆冬季节，西北风正盛，所以曹操预先对于火攻并没有在意和提防。原文中首先描写的是东风大作，表明影响战争胜负最重要的自然因素东风已经出现，为接下来的战争叙事作自然条件方面的铺垫；原文中的"看看月上，照耀江水，如万道金蛇翻波戏浪"，对当时江上的环境进行了描写，展现了战争爆发前的场景，除了风大浪急以外，在月光的照耀下，一切都很平静，与之后火烧连营的激烈战况及战后的狼藉形成了鲜明的对照；在月光下平静的自然环境，衬托出战争主角之一曹操掌控一切的心理，江面汹涌的波涛则是曹操心中壮志和抱负的一种写照和反映，这些描写都为接下来曹操的大笑和"自以为得志"作了极佳的铺垫，同时对于曹操当时的心理也是一种衬托，从而对于人物形象的塑造也起到了重要作用。

对于原文这一段自然环境的描写，两位母语译者和两位非母语译者的处理存在较大差异。在句式方面，母语译者和非母语译者存在差异。两位非母语译者的处理一致，两者都是使用两个主谓结构的句子和一个主从复合句，共3句来完成原文两个整句的翻译。第一句句子的结构为主语＋谓语＋宾语＋补语，第二句句子的结构为主语＋谓语＋宾语，第三句时间状语从句的结构为主语＋谓语＋状语，主句的结构为主语＋系动词＋表语。这3句的句式结构基本一致，结构相对比较单一。两位母语译者的句式结构相对比较复杂。邓译使用两句来完成原文两句的翻译,第一句为 and 连接的两个并列句,第一个分句的结构为主语+系动词+表语,第二个分句的结构为主语+谓语+状语;第二句的结构较为复杂,其主句的结构为主语+地点状语+方式状语+谓语+宾语,定语从句的结构为主语+谓语+地点状语+方式状语,而其方式状语是一个结构较为复杂的介词短语。整体来看,邓译的句式结构比两位非母语译者的句式结构更为复杂和灵活。罗译使用 4 句来完成原文两句的翻译,第一句的结构为时间状语+主语+系动词+表语,第二句的结构为主语+谓语+状语,第三句的结构为主语+谓语+宾语+并列谓语+宾语,第四句的结构为主语+谓语+地点状语+伴随状语;伴随状语是一个结构比较复杂的现在分词短语。整体来看,罗译的句式结构与两位非母语译者相比也更为复杂和灵活。

  从形式上来看,两位母语译者与两位非母语译者相比,对于原文的形式在某种程度上进行了再现。邓译的第一句较短,第二句较长,使其译文在整体形式上与原文具有某种相似性。从句子内部来看,邓译的第一句为两个结构较为简单的分句组成的并列句,与原文第一句的两个四字格为主构成的句子在形式上也具有某种相似性;邓译的第二句的句子成分多由介词短语、动宾结构、动词短语构成,这些句子成分内部的结构或短语长短大体相当,与原文第二句内部多由四字格构成在形式上也具有某种相似性。罗译的第一句较短,后面的三句句子成分内部多由名词短语、动宾结构、介词短语、分词短语构成,这些短语或结构长短也大体相当,与原文第二句在形式上也具有某种相似性。同时,由于形式上与原文的相似性,邓译和罗译在节奏方面某种程度上再现了原文四字结构所具有的节奏感。

  原文"自以为得志"是在自然环境描写的衬托下,直观描述战争主角之一的曹操认为自己即将实现生平"扫清四海,削平天下"的政治抱负时志得意满的心理状态。"自以为得志"至少包含两层意义:一是体现曹操对即将实现政治抱负的自信和得意,这层意义对于刻画曹操在小说中"奸雄"的人物形象具有重要作用;二是体现曹操对于在决战中战胜东吴的自信和得意,这层意义有助于刻画曹操性格中自负的一面。母语译者邓译对其的处理为 he was now to obtain his desire,罗译的处理为 thinking he would achieve his ambition;非母语译者杨译和张译都将其处理为 sure of success。两位非母语译者的处理略显倾向于缩小

· 238 ·

第五章　古典小说英译的母语译者和非母语译者的定性比较研究

原文意义的范围,对于人物展现即将实现政治抱负的自信和得意的再现略显不足;两位母语译者的处理都较为有效地再现了原文所包含的两层意义,从而比较成功地再现了原文对于人物形象和性格的刻画,与非母语译者相比,其对于原文意义、人物形象的塑造以及性格刻画显得更为充分和饱满。

5.6　本章小结

定量分析和定性分析两者相辅相成,互为支撑,定量分析使用语料库统计分析软件对特定文本进行统计和定量分析,其所得出的结论更为科学和客观;定性分析则对文本进行定性的性质分析,具有主观性和哲学思辨的性质。没有定性分析,定量分析就缺乏质性的判断和界定,其数据也失去意义,定性分析如果没有定量分析作支撑,就会滑向主观片面性。

本章的研究首先确定了研究方法、目标、范围以及步骤,旨在使用定性研究的方法从战斗场面描写、动词、否定词、自然环境描写4个有代表性的视角进行定性分析,从定性描写研究的视角来探讨母语译者相较于非母语译者的区别性特征,并用第四章定量分析的数据作支撑,从而使母语译者和非母语译者的比较研究更为全面和系统。在此基础上,本章研究对《三国演义》三个英文全译本和四个英文节译本的母语译者和非母语译者的译文进行了定性的对比分析,发现母语译者的译文相较于非母语译者在战斗场面描写、动词、否定词、自然环境描写方面具有一定的区别性特征,从而使对于《三国演义》三个英文全译本和四个英文节译本的母语译者和非母语译者的译文比较研究更为全面和系统,对于"母语优势"的验证也更为全面,并为后续的探究汉英翻译策略提供支持。

第六章 母语译者的区别性特征对汉英翻译策略的启示

6.1 词汇层面的特征

本研究的第四章、第五章的研究表明,古典小说《三国演义》三个英文全译本和四个英文节译本的母语译者和非母语译者之间存在较大差异。从定量分析的研究结果来看,母语译者相较于非母语译者在词汇、句子以及篇章三个层面存在区别性特征;从定性分析的研究结果来看,母语译者相较于非母语译者对原文的再现更为充实和自然。母语译者相较于非母语译者的这些区别性特征反映了母语译者在母语思维模式和母语文化的影响下在词汇、句子和篇章层面处理的一些特征,在一定程度上也反映了母语思维模式和母语语言使用习惯的某些特征。

词汇是组成文本的最基础的成分,其词汇使用的数量和类型特征很大程度上影响着文本的风格和特征,不论是句子层面还是篇章层面的特征最终都取决于词汇层面的某些特征,并由这些词汇层面的特征来反映和体现。母语译者相较于非母语译者在词汇层面的特征是母语优势在词汇层面的具体体现,一定程度上反映了母语思维模式和母语语言使用习惯的某些特征。下面本研究将从总体词汇、句法功能词、具体词汇三个方面来整理总结《三国演义》英译的母语译者相较于非母语译者的词汇特征。

第六章 母语译者的区别性特征对汉英翻译策略的启示

6.1.1 总体词汇

母语译者相较于非母语译者在词汇方面的一个重要特征是其译文的形符数和类符数都在一定幅度多于非母语译者。《三国演义》英文全译本和四个英文节译本母语译者的类符数都以较大幅度多于非母语译者;形符数方面,除了虞译的形符数以一定幅度多于罗译外,其余不论全译本还是节译本所有母语译者的形符数都以较大幅度多于非母语译者。虞译的形符数多于罗译本并不影响母语译者译文的形符数较多的倾向性。就虞译的形符数多于罗译的原因来说,从虞译本产生的时间和其译文具体内容与其他两位母语译者的译文相比较来看,笔者认为主要在于两个方面:一是随着时间的推移,随着我国翻译事业的发展和繁荣,随着我国翻译理论研究与实践的发展和进步,我国译者在汉籍英译方面出现某些母语译者在母语优势下的某些特征便成为可能;二是作为最晚出现的译本,虞译本应该参考了其他几个译本,避免或借鉴了其他译本的某些翻译策略和方法。本研究在第四章的4.2.1有关形符一节对其进行了详细分析,此处不再赘述。朱自清散文英译的母语译者的形符数和类符数都以一定幅度多于其他三位非母语译者。本研究第四章、第五章的研究结果表明除了虞译的形符数之外,《三国演义》和朱自清散文英译的母语译者的形符数和类符数都具有多于非母语译者的倾向性。

形符数与类符数相比,类符数具有更为基础性和决定性的意义。类符数的多少直接反映了译文所使用词汇种类的多少,是反映和体现译文词汇丰富与否的重要指标,在一定程度上影响并反映了译文对于原文风格再现的细腻程度和精确性。类符数在某种程度上也是影响形符数大小的一个重要因素,译文所使用的类符数的大小在一定程度上影响着其形符数的大小即译文的长度。

母语译者的类符数以一定幅度多于非母语译者是母语译者相较于非母语译者的一个重要特征。从《三国演义》三个英文全译本和四个英文节译本来看,母语译者除了总类符数较高之外,其类符数较高的特征还体现在动词、名词、副词、形容词以及介词和从属连词的类符数多于非母语译者。这说明《三国演义》英译的母语译者是从整体到各子类的类符数都多于非母语译者,这使母语译者不仅在译文的整体上由于类符数较高而更为细腻和精确,更重要的是由于其在名词、动词等各子类的类符数较高而使其对与原文相关的背景信息和人物行为动作等方面的再现也更为细腻和精确。

6.1.2 名词

就名词来说,《三国演义》母语译者的名词类符数都多于非母语译者。本研究在第四章所统计的《三国演义》的全译本和节译本的名词形符和类符数都是指除了人名之外的名词形符和类符数,所以母语译者名词类符数较高的特征对于其译文再现原文中相关的背景信息具有重要作用。我们有必要对母语译者名词类符数较高的具体体现和背后的原因进行梳理和探讨,以便为我们在汉译英时进行借鉴和参考。

从本研究第四章对《三国演义》全译本和节译本的统计来看,独特名词是体现母语译者名词类符数较高的一个重要指标。全译本两位母语译者使用频次合计 6 次以上的独特名词共 126 个,非母语译者使用频次 6 次以上的独特名词共 9 个;节译本两位母语译者的使用频次合计 5 次以上的独特名词共 53 个,两位非母语译者的使用频次合计 5 次以上的独特名词共 13 个。母语译者的独特名词以较大幅度多于非母语译者是母语译者名词类符数较多的具体体现。从全译本母语译者的独特名词中我们可以发现,与原文相关的政治背景信息词汇占有较大比重。笔者推测造成这一现象的一个重要原因是母语译者在母语思维模式和母语文化的影响下能够站在目的语读者的立场并用目的语读者的文化需求来审视译文中相关的政治背景信息,采取恰当的翻译策略使相关信息得以再现。

母语译者名词类符数较高的另外一个原因是母语译者对于原文中的某些词或短语多根据其上下文的语境进行灵活处理,而非母语译者多侧重原文词汇意义的再现,因而相同的词汇在不同上下文的语境中处理方式多数倾向于一致。母语译者的名词类符数多于非母语译者本身就是其对于相同词汇或短语在不同语境中使用不同方式处理的结果,同时也是母语译者对于原文的处理更为灵活细腻的体现。从第五章对于《三国演义》三个英文全译本和四个英文节译本的定性比较分析中,我们也可以发现在对原文战争场面描写、自然环境描写以及动词、否定词的英译中,母语译者的处理相较于非母语译者更为灵活和细腻,对于相同或

第六章 母语译者的区别性特征对汉英翻译策略的启示

相似的表达,在不同的语境中会使用不同的词汇或以不同的方式进行处理。需要指出的是,这并不意味着非母语译者对于原文相同或相似的词汇在不同的语境中就不会使用不同的词汇或不同的方式进行处理,而是指相对来说,非母语译者在更大概率上会侧重原文词汇意义的再现,从而在不同的语境中多数使用相同或相似的处理方式,与母语译者相比,相对缺乏灵活性。非母语译者的这种倾向性反过来又促成了其词汇类符数相对较少的现象和特征。

另一个原因是与非母语译者相比,母语译者在母语思维模式和母语文化的影响下对于目的语词汇和短语在不同上下文中的把握更为精确和细腻,对于原文中不同语境下的同义词或近义词以及同一表达法能使用意义和用法更为细腻的同义词或近义词以及不同的表达法进行处理,使其译文对于原文的再现更为精确和细腻。需要指出的是,母语译者由于母语思维模式好和母语文化的影响而对于目的语词汇和短语在不同上下文中的把握更为精确和细腻并不是指母语译者对于具体词汇或短语以及表达法的掌握好于非母语译者,或非母语译者的掌握好于母语译者,而是指在母语思维模式和母语文化的影响下,母语译者能够不受原文表层结构和词汇意义的约束,依据语境的变化恰当变换和调整词汇及其他表达方式的现象。造成母语译者名词类符数相对较高这一特征的深层次原因是母语译者在母语思维模式和母语译文化影响下充分发挥其译入语优势,灵活使用词汇和其他表达方式来再现原文的意义和风格。

6.1.3 动词

动词对于英语语言来说是极其重要的词类之一,实义动词主要用来表示人或事物的动作、行为、态度、存在、变化以及趋向等,是一个表达完整意义的句子不可或缺的重要词类;情态动词、系动词以及助动词最重要的作用之一则是其语法功能。对于文学作品来说,动词的使用情况对于整部作品都具有重要意义和影响。《三国演义》作为一部以政治军事斗争为主轴的历史小说,政治军事斗争的场景描写,尤其是战争场面的描写以及人物行为和动作的描写在整部小说中占有很大比重,因此译文如何处理这些包含大量动词的描写以及译文中动词的使用情况对于其再现原文中的这些包含大量动词描写的效果具有重要影响。考察并梳理《三国演义》三个英文全译本和四个英文节译本的母语译者相较于非母语译者的特征，对于我国古典小说以及文学作品的英译都具有一定的参考价值和借鉴意义。

《三国演义》三个英文全译本和四个英文节译本母语译者的动词类符数多于非母语译者是母语译者相较于非母语译者的重要区别性特征之一。从本研究第四章对《三国演义》全译本和节译本的统计来看，全译本两位母语译者使用频次合计4次以上的独特动词共计150个，非母语译者使用频次4次以上的独特动词共计9个；节译本两位母语译者使用频次合计4次以上的独特动词共计68个，两位非母语译者使用频次合计4次以上的独特动词共计39个，这在一定程度上反映了母语译者的动词类符数相较于非母语译者较高的特征。母语译者的这一特征使其译文对于原文中占有很大比重的政治军事斗争的场面描写尤其是人物的行为动作描写的再现相对更为精确和细腻，本研究在第五章已对此做过具体的比较分析。

母语译者的动词类符数较高原因与名词类符数较高的原因是一致的，包括母语译者能够站在目的语读者的立场审视译文，能够对原文相同的词汇依据语境的不同对词汇进行相对更为灵活的处理，以及对于译文词汇的把握更为精准和细腻等。从深层次的原因来说，母语译者在母语思维模式和母语文化的影响下，充分发挥译入语优势，灵活使用不同种类的动词对原文中人物的动作、行为、心理活动或事物的变化、发展等进行处理，从而对原文政治军事斗争等场面描写的再现更为细腻和精确。具体表现为对于原文中相同的动词在不同的语境中使用不同的动词或其他方式进行处理，而非母语译者往往受原文表层结构的约束较多，更侧重译文与原文词汇和意义的对等，处理方式相对没有母语译者灵活。母语译者和非母语译者的这一差异体现为母语译者的动词类符数以一定幅度多于非母语译者，以及母语译者的特色动词的数量也多于非母语译者。母语译者在动词类符数多于非母语译者的基础上，特色动词的数量也多于非母语译者，表明母语译者的译文相较于非母语译者对于动词的使用更为灵活和多样，从而在一定程度上影响了其对于原文政治军事斗争等场面描写的再现。

《三国演义》全译本母语译者的特色动词共计20个，非母语译者的特色动词共计4个；节译本母语译者的特色动词共计10个，非母语译者的特色动词共计6个。全译本非母语译者的特色动词包括

第六章 母语译者的区别性特征对汉英翻译策略的启示

challenge、stir、launch、revealed,节译本非母语译者的特色动词包括 kill、surrender、dare、defeat、hope、killed。从非母语译者的特色动词来看,多是原文中意义对等词汇的重复使用的结果,而母语译者对于其使用频次远少于非母语译者,是其依据语境的不同,使用不同的词汇或表达方式的结果,这也说明非母语译者更侧重于原文表层结构或词汇意义的对等。这一定程度上是非母语译者采用翻译策略的结果,但更深层次的原因是其在翻译的过程中受非母语思维模式影响的结果,尤其是几位非母语译者与几位母语译者相比较表现出相同的特征和倾向性,说明母语思维模式和母语文化的影响所起的作用相对更大。

6.1.4 具体词汇

母语译者在词汇层面相较于非母语译者的区别性特征除了整体类符数以及各子类包括名词、动词、形容词、副词、介词和从属连词等的类符数较高之外,还表现在某些具体词汇的使用上。本研究第四章的研究表明,母语译者对于某些词汇的使用具有明显不同于非母语译者的特征,这些词汇主要是母语译者受母语思维模式和母语文化影响的结果,是母语译者的母语思维模式和母语文化在词汇使用方面的突出体现,某种程度上体现了母语思维模式和母语文化在文学尤其是小说方面的用词特征和风格。这些词汇主要包括在母语译者相较于非母语译者的高频词和特色词当中。

根据本研究第四章的 4.2.3.1 小节高频名词的研究结果,time 的使用频次在《三国演义》三个英文全译本和四个英文节译本的名词类中都排第一位,这与 time 在 BNC 名词类中的排序是一致的,但其母语译者的使用频次要低于非母语译者的使用频次,其原因在于母语译者对于原文中的时间概念会依据不同的上下文语境使用不同的词汇或是表达方式进行翻译,使其译文当中对于时间概念的表述较为多样化,对于原文时间概念在不同语境中的细腻的差异进行了再现,而非母语译者多使用 time 来表达不同语境下的时间概念,缺少变化。

根据 BNC 的词频统计,have 的使用频次在动词类中排第一位,will 的使用频次在动词类中排第三位,两者在英语语言中都属于使用频次较高的动词。就高频动词来看,《三国演义》三个全译本和四个节译本的 have 和 will 都是使用频次排序靠前的动词,这与 BNC 的统计相吻合。《三国演义》全译本母语译者have的使用频次都高于非母语译者，对于will的使用频次略低于非母语译者；四个节译本中，除了罗译（节译）的have的使用频次（208~210次）略低于张译（节译）之外，其他三位母语译者have和will的使用频次都高于非母语译者，同时鉴于虞译本翻译完成的年代以及与两位母语译者的译本的比较来看，在某种程度上应该把对于will的使用频次较高看作是母语译者的一个特征。这说明have和will是英语语言中使用频次较高的动词，在进行汉英翻译尤其是文本较大的文学作品的汉英翻译时，应注意其在英语语言中较高频次使用的特征。

就特色词来说，《三国演义》母语译者值得注意的特色动词是begin（began/begun/beginning）和play（played/playing），其余的特色动词多数是与《三国演义》原文的描写内容相关性较为密切的动词。这两个动词在文本较大的文学作品中其使用受作品内容和题材的影响和约束相对较小，在英语语言中，其使用范围相对较广。母语译者对于begin（began/begun/beginning）和play（played/playing）的使用频次以较大幅度高于非母语译者，而且对于其相关的搭配使用频次也比较高，其中对于begin（began/begun/beginning）和play（played/playing）的相关搭配及常用句式的使用，不论是全译本还是节译本，母语译者都以一定幅度高于非母语译者。其中begin（began/begun）作为母语译者的特色动词还得到了《红楼梦》英译本霍译和杨译的支持，play（played/playing）的使用频次，霍译也以一定幅度高于杨译。

《三国演义》英文节译本母语译者值得注意的特色形容词是own和little，这两个词母语译者的使用频次以较大幅度高于非母语译者，在英文全译本中，母语译者对于little的使用频次也以一定幅度高于非母语译者，对于own的使用频次，全译本的邓译本与虞译本相接近，罗译本略低于虞译本，但罗译本own的排序要比虞译本的靠前。母语译者对于own和little的较高频次的使用也得到了参照语料库10部英文原创小说和《红楼梦》母语译者的支持。这两个形容词在文本较大的文学作品中的使用受作品内容和题材的影响和约束也相对较小，使用范围相对较广，其较高频率的使用对我们文学作品的汉英翻译具有一定的参考价值。

《三国演义》英文全译本和节译本母语译者值得注意的特色介词和从属连词包括upon、though、beyond，其中though同时是全译本和节

第六章 母语译者的区别性特征对汉英翻译策略的启示

译本母语译者的特色从属连词,beyond 是全译本母语译者的特色介词,upon 是节译本母语译者的特色介词,upon 和 beyond 作为特色介词得到了《红楼梦》英文全译本霍译的支持。母语译者对于 upon 和 beyond 以及 though 较高频率的使用对于我们文学作品的汉英翻译具有一定的参考价值。

另外一个值得特别关注的现象是否定词的使用,《三国演义》全译本和节译本的非母语译者对于情态动词、助动词以及系动词的否定缩写形式的使用频次远高于母语译者。在第五章否定词的英译一节,本研究对《三国演义》母语译者和非母语译者对原文否定词的处理进行了定性的比较分析,发现非母语译者多使用情态动词、助动词以及系动词的否定缩写形式来处理原文的否定词,而母语译者多根据原文上下文的语境以及说话人的语气和口吻进行灵活处理,相比较而言,对于原文说话人的语气和口吻的再现更为充实,更有助于译文对于原文人物形象的再现。

6.2 对汉英翻译策略的启示

母语译者相较于非母语译者在词汇层面的特征是母语优势在词汇层面的具体体现,一定程度上反映了母语思维模式和母语语言使用习惯的某些特征,这些特征对我们进一步认知汉英翻译目的语的特征和使用习惯并在翻译中完善翻译策略具有一定的参考和借鉴价值。下面本研究将在上一节对《三国演义》英译的母语译者相较于非母语译者的词汇特征的基础上,从总体词汇、名词、动词、具体词汇几个方面提出基于母语优势的汉英翻译的词汇策略。

6.2.1 总体词汇策略

《三国演义》三个英文全译本和四个英文节译本母语译者的类符数都以一定幅度多于非母语译者,母语译者的类符数较高是母语译者区别于非母语译者的一个重要特征。母语译者的这一特征使其译文从整体上来说对原文的再现相对更为充实。类符数是影响译文对于原文内容和风格整体再现效果的重要因素,母语译者类符数较高的特征对我们汉英文学翻译具有一定的参考价值,即在以再现原文的内容和风格为目标的基础上,应注重译文整体类符数的大小,尽可能提高译文的整体类符数,使译文对于原文内容和风格的再现更为充实。

6.2.2 名词策略

名词是文学作品中最重要的词类之一,是小说信息的重要载体,其使用情况反映了小说人物、政治背景、时代风貌、自然环境等重要信息。《三国演义》三个英文全译本和四个英文节译本的母语译者的名词类符较高是母语译者相较于非母语译者的一个重要区别性特征。基于母语译者的这一特征对其译文再现原文的内容和风格的重要作用,我们文学外译应该注重译文名词类符数的大小,应尽可能地提高译文的名词类符数,使译文对于原文人物、政治背景、时代风貌、自然环境等信息的承载更为详细和充实。

针对本章在上一小节名词部分所分析的母语译者名词类符数较高的原因,笔者提出以下具有针对性的文学外译的名词策略。首先应尽可能地转换思维模式,站在目的语读者的立场用目的语的文化来审视译文,一定程度上依据目的语读者对原文所承载信息的需要来引导译文名词的使用,注重译文的名词类符数,使译文对于原文相关的人物、政治背景、时代风貌、自然环境等信息的承载更为详细和充实。其次尽可能转换思维模式并用母语文化的视角去审视译文的上下文语境,对于原文中相同或相似的词汇依据不同的上下文语境恰当使用不同的词汇或表达方式进行处理以期译文效果更为充实和细腻。

6.2.3 动词策略

动词对于英语语言来说是其最为重要的词类之一,在文学作品中,动词的使用情况对于整部作品都具有重要意义和影响。《三国演义》母语译者的动词类符数较高也是其区别于非母语译者的一个重要特征,母语译者的这一特征对于其译文更好地再现原文政治军事斗争场面的描写具有重要作用。针对本章在上一小节动词部分所分析的母语译者动词类符数较高的原因,笔者提出以下有针对性的文学外译的动词策略。

第六章 母语译者的区别性特征对汉英翻译策略的启示

首先也应尽可能地转换思维模式,站在目的语读者的立场用目的语的文化来审视译文,依据原文词汇的不同上下文语境来使用不同的动词或其他表达方式来进行处理,注重译文的动词类符数,使译文对于原文相关动词和包含动词的描写再现得更为充实细腻。

6.2.4 具体词汇策略

母语译者除了在整体类符数以及各子类的类符数多于非母语译者外,在某些具体词汇的使用上也表现出明显不同于非母语译者的特征。这些词汇在上一节中已作了详细梳理,本小节将依据母语译者对这些词汇的使用特征提出文学外译中关于这些词汇的相关翻译策略。

《三国演义》英译本中体现母语译者词汇使用特征的具体词汇主要是母语译者的高频词、特色词和独特词,这些词主要包括高频名词 time,高频动词 have 和 will,特色动词 begin(began/begun/beginning)和 play(played/playing),特色形容词 own 和 little,特色介词 upon 和 beyond,特色从属连词 though。此外,相较于非母语译者对于情态动词、助动词以及系动词的否定缩写形式较低频率的使用,也是母语译者的具体词汇使用特征。

对于文本较大的文学作品来说,母语译者对于以上词汇较高频率的使用对于我们的文学外译具有一定的参考价值。对于 time 在注重其较高频次使用的同时,要注意对原文中的时间概念应依据不同的上下文语境使用不同的词汇或是表达方式进行处理,增强时间概念表达的多样化,以期更为有效地再现原文中的时间概念。在较大文本文学作品的汉英翻译中,注重 have 和 will 较高频次的使用,使译文中 have 和 will 的使用更为接近原创文本的使用特征,从而在整体上有助于增强译文的地道性;注重在译文中对于 begin(began/begun/beginning)和 play(played/playing)及其相关搭配或句式的较高频率的使用,注重形容词 own 和 little 的较高频次的使用,注重介词 upon 和 beyond 以及从属连词 though 的较高频次的使用,使译文更为接近英语的语言使用习惯,以期使其语言更为地道和自然。此外,注重对于原文中否定词的翻译,要依据上下文的语境灵活使用情态动词、助动词以及系动词的否定缩写形式或其他否定形式和表达法进行处理,以期更为有效地再现原文的语气和口吻。

6.3　句子层面的特征及翻译策略

《三国演义》英文全译本和节译本母语译者在句子层面相较于非母语译者也存在一定的区别性特征。其区别性特征主要表现在对于句首词 and、非谓语动词的 ing 形式以及逗号的较高频次的使用三个方面。母语译者对于句首词 and 较高频次的使用使其译文相较于非母语译者的译文句子之间和语篇整体更为衔接和连贯；对于逗号和非谓语动词 ing 形式较高频次的使用一定程度上表明其译文的句子结构相较于非母语译者的译文更为复杂，在一定程度上有助于避免其译文句式结构的相对单一性。

《三国演义》英文全译本和节译本母语译者在句子层面相较于非母语译者的区别性特征体现了母语译者在母语思维模式的影响下在句子层面相对较少受原文表层结构的影响，充分发挥译入语优势，使其译文在句子结构方面相较于非母语译者的译文更为复杂，避免了句子结构的相对单一性。参照母语译者在句子层面的特征，我们在进行文学外译时，尽可能地转换思维模式，避免原文表层结构的影响和约束，在以有效再现原文的内容和风格为目的的同时，应尽可能通过较高频次地使用逗号和非谓语动词的 ing 形式，增强句子结构的复杂性，避免句子结构的相对单一性，同时应尽可能通过句首词 and 较高频次的使用以期增强句子之间和篇章整体的衔接性和连贯性。

6.4　篇章层面的特征及翻译策略

母语译者在篇章层面的特征主要表现为对于代词 it 和 its 相较于

第六章 母语译者的区别性特征对汉英翻译策略的启示

非母语译者较高频次的使用,母语译者的这一特征增强了其译文的语篇衔接性和连贯性。参照母语译者在语篇层面的这一特征,我们在进行文学外译时应尽可能地转换思维模式,避免原文表层结构的影响和约束,在以有效再现原文的内容和风格为目的的同时,尽可能通过对于代词 it 和 its 较高频次的使用来增强语篇整体的衔接性和连贯性。

6.5 本章小结

本章研究主要在第四章和第五章研究结果的基础上,对《三国演义》三个英文全译本和四个英文节译本的母语译者在词汇、句子、篇章层面的特征进行了概括总结,进而在此基础上提出了我国文学的汉英翻译策略。在词汇层面主要基于母语译者类符数较高的特征提出汉英翻译时注重提高类符数的策略,类符数的大小对于译文再现原文从意义到风格的所有内容都具有重要影响。母语译者和非母语译者在类符数方面的差异主要体现和反映了两者在翻译观、翻译策略、思维模式和语言使用习惯等方面的差异,母语译者更多体现和反映了其母语思维和母语语言习惯的特征,非母语译者则表现为受原文表层结构的约束程度较深。所以翻译中类符数较高是表现和结果,翻译策略和方法是转变思维模式,发挥目的语语言使用习惯的优势,尽可能地再现原文从意义到风格的所有内容。

在句子层面,基于母语译者的句子特征提出了句子层面的翻译策略。母语译者在句子层面的特征表现为句子结构相对比较复杂,主要表现为句首词 and、逗号、非谓语动词 ing 形式的使用频次比较高,所以在汉英翻译时,要转换思维模式,通过使用句首词 and、逗号、非谓语动词 ing 形式等方法,提高句子的复杂度,增强译文的衔接性和流畅性。

在篇章层面,基于母语译者篇章层面的特征提出了篇章层面的翻译策略。母语译者在篇章层面的特征主要表现为对于代词 it 和 its 较高频次的使用,母语译者的这一特征增强了其译文的语篇衔接性和连贯性。参照母语译者在语篇层面的这一特征,我们在进行文学外译时应尽可能地转换思维模式,避免原文表层结构的影响和约束,在以有效再现原文的内容和风格为目的的同时,尽可能通过对于代词 it 和 its 较高频次的使用来增强语篇整体的衔接性和连贯性。

第七章 结 论

本研究在语料库翻译学的框架下,借助语料库统计分析软件对《三国演义》的 3 个译文全译本和 2 个英文节译本的母语译者和非母语译者的译文进行了定量研究和定性研究。本研究通过定量研究发现母语译者与非母语译者在词汇、句子、篇章层面上都存在较为明显的区别性特征;定性研究的范围涉及战斗场面描写、动词、自然环境描写以及否定词共 4 个有代表性的方面,为定量研究的数据进行了阐释和补充。在母语译者相较于非母语译者区别性特征的基础上对我国文学外译的翻译策略进行了探讨并提出建议,以期为我国的文学外译提供一些参考和启示。

7.1 研究结论

本研究主要以《三国演义》的英译为例,通过定量研究和定性研究来探究母语译者相较于非母语译者的区别性特征,并在此基础上探讨我国文学外译的翻译策略,为我国的文学外译提供一些参考和启示。本研究的研究内容和研究结论简要归纳如下。

7.1.1 母语译者的区别性特征

通过定量研究和定性研究,本研究发现母语译者相较于非母语译者在词汇、句子、篇章层面存在较为显著的区别性特征。

7.1.1.1 词汇层面

形符类符的统计结果显示:《三国演义》母语译者的形符数和类符数都以一定幅度多于非母语译者。《三国演义》的三个英文全译本和四个英文节译本母语译者的类符数都以较大幅度多于非母语译者;形符数方面,除了虞译的形符数以一定幅度多于罗译外,其余不论全译本还是节译本所有母语译者的形符数都以较大幅度多于非母语译者。虞译本的形符数多于罗译本并不影响母语译者译文的形符数较多的倾向性。母语译者的类符数较多是母语译者相较于非母语译者在词汇层面最为显著的特征之一,全译本中的邓译本和罗译本的类符数都以较大幅度多于虞译本,邓译本和罗译本的第 43-50 回内容的类符数也以较大幅度多于杨译本和张译本。母语译者类符数较多的特征除了表现为类符数的总量较多之外,还表现为其动词、名词、形容词、副词、介词和连词的类符数也多于非母语译者。这说明母语译者所使用的词类更为丰富,从词汇丰富的角度来说,对于原文的再现更为细腻。

结论:母语译者的形符数具有高于非母语译者的倾向性,类符数都以较大幅度多于非母语译者。

高频词的统计结果显示:《三国演义》的三个英文全译本和四个英文节译本的母语译者和非母语译者排前 10 位的高频词大体一致。就高频名词来说,不论是三个英文全译本还是四个英文节译本,母语译者对于 time 的使用频次都要少于非母语译者对于 time 的使用频次,而且差异比较显著。其原因在于两者对于原文中的时间概念的翻译采用了不同的翻译方法和策略。

结论:总体来说,母语译者和非母语译者之间在高频词方面并不存在显著的差异。高频词更多反映和体现的是英语语言的某些词汇使用特征以及原作内容和语言风格的某些特征。

特色词的统计结果显示:《三国演义》的三个英文全译本和四个英文节译本的母语译者和非母语译者在用词方面存在显著差异,母语译者的特色词是其区别于非母语译者最主要的特征之一。就特色动词来说,全译本和节译本母语译者特色动词的数量都多于非母语译者的特色动词数量。《三国演义》全译本母语译者的特色动词数为 20 个,非母语译者的特色动词数为 4 个;《三国演义》节译本母语译者的特色动词数为10个,非母语译者的特色动词数为6个。母语译者在动词类符数较多的情况下,其特色动词数多于非母语译者,反映了其动词使用具有较为显著的特色。母语译者值得关注的特色动词主要有played和began(begun),母语译者对于特色动词相关搭配的使用频次也远高于非母语译者,母语译者的特色动词及其相关搭配较高频次的使用得到了《红楼梦》母语译者霍克斯译本和参照语料库10部英文小说原著的有力支持。就特色名词来说,母语译者的特色名词数多于非母语译者的特色名词数,全译本母语译者的特色名词数为4个,非母语译者相较于母语译者的特色名词数为零,节译本母语译者的特色名词数为7个,非母语译者的特色名词数为2个。母语译者值得关注的特色名词有moment和point,母语译者对于moment和point及其相关搭配的较高频次的使用得到了参照语料库10部英文小说原著的有力支持。

就特色副词来说,母语译者和非母语译者的数量都比较少,全译本母语译者的特色副词共2个,非母语译者的特色副词共4个,节译本母语译者的特色副词共1个,非母语译者则没有特色副词。这些特色词中值得关注的是全译本非母语译者的特色副词besides,extremely,deliberately,非母语译者对于besides,extremely,deliberately的使用频次分别为远多于母语译者的使用频次,母语译者对于besides,extremely,deliberately较低频次的使用得到了参照语料库10部英文小说原著的有力支持。就特色形容词来说,母语译者和非母语译者的数量都比较少,全译本母语译者的特色副词共3个,非母语译者的特色形容词共2个,节译本母语译者的特色形容词共4个,非母语译者的特色形容词共2个,母语译者对于特色形容词相关搭配的使用频次高于非母语译者。母语译者值得关注的特色形容词有own和little,母语译者对于own和little较高频率的使用得到了参照语料库10部英文小说原著和《红楼梦》英文全译本母语译者霍克斯译本的有力支持。就特色介词和从属连词来说,母语译者的特色介词和从属连词数略多于非母语译者的特色介词和从属连词数,全译本母语译者的特色介词和从属连词共2个,非母语译者的特色介词和从属连词共1个,节译本母语译者的特色介词和从属连词共4个,非母语译者的特色介词和从属连词共1个。母语译者值得关注的特色介词有upon和beyond,母语译者对于这两个介词较高频率的使用得到了参照语料库《红楼梦》母语译者霍克斯译本的有力支持。

结论：母语译者特色词的数量多于非母语译者特色词的数量，母语译者的特色词及其相关的搭配的较高频率的使用得到了参照语料库的有力支持，这说明母语译者的对于特色词的使用在很大程度上是其母语思维模式影响的结果；而非母语译者的特色词反映了译者受原文字面意义的约束程度较大。

独特词的统计结果显示：《三国演义》三个英文全译本和四个英文节译本母语译者和非母语译者在用词方面存在显著差异，语译者的独特词在数量上远多于非母语译者，母语译者的独特词是其区别于非母语译者最主要的特征之一。就独特名词来说，全译本和节译本母语译者独特名词的数量都远多于非母语译者的独特名词的数量，全译本两位母语译者总计使用频次超过 6 次的独特名词共 126 个，非母语译者总计使用频次超过 6 次的独特名词共 9 个，节译本两位母语译者总计使用频次超过 5 次的独特名词共 53 个，两位非母语译者总计使用频次超过 5 次的独特名词共 13 个，差异比较显著。不论是全译本还是节译本母语译者的独特名词绝大多数都是与小说原文题材相关的政治军事词汇，这说明母语译者使用的名词词类更为丰富，对于与原文题材相关的信息处理得更为细腻。就独特动词来说，全译本和节译本母语译者独特动词的数量都远多于非母语译者的独特动词的数量，全译本两位母语译者总计使用频次超过 4 次的独特动词共 150 个，非母语译者总计使用频次超过 4 次的独特动词共 3 个，节译本两位母语译者总计使用频次超过 4 次的独特动词共 68 个，两位非母语译者总计使用频次超过 4 次的独特动词共 34 个，差异比较显著。全译本和节译本母语译者的独特动词绝大多数都是原文题材相关的政治军事斗争词汇，这说明母语译者使用的动词词类更为丰富，对原文相关信息的处理更为细腻。

就独特副词来说，全译本和节译本母语译者独特副词的数量都多于非母语译者的独特副词的数量，全译本两位母语译者总计使用频次超过 2 次的独特副词共 54 个，非母语译者总计使用频次超过 1 次的独特副词共 42 个，节译本两位母语译者总计使用频次超过 3 次的独特副词共 24 个，两位非母语译者总计使用频次超过 3 次的独特副词共 7 个，差异比较显著。母语译者值得关注的独特副词包括：thence 和 surely，母语译者对于这两个独特副词的使用频次排在全译本和节译本所有独特副词的首位，而且其使用频次得到了参照语料库 10 部英文小说原著的有力支持，thence 的使用频次同时还得到了《红楼梦》母语译者霍克斯译本的有力支持。就独特形容词来说，全译本和节译本母语译者独特形容词的数量都多于非母语译者的独特形容词的数量，全译本两位母语译者总计使用频次超过 5 次的独特形容词共 51 个，非母语译者总计使用频次超过 5 次的独特形容词共 5 个，节译本两位母语译者总计使用频次超过 4 次的独特形容词共 26 个，两位非母语译者总计使用频次超过 4 次的独特形容词共 8 个，差异比较显著。从独特形容词的数量来说，母语译者对于原文相关信息的翻译更为细腻。母语译者值得关注的独特形容词为 especial，母语译者对于 especial 的使用频次得到了参照语料库 10 部英文小说原著和《红楼梦》母语译者霍克斯译本的有力支持。

结论：母语译者独特词的数量大于非母语译者独特词的数量，母语译者的独特词及其相关搭配较高频率的使用得到了参照语料库的有力支持，这说明母语译者的对于独特词的使用在很大程度上是其母语思维模式影响的结果；而非母语译者的独特词反映了译者受原文字面意义的约束程度较大。

7.1.1.2 句子层面

句首词 and 的统计结果显示：《三国演义》英文全译本和节译本的母语译者对于句首词 and 的使用频次以较大幅度高于非母语译者。全译本母语译者对于句首词 and 的使用频次邓译为 838 次，罗译为 806 次，非母语译者虞译对于句首词 and 的使用频次为 556 次；节译本母语译者对于句首词 and 的使用频次邓译为 46 次，罗译为 67 次，非母语译者对于句首词 and 的使用频次杨译为 17 次，张译为 18 次。

结论：《三国演义》英文全译本和节译本的母语译者对于句首词 and 的使用频次以较大幅度高于非母语译者。从 and 的使用角度来看，母语译者对于句首词 and 较高频次的使用使其译文增强了句子之间的衔接性和流畅性。

标点符号的统计结果显示：《三国演义》英文全译本和节译本的母语译者对于逗号的使用频次都以较大幅度高于非母语译者。全译本母语译者平均每句使用逗号的频次邓译为 0.949 次，罗译为 0.860 次，非母语译者虞译平均每句使用逗号的频次为 0.790 次；节译本母语译者平均每句使用逗号的频次邓译为 0.955 次，罗译为 0.901 次，非母语译者平均每句使用逗号的频次杨译为 0.783 次，张译为 0.766 次。母语译者平均每句使用逗号的频次高于非母语译者。

结论：从平均每句使用逗号的频次的视角来说，母语译者平均每句使用逗号的频次高于非母语译者表明一定程度上母语译者的句子结构与非母语译者相比更为复杂。

非谓语动词的 ing 形式的统计结果显示：《三国演义》英文全译本的母语译者邓译对于非谓语动词 ing 形式的使用平均每句为 0.08787 次，罗译为平均每句 0.09738 次，非母语译者虞译对于非谓语动词 ing 形式的使用平均每句为 0.09432 次；英文节译本母语译者对于非谓语动词 ing 形式的使用邓译为平均每句 0.1760 次，罗译为 0.2056 次，非母语译者对于非谓语动词 ing 形式的使用杨译为平均每句 0.1751 次，张译为平均每句 0.1718 次。全译本母语译者罗译平均每句使用 ing 形式的次数最高，母语译者邓译最低，非母语译者虞译介于两者之间；节译本母语译者平均每句使用非谓语动词 ing 形式的次数都以一定幅度多于非母语译者。

结论：除了邓译低于虞译之外，母语译者总体上平均每句对于非谓语动词 ing 形式的使用次数多于非母语译者，从非谓语动词 ing 形式使用次数的角度来看，母语译者的句子结构与非母语译者相比更为复杂。

7.1.1.3 篇章层面

代词 it 和 its 的统计结果显示：《三国演义》英文全译本和节译本的母语译者对于代词 it 和 its 的使用频次在译文中的占比以一定幅度大于非母语译者。全译本母语译者对于代词 it 和 its 的使用频次在译文中的占比邓译为 0.0047，罗译为 0.0046，非母语译者虞译为 0.0045；节译本母语译者对于代词 it 和 its 的使用频次在译文中的占比邓译为 0.0055，罗译为 0.0052，非母语译者对于代词 it 和 its 的使用频次在译文中的占比杨译为 0.0045，张译为 0.0044。

结论：从对于代词 it 和 its 的使用频次在译文中的占比的视角来看，母语译者与非母语译者相比，其 it 和 its 的在译文中的较高占比有助于增强其译文的衔接性和连贯性。

第七章 结 论

7.1.2 对汉英翻译策略的启示

7.1.2.1 词汇层面

母语译者的类符数较高是母语译者区别于非母语译者的一个重要特征。母语译者的这一特征使其译文从整体上来说对原文的再现相对更为充实。类符数是影响译文对于原文内容和风格整体再现效果的重要因素,母语译者类符数较高的特征对我们汉英文学翻译具有一定的参考价值,即在以再现原文的内容和风格为目标的基础上,应注重译文整体类符数的大小,尽可能提高译文的整体类符数,使译文对于原文内容和风格的再现更为充实。

7.1.2.2 句子层面

参照母语译者在句子层面的特征,我们在进行文学外译时,尽可能地转换思维模式,避免原文表层结构的影响和约束,在以有效再现原文的内容和风格为目的的同时,应尽可能通过较高频次地使用逗号和非谓语动词的 ing 形式,增强句子结构的复杂性,避免句子结构的相对单一性,同时应尽可能通过句首词 and 较高频次的使用以期增强句子之间和篇章整体的衔接性和连贯性。

7.1.2.3 篇章层面

母语译者在篇章层面的特征主要表现为对于代词 it 和 its 相较于非母语译者较高频次的使用,母语译者的这一特征增强了其译文的语篇衔接性和连贯性。参照母语译者在语篇层面的这一特征,我们在进行文学外译时应尽可能地转换思维模式,避免原文表层结构的影响和约束,在以有效再现原文的内容和风格为目的的同时,尽可能通过对于代词 it 和 its 较高频次的使用来增强语篇整体的衔接性和连贯性。

7.2　研究价值

本研究的研究价值主要体现在三个方面。

第一,使用实证研究的方法,通过对我国古典小说《三国演义》公认的有影响力的母语译者和非母语译者的译文进行比较研究,探索发现两者译文风格的差异,进一步验证学界传统所认知的"母语优势"。

第二,对母语译者的风格特征和非母语译者的风格特征进行梳理,进一步厘清母语译者在词汇、句子、篇章层面的特征。这些通过语料库统计分析,并结合定性分析所探究的母语译者的风格特征以及非母语译者的风格特征是建立在实证研究基础上所得出的数据资料,可以为翻译理论研究进行研究探索以及翻译实践提供一定的可资借鉴和参考的数据支持。

第三,在进一步厘清母语译者的风格特征的基础上,探索研究母语优势下的翻译策略,为我国的文化走出去和文学外译提供翻译策略方面的参考和支持。

7.3　研究局限与展望

本研究的局限性主要有三个方面。

第一,本研究重点对《三国演义》的两位母语译者和三位非母语译者的共三个英文全译本和四个英文节译本进行了统计分析和比较研究,发现了母语译者相较于非母语译者的区别性特征,研究发现也得到了参照语料库10部英文小说原著和《红楼梦》母语译者霍克斯译本的有力支持。但研究语料比较缺乏,现存的我国经典名著的译本大多是英语母语译者的译本,我国译者的译本尤其是有影响力的译本还不多见,本研

第七章 结 论

究的研究语料有待于进一步丰富,研究范围还有待于进一步扩大,以期本研究的研究结论获得更大范围更为丰富的语料支持。

第二,本研究在母语译者相较于非母语译者的区别性特征的基础上提出了我国文学外译的翻译策略建议,这些策略所给出的建议属于具有指导性质的原则和要求,相对比较宏观。而母语译者相较于非母语译者的区别性特征主要体现和反映了母语思维模式和母语语言的使用习惯,这些母语思维模式和语言使用习惯还有待于使用更大范围的语料作进一步的研究;母语译者和非母语译者各自的思维模式和语言使用习惯具体是如何影响其翻译策略的;母语译者和非母语译者各自特征的差异所体现的两种语言的深层次差异以及这种深层次差异对两种语言之间的翻译的影响还有待于进一步的研究和探讨。

第三,由于本研究的重点是探讨母语译者相较于非母语译者的区别性特征,许渊冲的翻译理论和高健的语言个性理论对于进一步认知目的语的优势和特征的要求仅作了简要的阐述,还有待于进行深层次的研究。

本研究的发展空间主要有三个方面。

第一,本研究通过对《三国演义》的三个英文全译本和四个英文节译本进行了统计分析和比较研究,发现了其母语译者相较于非母语译者的区别性特征。这些区别性特征对于文学领域的其他文体外译以及政治军事等领域的外译研究都具有借鉴意义,同样的研究方法可以应用到上述领域进行外译研究,为翻译研究提供借鉴和参考。

第二,母语译者相较于非母语译者的区别性特征的研究对于翻译策略的研究,尤其是直译和意译,归化和异化的深入研究具有一定的参考价值,具有较大的研究空间。

第三,母语译者和非母语译者各自的思维模式和语言使用习惯具体是如何影响其翻译策略,母语译者和非母语译者各自特征的差异所体现的两种语言的深层次差异以及这种深层次差异对两种语言之间的翻译的影响还有待进一步的研究和探讨。

参考文献

[1] Bacon, Francis. The Essays of Francis Bacon[M].General Books LLC, 2009.

[2] Beeby Lonsdale, Allison.Direction of Translation[A].In Mona Baker（ed.）.Routledge Encyclopedia of Translation Studies [C].London, New York: Rout-ledge,1998.

[3] Brewitt-Taylor, C. H. San Kuo or Romance of the Three Kingdoms[M] Shanghai, Hong Kong and Singapore: Kelly & Walsh Limited,1925.

[4] Campbell, Stuart. Translation into the Second Language. London and New York: Longman,1998.

[5] Cannon. I. C. Public Success, Private Sorrow: The Life and Times of Charles Henry Brewitt-Taylor（1857-1938）.China Customs commissioner and pioneer translator [M] Hong Kong: Hong Kong University Press. 2009

[6] Cao Xueqin and Gao E.A Dream of Red Mansions[M].Trans.Yang Xianyi and Gladys Yang.Beijing: Foreign Languages Press,1978-1982.

[7] Cao Xueqin and Gao E.The Story of the Stone[M].Trans.David Hawkes and John Mindford.London: Penguin Group,1973-1986.

[8] Charles Dickens. A Tale of Two Cities [M]. 北京：外语教学与研究出版社, 2007.

[9] Charles Dickens. David Copperfield [M]. 北京：外语教学与研究出版社, 2007.

[10] Charlotte Bronte. Jane Eyre[M]. 呼和浩特：远方出版社,2005.

参考文献

[11] Daniel Defoe. Robinson Crusoe [M]. 北京：外语教学与研究出版社，2007.

[12] Halliday，M.A.K. & Hasan，R. Cohesion in English [M]. London：Longman，1977.

[13] Jane Austen. Pride And Prejudice [M]. 北京：人民日报出版社，2017.

[14] Mark Twain. The Adventures of Tom Sawyer [M]. 北京：中央编译出版社，2010.

[15] Nathaniel Hawthorne. The Scarlet Letter [M]. 北京：外语教学与研究出版社，2007.

[16] Newmark，Peter. Textbook of Translation [M]. 上海：上海外语教育出版社，2001.

[17] Newmark，Peter. Approaches to Translation [M]. Oxford/New York：Pergamon-Press，1981.

[18] Pokorn，Nike K. Challenging the Traditional Axioms：Translation into a Non-Mother Tongue [M]. Amsterdam & Philadelphia：John Benjamins，2005.

[19] Robert Louis Stevenson. Dr. Jekyll and Mr. Hyde [M]. 北京：人民日报出版社，2017.

[20] Shuttleworth，Mark & Moira Cowie. Dictionary of Translation Studies [Z]. 上海：上海外语教育出版社，2004.

[21] S.M. Lau and Howard Goldblatt（eds）. The Columbia Anthology of Modern Chinese Literature [M]. New York：Columbia University Press，1995.

[22] The New Oxford English-Chinese Dictionary[M]. Shanghai：Shanghai Foreign Language Education Press，2007.

[23] Theodore Dreiser. Sister Carrie [M]. 北京：中译出版社，2017.

[24] Thomas Hardy. Tess of the D'Urbervilles [M]. 北京：商务印书馆，1997.

[25] Yang Xianyi and Gladys Yang. Excerpts from three classical Chinese novels [M]. Nanchang：Panda Books，1981.

[26] 曹雪芹，高鹗. 红楼梦 [M]. 北京：人民文学出版社，1964.

[27] 陈琳. 翻译中语篇指示语与语篇衔接重构 [J]. 外语与外语教学, 2001（7）.

[28] 陈甜.《三国演义》英译与传播研究 [M]. 开封：河南大学出版社, 2019.

[29] 陈晓莉, 张志全.《三国演义》两个英译本中回目的翻译 [J]. 重庆大学学报(社会科学版), 2011（4）.

[30] 程永生. it 的翻译与语篇 [J]. 上海科技翻译, 1995（2）.

[31] 党争胜, 冯正斌. 师从先贤, 潜心翻译——纪念杨宪益先生 [J]. 外国语言与文化, 2019（6）.

[32] 董晓波. 英汉比较与翻译 [M]. 北京：对外经济贸易大学出版社, 2013.

[33] 董琇. 译者主体性与翻译风格——以赛珍珠的《水浒传》和罗慕士的《三国演义》英译本为例 [M]. 北京：外语教学与研究出版社, 2018.

[34] 董琇. 罗慕士英译《三国演义》风格之探析——以邓罗译本为对比参照 [J]. 中国翻译, 2016（7）.

[35] 冯庆华. 母语文化下的译者风格 [M]. 上海：上海外语教育出版社, 2008.

[36] 冯庆华. 思维模式下的译文词汇 [M]. 上海：上海外语教育出版社, 2012.

[37] 冯庆华. 思维模式下的译文句式初探——以《红楼梦》的霍译与杨译为例 [J]. 外语电化教学, 2014（6）.

[38] 高健. 语言个性与翻译 [J]. 外国语, 1999（4）.

[39] 管新潮, 陶友兰. 语料库与翻译 [M]. 上海：复旦大学出版社, 2017.

[40] 郭立秋, 范守义, 贾令仪. 语篇翻译中的衔接问题：理论解读与翻译应用 [J]. 上海翻译, 2011（4）.

[41] 郭昱. 邓罗对《三国演义》的译介 [J]. 中国翻译, 2014（1）.

[42] 贺显斌. 从《三国演义》英译本看副文本对作品形象的建构 [J]. 上海翻译, 2017（12）.

[43] 胡开宝. 语料库翻译学概论 [M]. 上海：上海交通大学出版社, 2011.

[44] 胡开宝. 语料库翻译学：内涵与意义 [J]. 外国语, 2012（5）.

参考文献

[45] 胡开宝，李晓倩．语料库批评译学：内涵与意义 [J]．中国外语，2015（1）．

[46] 黄立波．译出还是译入：翻译方向探究——基于语料库的翻译文体考察 [J]．外语教学，2011（2）．

[47] 黄立波．翻译研究的文体学视角探索 [J]．外语教学，2009(5)．

[48] 黄艳春，黄振定．英汉语指称照应对比与翻译 [J]．外语教学，2006（1）．

[49] 胡壮麟．语篇的衔接与连贯 [M]．上海：上海外语教育出版社，1994．

[50] 李伶伶，王一心．五味人生 杨宪益传 [M]．哈尔滨：北方文艺出版社，2015．

[51] 李伶伶．译界泰斗 杨宪益传 [M]．南京：江苏人民出版社，2011．

[52] 李美．母语与翻译 [M]．上海：上海外语教育出版社，2008．

[53] 李养龙．翻译过程中的主体间性研究：以罗译《三国演义》为例 [M]．北京：外语教学与研究出版社，2013

[54] 连淑能．英汉对比研究 [M]．北京：高等教育出版社，1993．

[55] 梁茂成，李文中，许家金．语料库应用教程 [M]．北京：外语教学与研究出版社，2010．

[56] 梁茂成．语料库语言学研究的两种范式：渊源、分歧及前景 [J]．外语教学与研究，2012（5）．

[57] 刘瑾，罗慕士．钻研中国文化 倾情翻译中国——《三国演义》英译者罗慕士访谈录 [J] 东方翻译，2018（8）．

[58] 刘爱军．基于语料库的译者风格比较研究——以朱自清散文英译为例 [J]．外学电化教学，2020（4）．

[59] 刘爱军．《红楼梦》英译本中母语译者与非母语译者 it 使用情况对比分析 [J]．西安外国语大学学报，2020（2）．

[60] 刘爱军．基于语料库的《三国演义》英译本比较研究 [J]．运城学院学报，2022（5）．

[61] 刘爱军．基于语料库的《三国演义》英译本比较研究——以杨宪益译本、张亦文译本、邓罗译本、罗幕士译本为例 [J]．运城学院学报，2023（6）．

[62] 刘克强.《三国演义》诗词英译 [M]. 北京：中央编译出版社，2015.

[63] 刘宓庆. 文体与翻译 [M]. 北京：中国对外翻译出版公司，1998.

[64] 刘明东. 语篇层面汉译英的衔接性标准 [J]. 中国翻译，2001（5）.

[65] 刘士聪. 英汉·汉英美文翻译与鉴赏 [M]. 南京：译林出版社，2011.

[66] 刘士聪. 介绍一部中国散文经典译作——兼谈 David Pollard 的汉英翻译艺术 [J]. 中国翻译，2005（2）.

[67] 刘士聪. 散文的"情韵"与翻译 [J]. 中国翻译，2002（2）.

[68] 罗贯中.《三国演义》汉英对照版（套装全5卷）[M]. Moss Roberts 罗慕士 [译]. 北京：外文出版社，2000.

[69] 罗贯中.《三国志演义》（第四十三至五十回）中英对照版 [M]. 张亦文 [译]. 北京：中国友谊出版公司，1985.

[70] 罗贯中. Three kingdoms. 1，The Sacred Oath[M]. 虞苏美 [译]，上海：上海外语教育出版社，2017.

[71] 罗贯中. Three kingdoms. 2，The Sleeping Dragon[M]. 虞苏美 [译]. 上海：上海外语教育出版社，2017.

[72] 罗贯中. Three kingdoms. 3，Welcome the Tiger[M]. 虞苏美 [译]. 上海：上海外语教育出版社，2017.

[73] 马士奎. 从母语译入外语：国外非母语翻译实践和理论考察 [J]. 上海翻译，2012（3）.

[74] 潘文国. 汉英语对比纲要 [M]. 北京：北京语言大学出版社，1997.

[75] 潘文国. 译入与译出——谈中国译者从事汉籍英译的意义 [J]. 中国翻译，2004（2）.

[76] 秦洪武，王克非. 基于对应语料库的英译汉语言特征分析 [J]. 外语教学与研究，2009（2）.

[77] 裘克安（译）. 关于翻译工作者和翻译作品的法律保护以及改善翻译工作者地位的实际方法的建议书 [J]. 中国翻译，1984（6）.

[77] 汪世蓉.《三国演义》传统文化事象的多视角英译研究 [M]. 北京：中国社会科学出版社，2015.

[79] 王承时. 翻译工作者宪章 [J]. 中国翻译, 1985（6）.

[80] 王瑢, 陈铸芬. 英汉翻译中的隐性衔接与连贯问题 [J]. 外语研究, 2009（3）.

[81] 王恩冕. 从母语译入外语：东亚三国的经验对比 [J]. 中国翻译, 2008（1）.

[82] 王建国, 何自然. 重过程, 还是重结果？——译者的母语对英译文本的影响 [J]. 上海翻译, 2014（2）.

[83] 王建开. 母语者还是外语者：中国文学对外传播的译者资格之争——兼谈高校英语教师的能力转型 [J]. 外国语文, 2016（3）.

[84] 王克非. 语料库翻译学探索 [M]. 上海：上海交通大学出版社, 2012.

[85] 王克非. 语料库翻译学——新研究范式 [J]. 中国外语, 2006（3）.

[86] 王丽娜, 杜维沫.《三国演义》的外文译文 [J]. 明清小说研究, 2006（4）.

[87] 王学功. 近五年国内《三国演义》英译研究 [J]. 中华文化论坛, 2016（7）.

[88] 王燕. 19世纪三国演义英译文献研究 [M]. 北京：中国社会科学出版社, 2018.

[89] 文军, 潘月.《母语向第二语言的翻译》评介 [J]. 中国科技翻译, 2003（8）.

[90] 许宏. 衔接手段与汉译英译文质量 [J]. 解放军外国语学院学报, 2003（1）.

[91] 徐英才. 英译中国经典散文选 [M]. 上海：上海外语教育出版社, 2014.

[92] 许渊冲. 翻译的艺术 [M]. 北京：五洲传播出版社, 2007.

[93] 许渊冲. 新世纪的新译论 [J]. 中国翻译, 2000（3）.

[94] 许渊冲. 再谈《竞赛论》和《优势轮》——兼评《忠实是译者的天职》[J]. 中国翻译, 2001（1）.

[95] 许渊冲. 再谈中国学派的文学翻译理论 [J]. 中国翻译, 2012（4）.

[96] 许渊冲. 有中国特色的文学翻译理论 [J]. 中国翻译, 2016（5）.

[97] 杨平. 名作精译《中国翻译》汉译英选萃 [M]. 青岛：青岛出版

社,2003.

[98] 杨宪益.杨宪益自传[M].北京:人民日报出版社,2010.

[99] 余高峰.语篇衔接连贯与翻译[J].语言与翻译,2009(4).

[100] 余静.《挑战传统原则——译入非母语》述评[J].中国翻译,2011(1).

[101] 张梦井,杜耀文.中国名家散文精译[M].青岛:青岛出版社,1999.

[102] 张培基.英译中国现代散文选(一)[M].上海:上海外语教育出版社,2007.

[103] 张琦.英汉衔接手段对比及其翻译[J].中国翻译,1999(1).

[104] 周燕,周维新.评《三国演义》的英译本——兼谈中国古典小说的翻译[J].外国语,1988(6).

[105] 朱振武.《汉学家的中国文学英译历程》[M].上海:华东理工大学出版社,2017.

[106] 朱振武.《三国演义》的英译比较与典籍外译的策略探索[J].上海师范大学学报(哲学社会科学版),2017(11).

[107] 朱自清.背影·匆匆朱自清的散文[M].北京:中国对外翻译出版公司,2005.

[108] 左岩.汉英部分语篇衔接手段的差异[J].外语教学与研究,1995(3).